Josephine Pollard

The Wonderful Story of Jesus Told in Simple Language

in words of easy reading for the young

Josephine Pollard

The Wonderful Story of Jesus Told in Simple Language
in words of easy reading for the young

ISBN/EAN: 9783337390075

Printed in Europe, USA, Canada, Australia, Japan

Cover: Foto ©Lupo / pixelio.de

More available books at **www.hansebooks.com**

The Wonderful Story of Jesus

TOLD IN SIMPLE LANGUAGE

IN WORDS OF EASY READING FOR THE YOUNG.

THE SWEET STORY

——OF THE——

PRINCE OF PEACE

FROM THE MANGER TO THE CROSS

MADE CLEAR TO THE MIND AND HEART OF THE LITTLE ONES

——WITH THE AID OF MORE THAN——

TWO HUNDRED PICTURES

COPIES OF WORLD-FAMOUS WORKS OF ART

SHOWING FORTH IN-DOOR AND OUT-DOOR SCENES IN THE HOLY LAND WHILE OUR LORD JESUS CHRIST WAS ON EARTH.

——BY——

JOSEPHINE POLLARD,

Author of "History of the Old Testament," "History of the New Testament," "Young Folks' Bible," "The Bible and its Story," etc., etc., etc.

NEW YORK AND ST. LOUIS:
N. D. THOMPSON PUBLISHING CO.
1890.

COPYRIGHTED 1890 BY N. D. THOMPSON PUBLISHING CO.

A WORD TO THE READER.

A piece of cloth was once brought to a man, who was told to take out of it all the threads of gold that shone there-in, and weave them in-to a web of their own. This seemed at first not a hard task, for the bright threads shone out so that the eye could not fail to see them. But it was found that each gold thread was so much a part of the warp and the woof that he must take great care who would weave them a-new, lest the web should be spun wrong, and the bright gold marred.

With some such thought as this in my mind I sat down to write The Life of Christ. The New Tes-ta-ment is full of Him. He is the Good News. But how can it be made clear to the mind of the young child who has just learned to read, and must take short steps?

Well do I call to mind the snarl it seemed to me when I was young, and how hard I tried to get things straight and smooth. We were blind then and groped in the dark. We had not such help as young folks have now-a-days.

Mat-thew, Mark, Luke and John were with Je-sus when He was on earth, and each one told in his own way the things that he had seen and heard. If we read them with-out the light thrown on the page, we are lost in a maze of doubt and can-not tell when the things took place, or if Je-sus spoke the same words twice or not.

It has been the au-thor's aim to take the bright threads that these four men wove in-to their web, and so weave them that they shall shine out for young eyes, and for old eyes too, and be to them like a great piece of Cloth of Gold.

The light of the great star shines out on the night. Come, let us go with the wise men of the East who set out to find Je-sus. We will see him as a young child and as a boy in his home on the hill-side, and read of all the great works he did in his short life-time. Here is a dark page where Je-sus was put to death by his foes, but on it shines the Cross with a great blaze of light. He must have a heart of stone who can read of these things and not feel drawn to Je-sus, who came in-to the world to save us and who laid down His life for us.

That those who read this book may learn to love Him more and more, and grow to be more Christ-like each day of their lives, more brave and true—glad to bear the Cross, and to do good in His name—with-out fear of loss or hope of gain, is the fond wish of their friend,

THE AUTHOR.

CONTENTS.

CHAPTER I.
	PAGE.
The Birth of Je-sus,	33

CHAPTER II.
| The Home at Naz-a-reth, | 52 |

CHAPTER III.
| Je-sus and John Preach and Teach, | 79 |

CHAPTER IV.
| Je-sus at the Well, | 95 |

CHAPTER V.
| The Ser-mon on the Mount, | 115 |

CHAPTER VI.
| Je-sus at Nain, | 134 |

CHAPTER VII.
| Je-sus by the Sea-Side, | 142 |

CHAPTER VIII.
| Je-sus at Ca-per-na-um, | 156 |

CHAPTER IX.
The Pool of Be-thes-da.—Je-sus in Je-ru-sa-lem.—Death of John the Bap-tist, ... 173

Contents.

CHAPTER X.
FIVE THOUS-AND FED.—JE-SUS WALKS ON THE SEA.—HE WARNS JU-DAS, ... 186

CHAPTER XI.
THE LORD'S PRAYER.—THE LAW-YER.—THE RICH FOOL.—JE-SUS TALKS TO THE CROWD, AND BIDS THEM WATCH, ... 206

CHAPTER XII.
JE-SUS GOES TO TYRE AND SI-DON.—HEALS THE CHILD OF THE GREEK WOM-AN.—GIVES THE BLIND MAN SIGHT.—HIS CHARGE TO PE-TER, 217

CHAPTER XIII.
JE-SUS IS TRANS-FIG-URED.—THE LIT-TLE CHILD IN THEIR MIDST.—HOW TO FOR-GIVE DEBTS, ... 228

CHAPTER XIV.
THE TEM-PLE TAX.—THE GREAT FEAST OF THE JEWS.—JE-SUS GOES NOT UP WITH HIS KINS-FOLK.—"I AM THE LIGHT OF THE WORLD."—THE MAN BORN BLIND, ... 241

CHAPTER XV.
JE-SUS LEAVES GAL-I-LEE.—SENDS OUT THE SEV-EN-TY.—HEALS TEN LEP-ERS.—THE WOM-AN BOWED DOWN.—PAR-A-BLE OF THE KING'S WED-DING FEAST, ... 264

CHAPTER XVI.
THE UN-JUST STEW-ARD.—THE RICH MAN AND LAZ-A-RUS.—THE GOOD SA-MAR-I-TAN.—THE PROD-I-GAL SON.—THE LOST SHEEP.—THE LOST PIECE OF SIL-VER, ... 282

CHAPTER XVII.
MARY'S CHOICE.—THEY BRING YOUNG CHIL-DREN TO JE-SUS.—THE YOUNG RUL-ER.—THE WORK-MEN IN THE VINE-YARD.—THE HIGH PRIEST TELLS THAT JE-SUS MUST DIE, ... 298

Contents.

CHAPTER XVIII.

THE PASS-O-VER FEAST.—BLIND BAR-TI-ME-US.—ZAC-CHE-US CLIMBS A TREE.—JE-SUS ON THE WAY TO JE-RU-SA-LEM.—THE FEAST AT BETH-A-NY, ... 314

CHAPTER XIX.

JE-SUS LEAVES BETH-A-NY.—SONGS OF PRAISE, AND PALMS OF JOY.—HE SPEAKS IN THE TEM-PLE.—A VOICE FROM ON HIGH.—THE FIG TREE THAT BORE NO FRUIT, ... 326

CHAPTER XX.

LAST DAYS.—WHAT THE SIGNS SHALL BE.—THE TEN VIR-GINS.—THE TEN TAL-ENTS, ... 344

CHAPTER XXI.

JU-DAS PLOTS TO SELL HIS LORD.—THE LAST SUP-PER.—JE-SUS WASHES THE DIS-CI-PLES FEET.—LORD IS IT I? 359

CHAPTER XXII.

WITH JE-SUS IN THE UP-PER ROOM, ... 371

CHAPTER XXIII.

JE-SUS IN THE GAR-DEN OF GETH-SEM-A-NE.—THE JU-DAS KISS.—IN THE HANDS OF HIS FOES.—HE IS BROUGHT BE-FORE THE HIGH PRIEST, AND THEN SENT TO PI-LATE.—PE-TER DE-NIES HIS LORD, . 387

CHAPTER XXIV.

JE-SUS ON THE CROSS, AND IN THE GRAVE.—AN AN-GEL ROLLS THE STONE A-WAY.—"HE IS NOT HERE, HE HAS RIS-EN," . . 415

CHAPTER XXV.

THE WALK TO EM-A-US.—JE-SUS IS SEEN BY THOSE WHO LOVE HIM.—THE LAST FARE-WELL.—A CLOUD HIDES HIM FROM SIGHT, . 436

Illustrations

	PAGE
Let the lit-tle ones come un-to me,	32
Beth-le-hem and the tombs of the monks,	38
Con-vent that marks the birth-place of Je-sus,	39
I bring you good news,	40
The first Christ-mas,	41
The Christ-child,	43
The wise men and the star,	45
Rich gifts they brought,	47
Sim-e-on gives thanks to God,	48
The flight in-to E-gypt,	50
Hous-es in Naz-a-reth,	52
Naz-a-reth,	53
Car-pen-ter's shop,	54
His hum-ble trade,	55
Christ brought by his par-ents,	56
Booths or tents used in the East,	57
Taught from the Word of God,	58
Je-sus in the tem-ple,	60
Palms and fruits of Pal-es-tine,	61
Figs and date palms,	62
The rol-ler bird,	63
John the Bap-tist,	64
Fords of the Jor-dan,	65
Wild-er-ness of Ju-de-a,	66
Banks of the Jor-dan,	69

Illustrations.

	PAGE
One of the fords of the Jor-dan,	70
The riv-er Jab-bok,	71
On the Dead Sea,	72
Dead Sea,	73
Dead Sea by moon-light,	74
Temp-ta-tion in the des-ert,	75
Temp-ta-tion on the moun-tain,	76
The Jor-dan val-ley,	80
Come with me,	82
Boat in Sea of Gal-i-lee,	83
Ca-na in Gal-i-lee,	84
Fill the wa-ter pots,	86
Je-sus turns wa-ter in-to wine,	87
Ruins of Ca-na of Gal-i-lee,	88
Take these things from God's house,	90
Je-sus and Nic-o-de-mus,	92
Sy-char,	96
An old well,	97
Ruins of tem-ple of Man-as-seh,	98
Mount Ger-i-zim,	99
Foot of Mount Ger-i-zim,	100
Top of Mount Ger-i-zim,	101
Gal-i-lee,	103
Gal-i-lee,	104
Street in Naz-a-reth,	105
A Jew-ish syn-a-gogue,	106
Hills a-round Naz-a-reth,	108
Christ heal-ing the sick,	111
Fish from the Sea of Gal-i-lee,	112
The draught of fish-es,	113
A man named Mat-thew,	114
Ti-be-ri-as,	116
The Ser-mon on the mount,	118
Gol-den can-dle stick,	119
The part-ridge that feeds on poor soil,	122
The part-ridge that feeds on rich soil,	123

Illustrations.

	PAGE.
Storks—Quail,	124
The Gal-li-nule,	125
Flow-ers of the field,	126
Wall of Je-ru-sa-lem,	127
Da-mas-cus gate, Je-ru-sa-lem,	128
Ro-man Cen-tu-ri-on,	129
Speak but the word,	131
Nain,	133
The wid-ow's son,	134
Plains of Gal-i-lee,	135
House of a rich man,	136
East-ern san-dals,	137
Couch used at meals,	138
She bowed her head with shame,	139
Spike-nard,	140
Je-sus teach-ing by the sea-side,	143
An east-ern sow-er,	144
The wheat and the tares,	146
Great spot-ted cuck-oo,	148
Lord, save us!	151
Tombs,	152
Be-hold, I stand at the door,	154
Where the Jews went to weep and wail,	163
The daugh-ter of Ja-i-rus,	165
Rise, my child!	167
Brought him the dumb,	169
View in Da-mas-cus,	170
Pool of Be-thes-da,	174
An an-gel stirred the pool,	176
Pool of Sol-o-mon,	178
Pool of Hez-e-ki-ah,	179
East-ern flute play-er,	184
Map of the Sea of Gal-i-lee,	187
Christ feed-ing the mul-ti-tude,	189
Je-sus walks on the sea,	193

Illustrations.

	PAGE
Ru-ins of a syn-a-gogue,	201
In the corn-field,	202
Wom-en grind-ing corn,	203
Ta-ble of shew-bread,	204
Wild with rage,	205
Wash-ing hands,	208
Fish-hawk,	212
Young ra-vens,	212
Cor-mo-rant,	212
Ra-ven,	213
Ru-ins of Tyre,	217
Si-don,	218
Send her a-way,	219
He sat down to rest and pray,	221
Mag-da-la,	223
Lake, or Sea of Gal-i-lee,	224
Ru-ins at Cæs-a-re-a, Phil-ip-pi,	225
Mount Her-mon,	226
The trans-fig-ur-a-tion,	229
Rest and shade,	230
Mount Tabor,	231
Sor-row for sin,	236
The sheep that was lost,	238
Shouldst thou not for-give,	241
Mount of Ol-ives,	248
Vil-lage of Si-lo-am,	255
Pool of Si-lo-am,	256
The man born blind,	258
The good shep-herd,	262
A bird of prey,	263
Ru-ins on site of Cho-ra-zin,	265
Ru-ins at Cho-ra-zin,	266
Ru-ins of temple at Ger-a-sa	267
Ru-ins of Ger-a-sa,	268
Tow-er of An-to-ni-a,	269
Ro-man sol-diers,	270

Illustrations.

	PAGE.
Ro-man arms,	271
Group of Sa-mar-i-tans,	272
Lep-ers out-side the gate,	273
Je-sus preach-ing in syn-a-gogue,	275
Ru-ins of syn-a-gogue,	276
The wed-ding feast,	281
The beg-gar at the rich man's gate,	285
Jew-ish priest,	288
A Le-vite,	288
Rob-bers on the road to Jer-i-cho,	289
Half dead by the road-side,	290
Palms and plains of Jer-i-cho,	292
Wom-an of Naz-a-reth,	295
Beth-a-ny,	299
Ma-ry hath cho-sen the good part,	301
Then the Jews took up stones,	303
Ma-ry bathes the feet of Christ,	307
Laz-a-rus raised from the dead,	311
Jew-ish high priest,	312
Je-sus on the way to Je-ru-sa-lem,	315
On the way to Je-ru-sa-lem,	316
Je-ru-sa-lem from the south,	317
Sup-posed site of Jer-i-cho,	319
Mount at Jer-i-cho,	320
Zac-che-us called by Christ,	321
Square ru-in at Jer-i-cho,	322
On the road to Beth-a-ny,	325
View in Je-ru-sa-lem,	327
Beth-page,	328
Where Beth-page once stood,	329
East-ern ass-es,	330
En-try in-to Je-ru-sa-lem,	331
Je-ru-sa-lem from Mount of Ol-ives,	332
Christ weep-ing o-ver Je-ru-sa-lem,	333
Sir, we would see Je-sus,	335
Fig tree,	337

Illustrations

	PAGE.
Look-ing down on Beth-a-ny,	338
Street in Je-ru-sa-lem,	342
Friend, how didst thou come in?	343
Day-break at Je-ru-sa-lem,	345
Gold-en gate,	346
Whose face is on the coin?	347
The wid-ow's mite,	351
Ru-ins of an arch,	353
Lord, let us in,	355
Ju-das plots with the foes of Je-sus,	361
Brook Ked-ron,	362
The last sup-per,	364
Je-sus wash-es the dis-ci-ples' feet,	367
Is it I?	370
Tomb of Da-vid,	373
Church of the Ho-ly Sep-ul-chre,	375
The way of grief,	378
The place where Pi-late said, This is the man,	381
Carved tomb,	384
Slopes a-bove the Ked-ron,	387
Moon-light on Mount of Ol-ives,	388
Vale of the Ked-ron,	389
Ol-ive grove,	390
Ol-ive press,	391
Christ on the Mount of Olives,	392
Geth-sem-a-ne,	393
Scene at Geth-sem-a-ne,	394
Gar-den at Geth-sem-a-ne,	395
The Ju-das kiss,	397
Je-sus be-fore the high priest,	399
The chief priests tell what Je-sus has done,	400
Pe-ter de-nies his Lord,	402
The price of blood,	404
The field of blood,	406
What shall I do with Je-sus?	408
Scourg-ing Christ,	410

Illustrations.

	PAGE
Crown of thorns,	412
Then Je-sus came forth,	414
Not this man,	416
Je-sus falls be-neath the cross,	418
On the cross,	420
The Marys at the cross,	422
Veil of temple rent in twain,	423
They took Je-sus down,	424
He was borne to the tomb,	426
Sep-ul-chre, or tomb,	427
Friends of Je-sus,	428
The guards at the tomb,	429
Je-sus shows him-self to Mary,	432
He is not here,	434
Em-a-us,	437
Je-sus shows him-self to his dis-ci-ples,	439
He shows them his hands,	442
Sea of Gal-i-lee,	443
Cast-ing the net,	444
The net did not break,	445
Je-sus takes bread and gives to them,	447
Brow of the Mount of Ol-ives,	449
The as-cen-sion,	451
He has balm for all our wounds,	452
The mosque of O-mar,	453
Je-sus my king,	454

THE SHEP-HERDS COME TO SEE JE-SUS.

The Story of Jesus.

CHAPTER I.

THE BIRTH OF JE-SUS.

In those dim old days, far back in the past, men did not live as they do now. They formed them-selves in-to tribes, and each tribe dwelt by it-self in tents made of the skins of beasts. They kept the old laws that Mo-ses gave them when he led the twelve tribes out of the land of E-gypt, and through the Red Sea, and by the food they ate, the way they lived, and the forms they made use of, showed that they were of the race of Jews, whom God had set a-part to do His will.

In time they learned how to build homes for them-selves out of wood and stone, and some of the Jews grew rich, and lived in fine style. But a large part of them were poor, and all had to pay a large tax to this King or that King, who looked up-on them as his slaves.

It was hard for the Jews to bear this yoke, and as far back as the days of Mo-ses they longed to be free; and hopes were held out to them that they should have a King of their own. They did not think that their chief yoke was their sins; and when A-bra-ham, Jo-seph, Josh-u-a and Da-vid spoke of One who was to save them, they looked for a great King, rich, strong and brave, who would lead them to war and put all their foes to flight.

For a long time the wise men of the Jews had thought it would be well to have one great church or tem-ple, where all could meet on feast days and fast days, and where the ark of God could be kept. This was the chief wish of King Da-vid's heart, but though he lived to build the great town of Je-ru-sa-lem, he died ere the Tem-ple could be built. This work was done by his son, Sol-o-mon, who was so rich and so wise that his fame spread far and wide, and men from all parts of the then known world came to see him, and to bring him rich gifts.

Proud were the Jews who could boast that they were of the tribe of Ju-dah, and in King Da-vid's line, for this gave them high rank though they might not have much of this world's goods. And it is a cause for pride to be well-born; not the wrong kind of pride that puts on airs and turns up its nose, but the right kind of pride that keeps one clean and true, and makes him loath to do aught that will soil the name he bears.

Now in the days when Her-od was King of Ju-de-a, and in the pay of the King of Rome, there lived a priest named Zach-a-ri-as and his wife E-liz-a-beth, and it was a great grief to them that they had no child. Each priest had his own work to do in the church of God, and Zach-a-ri-as had charge of the al-tar of in-cense where woods and gums were burned that filled the whole place with a sweet smell, and the smoke of which rose to God like prayers from the hearts of men.

One day, when this priest stood by the al-tar, an an-gel came to him, and said, Fear not, Zach-a-ri-as, for thy prayer is heard. God will give to thee a son, and thou shalt call his name John. And he shall be great in the sight of the Lord, and shall drink no wine nor strong drink. He shall turn the hearts of the Jews to the Lord their God, and fit them for their Lord and King who is to come.

The priest said to the an-gel, By what sign shall I know this? for I am an old man, and my wife is well on in years. The an-gel said to him, I am sent to speak to thee, and to bring thee these good news. And thou shalt be dumb till the day that these things come to pass, be-cause thou didst not have faith in me, and be-lieve that my words were true.

When the priest came out of the sa-cred place, it was seen by those who were in wait for him that he was both deaf and dumb. He could not speak or hear, but tried to tell them by signs what he had seen, and still kept at his tasks.

In due time God gave to E-liz-a-beth a son, and there was great joy at his birth, and the friends came to show how glad they were. They called the babe Zach-a-ri-as, for they said it was but right that he should have the same name as his fa-ther. But his mo-ther said, Not so; but he shall be called John. They said to her, There is none of thy folks called by this name. And they asked the fa-ther by signs how he would have him called.

The priest took up a tab-let smeared with wax, which was the kind of slate used in those days, and wrote on it, His name is John. And the friends thought it strange, for as he was deaf he could not have heard what his wife had said. And at once his tongue was loosed, and he spake, and gave praise to God.

And great fear came on all those who dwelt near them, and these things were much talked of in all that part of Ju-de-a. And all they that heard them laid the words up in their hearts, and said from time to time, What then shall this child be? For the hand of the Lord was with him. And the child grew in size and strength, and through all the days of his youth led a calm life, far from the haunts of men, that he might have time to think and to fit him-self for the life he was to lead when a full grown man.

Those who are to do a great work need time to think and pray. God sets them off from the world for a while, so that the things of the world shall not clog their mind. If John had staid a-mong men, his words would not have had so much weight with them, for they would have said to them-selves, We know this man—we went to school with him, and played with him when he was a boy, and it can-not be that he knows more than the rest of us. And they would not have cared so much to hear him preach.

God fits men for their work, and if they pay heed to Him, and o-bey His will they are sure to come out all right. The food John ate was to keep him in health. He did no hard work, and so did not need strong meat, and he drank from the clear streams that gushed forth from the rocks. He was taught of God in ways that we know not of; for we are not told of his boy-hood or man-hood, from his birth up to the time that he be-gan to preach. All that we know is that he led an out-of-door life. And men went to him to hear what he had to say.

Now ere the year was out the same an-gel that came to the priest, was sent from God to a town in Gal-i-lee, named Naz-a-reth, where lived a man named Joseph and Ma-ry his wife. And he came where Mary was, and said to her, Hail, thou that art loved with a great love! The Lord is with thee! And when she heard these words she knew not what to say or do.

And the an-gel said to her, Fear not, Ma-ry; for thou hast found favor with God, and he will give thee a son, and thou shalt call his name Je-sus. He shall be great, and shall be called the Son of the Most High, and God will set him on Da-vid's throne, and he shall be King of the Jews, and there shall be no end to his reign.

Ma-ry said, how can this be? The an-gel said, God can do all things. Then said Ma-ry, Let His will be done in me; and the an-gel left her.

Now in these days word was sent out from Rome that all the world should be taxed. Ro-mans and Jews were to go to the town from whence their tribe first came, and give in their names that they might be put on the tax-lists. And Jo-seph and Ma-ry went to Beth-le-hem, for both were of the house of Da-vid, who was born there.

Their way led up a hill, on top of which the town of Beth-le-hem was built, and as they were forced to walk slow, it was late when they reached there, and there was no room for them in the inn. The night was cold, and they were in need of rest, but the town was full, and the inn was full and they sought in vain for a place to lay their heads. Some of the large inns had court-yards, and a host who took care of his guests; but this way-side inn was just a place where rooms

BETH-LE-HEM, AND THE HOMES OF THE MONKS.

were let, and those who stopped there brought their own food, and took care of such cat-tle as they might have with them.

As the town of Beth-le-hem was on a hill, the cat-tle sheds were cut out of the lime-stone rock, and in one of these, in the midst of the hay and straw spread out there, Christ was born.

THE CON-VENT THAT MARKS THE BIRTH-PLACE OF JE-SUS.

The word Beth-le-hem meant THE HOUSE OF BREAD, but those who gave that name to the small town, five miles south of Je-ru-sa-lem, did not know that the time would come when it would be more thought of than Je-ru-sa-lem it-self. It was part of God's plan that He who brought the bread of life to feed the soul of man, should be born in Beth-le-hem, The House of Bread.

The Church of Rome has built a con-vent, that is, a home for monks, or nuns—to mark the spot where Je-sus was born, and to keep it safe from harm.

The Birth of Je-sus.

Ma-ry had no one to help her, and with her own hands she wrapped the babe in the swad-dling clothes, or bands,

I BRING YOU GOOD NEWS.

which are put on a child at its birth, and laid him in the trough, or box, from whence the cat-tle took their food.

The Birth of Je-sus.

It was a rough place. It may have been a cave, or a shed. That we do not know, for it was not thought worth while to tell just how it was built. But when Christ was born in it, there was no place in all the world so full of light and joy.

THE FIRST CHRIST-MAS.

The soul of man is like an inn. All sorts of folks stop there. Those that have wealth get the best rooms, and keep them-selves well in the fore-ground. The love of gold, love of dress, and show, pride, and love of self, fill the whole space. Their thoughts are all on what they shall eat, what they shall drink, and what they shall wear. The crowd is great. In vain does Christ stand out-side the door, and knock. There is no room for Him in the inn.

But there is a poor soul near whose lot is a low one. The rich turn from her as if she was no more to them than the beast of the field. Her heart is like a shed, in-to which the winds and rains pour, and storms beat on the roof from day to day. Hay and straw are all a-round her. But in the midst of it all she keeps a clean swept place. And one night, when her heart was full of gloom, the noise of those at the inn made her feel as if she was shut out from all the good things of life.

One night as she lay in her shed she clasped her hands, and raised her eyes, and there—there—through a chink in the roof, she caught sight of a star! What did it mean? Some good was on its way to her; she knew it by the strange thrill in her heart, the fresh hope and strength, the calm trust in God's will. Her sins had kept her where she was. Her heart was full of chaff, a place where beasts of the field were fed. It should be so no more. And then Je-sus was born! There was not room for Him in the inn, but there was room for Him in her heart, and the light that shone from His face, made all the place seem as if lit by the sun.

None are so poor that they can-not make room for Je-sus—if they will. If your heart is like an inn, where all sorts of things crowd in, and crowd Him out, you will miss the joy of life, and shut out that which is more to you than sun-light. Make room for Je-sus. Let Him be your guest.

Now there were in Ju-de-a some shep-herds who watched their flocks by night lest the wild beasts should come and slay them. And while they kept watch through

The Birth of Je-sus. 43

the dark hours, an an-gel came and stood by them, a bright light shone round them, and they were in great fear. The an-gel said to them, Fear not, for to you and to all I bring glad news. For Christ the Lord, who is to save you from your sins, is born this day in the town of Beth-le-hem. And this shall be the sign to you: Ye shall find a babe wrap-ped in swad-dling clothes and ly-ing in a man-ger. And as he ceased to speak a host of white-robed an-gels stood round him, and all sang a hymn of praise to God, and said, Praise be to God most high, and on earth peace and good will to men.

THE CHRIST-CHILD.

When the an-gels had left them, the shep-herds said to each oth-er, Let us go to Beth-le-hem and see this thing which has come to pass and which the Lord hath made known to us. And they came with haste, and found Ma-ry and Jo-seph, and the babe lying in a man-ger, just as the an-gel had said. And when they had seen it, they spread the glad news, and all they that heard were awe-struck at the things that were told them by the shep-herds. Ma-ry spoke not a word, but kept all these things in her heart; and the shep-herds went back to their homes, and gave thanks to God for all that they had seen and heard.

Now there were in the East at the time of King Her-od's reign, some priests who gave much time and thought to the stars. The sky was like a book to them, and each night they would gaze, and gaze, and read the signs on the broad page spread out be-fore their eyes. These men were so wise, and were so much thought of, that they were called Kings; and three of them had seen the strange star that shone on the shep-herds who watched their flocks by night.

These three Kings set out from their homes and came to Je-ru-sa-lem, and asked of all whom they met, Where is he that is born King of the Jews? for we have seen his star in the east and have come to worship him. When Her-od, the King, heard it, he was in great fear lest he should lose his throne; and all Je-ru-sa-lem was in a state of dread, for they knew not what Her-od might do. When he had brought all the chief priests to one place, he asked them where the Christ should be born. And they said, In Beth-le-hem of Ju-de-a, for so had it been fore-told.

Then Her-od had a talk with the wise men, and found out what time they first saw the star. And he sent them to Beth-le-hem and said, Go and search well for the young

THE WISE MEN AND THE STAR.

child, and when ye have found him bring me back word that I may come and bow down at his feet.

Then they went on their way, and lo, the star which they saw in the east went on with them till it came to the house where Je-sus was, and there it stood still. The sight of the star gave them great joy, and when they came in-to the house they saw the young child, with Ma-ry his mo-ther, and they bowed down be-fore him who was the King of Kings, and Lord of Lords. Then they gave to him the rich gifts they had brought, of gold, and rare gums such as they were wont to give to kings, and gods.

God warned the wise men in a dream not to go back to king Her-od, so they went to their own land by a way that led not near Je-ru-sa-lem.

On the eighth day the child was named, and he was called Je-sus; and when he was for-ty days old Ma-ry and Jo-seph took their first born son and went up to the Tem-ple at Je-ru-sa-lem. It was a law of the Jews that each first born male—both of man and of beast—was to be brought to God. A vow was made that the child would be brought up to do God's will, and be taught all God's laws as they had been made known to men. Those who were rich were to bring a lamb, which was slain on the al-tar and burned there, and the lamb thus slain was a sign that One was to come, and by His death take all the sins of the world a-way.

Those who were poor brought a pair of young doves, and with these and the young babe—who was him-self the Lamb of God—Jo-seph and Ma-ry went up to the priest in the Tem-ple.

RICH GIFTS THEY BROUGHT.

Now there was in Je-ru-sa-lem a good old man named Sim-e-on, who was well read in the law, and had long looked for One who was to come and save the Jews, as the wise men had fore-told. And it was shown to him in a dream that he should not die till he had seen the Lord's Christ—And he came to the Tem-ple at the same time that the par-ents brought in the child Je-sus, that they might do for him as they were taught in the Law.

SIM-E-ON GIVES THANKS TO GOD.

As soon as Sim-e-on saw the child, he took it in his arms, and burst forth in a grand song of praise to God, and said, Now let Thou Thy ser-vant go, O Lord, in peace as Thou hast said; for mine eyes have seen Him whom Thou hast sent to save men from their sins, and to be a light to all the world. Jo-seph and Ma-ry did not know what was meant by the strange words he spoke. And Sim-e-on blest them, and said to Ma-ry, This child is set for the fall and rise of men—and for a sign that shall be looked on as a mark of shame. Yes, a sword shall pierce through thy own soul, and His grief shall be thine. In these words he showed forth the life and death of Je-sus. Men were to be brought down by a sense of sin, and were to be raised up through faith and a good life. His life on earth was to end on the cross—on which none but the worst of men were put to death—and the sword would pierce her heart then and there, and test the faith of all the world.

And there was one An-na, a wise wom-an who foretold strange things that were to take place. Her hus-band was dead, and she was now four-score and four years old, and she lived in the Tem-ple and took part in all the feasts and fasts that were held there, night and day. And at the same hour that Sim-e-on took the child in his arms, An-na gave thanks to God that He had come who was to save the world from its sins and to be the King of the Jews. And she spoke of Him to all those who stood near her.

When they had done all that they came to do, Jo-seph and Ma-ry went back to the house in which they now lived at Beth-le-hem. And it was not long ere an an-gel came to Jo-seph in a dream, and said to him, Rise, and take the young child and his moth-er, and flee to E-gypt, and stay thou there till I tell thee to leave. For Her-od will seek the young child to kill him. Jo-seph rose at once, and took the young child and his moth-er, and set

50   *The Birth of Je-sus.*

out the same night for the land of E-gypt, and was there till the death of Her-od, that the words which a wise man

THE FLIGHT IN-TO E-GYPT.

of old had said might come true. And these words were, Out of E-gypt I have called my son.

It is worth while to pause here, and let our thoughts rest a-while on the great faith shown by Jo-seph and Ma-ry. What God told them to do they did at once. They did not wait, or stop to find fault with the task, or to speak of the hard-ships of their lot; but left all, and set forth with speed. God had bid them go, and they could not stay. He would take care of them, and keep them from all harm; for there is no place in the world where He is not.

Her-od was wroth when he found out how he had been mocked by the three wise men from the east. He was full of craft him-self, but he did not wish men do to him as he did to them. So he sent out to Beth-le-hem and the coasts a-round, and had all the boys put to death that were two years old or less. And there was great grief in the land.

But Her-od was struck down in the midst of his crimes; and one night an an-gel came to Jo-seph, and said, Rise, and take the young child and his moth-er and go to their own land, for they are dead who sought the young child's life. And he rose, and took the young child and his moth-er, and set out for Beth-le-hem. On the way he was met with the news that the worst of Her-od's four sons was on the throne, and he feared for his child's life, and went to Gal-i-lee and to a place called Naz-a-reth, for God so willed it.

CHAPTER II.

THE HOME AT NAZ-A-RETH.

THERE is not one of us but would like to know how Jesus looked when a child. His home was in Gal-i-lee in the midst of a poor class of Jews, and of Greeks and Arabs that were not thought much of by the rest of the world. Here he lived, and we are left to think that he

HOUS-ES IN NAZ-A-RETH.

played like the rest of boys of his age, but in a sweet mild way. For we are told that he loved all men, and all men loved the pure child who showed by all his acts that he had a kind heart, and a fine mind.

Naz-a-reth stood on high ground, as did most, if not all, the towns of the East, and was shut in by the hills a-round. There were no schools here, and no chance for boys or girls to learn much out-side of their own homes. For they would have to pay those who taught them, and were too

NAZ-A-RETH.

poor to do that. But each man was as a priest in his own house, and taught his boys to read, or read to them from the Books of the Law.

These books were called Scrolls, and were made of parch-ment. Parch-ment is made from the skin of calves, kids, and lambs, and is so tough and strong that it will last for a long long time. The men who wrote out and taught the Laws, that had come down to the Jews from the time of Mo-ses, were known as Scribes. Ink, such as we use, was not known of in those days, and some times the Scribes smeared a board with thin wax and wrote out with a sharp tool the words they wished to have read. Then this wax could be rubbed smooth, and not a trace be left of the words that were there; and Da-vid had this in mind when he wrote in one of his Psalms, O God, blot out my sins. And we are told that God said to Moses, He who hath sinned, him will I blot out of my book.

CAR-PEN-TER'S SHOP.

But this wax could not be rolled up and put a-way as the

HIS HUMBLE TRADE.

scrolls were; and on those some sort of juice must have been used that left a stain that would not wash out.

Jo-seph had to work at his trade, and Ma-ry had her hands full of house-hold cares, and Je-sus no doubt helped both of them at their tasks, and then went with them to church on the Sab-bath day.

CHRIST BROUGHT BY HIS PAR-ENTS.

It was the rule a-mong all the Jews, rich and poor, to have their sons taught some kind of a trade when they were twelve years of age, so that they could take care of them-selves when they were grown up. As Jo-seph was a car-pen-ter, we can but think that Je-sus learned the same trade, and worked at it for quite a long term of years. All the boys too were well taught in the Law, and knew all the feast days and fast days, and not a few of the Psalms of Da-vid.

Once a year, the Jews went up to Je-ru-sa-lem to keep the feast of the pass-o-ver. The time for this is in the spring of the year, and when Jo-seph and Ma-ry went they took Je-sus with them. He was then twelve years old.

FORMS OF TAB-ER-NA-CLES, BOOTHS, OR TENTS, USED IN THE EAST.

The feast was kept up for a week, and the crowds that flocked there were so great that there was not room for them in the town. So they made booths of mats, boughs, and leaves, which gave them a place to rest in by night or day.

When the feast was at an end, Jo-seph and Ma-ry set out for their home, with the rest of the Jews that came

TAUGHT FROM THE WORD OF GOD.

from the same town, or those near at hand. As thieves lay in wait on the road to rob, and if need be, to kill those who came their way, it was not safe for men to go off a-lone. But they all went in one great band, and marched to the sound of drums and sweet toned bells, and stopped now and then to eat some of the dates, or cool fruits, and to drink from the wells and streams that sprang up in their path.

The wom-en and the old men rode on horse-back, or on mules, while the young men, with long sticks in their hands, led by a string the beasts whose backs were well packed with jugs and all sorts of house-hold goods. The boys and girls would some-times walk by the side of their par-ents, and when they were tired get a lift on horse and mule.

Jo-seph and Ma-ry thought, of course, that Je-sus was with the rest of the young folks, or with some group of friends; but when night came and they could not find him they were in great grief. The next day they left their friends, and went back to Je-ru-sa-lem, and searched for him on the way, but he was not to be seen, and for three days they sought for him in vain.

At last they went up in-to a porch of the Tem-ple, where some of the Rab-bis—or learned Jews—had their schools, and there they found him calm and well-pleased in the midst of the great priests, and seemed more wise than they.

Jo-seph and Ma-ry were awe-struck at the sight, for they did not think that a child of theirs would be so bold. Ma-ry was grieved too that so good a boy should cause them so much pain, and she said to him, Child, why hast thou

JE-SUS IN THE TEM-PLE.

The Home at Naz-a-reth.

thus dealt with us? Thy fath-er and I sought thee with tears.

Je-sus said to them, Why did ye seek me? Did ye not know that I am where my Fa-ther meant me to be? They did not know what he meant by these words, and thought it strange that he should speak thus. And he went down with them, and came to Naz-a-reth, and was a good son in whom no fault could be found.

He learned to read and to write, but more than all that he learned to do God's will. Home is the school of life. Here we are placed to learn to give up all thoughts of self, to think more of oth-ers, to fix our hearts up-on things that are good and pure, and to grow each day more and more like Je-sus.

PALMS AND FRUITS OF PAL-ES-TINE.

The Home at Naz-a-reth.

There were no schools at Naz-a-reth, but if there had been Je-sus could not have gone to one, for he was a poor lad.

FIGS AND DATE PALMS.

But he learned more than could be taught in the schools, and there was not an hour of the day that he did not fit him-self for his life work. He took note of the birds, and knew their ways, and what they were sold for. He knew all a-bout the trees, and fruits, and when was the time to look for figs. He saw, too, how the folks lived, and what was the cause of much of their strife and ill-will. He knew all a-bout seed-time and har-vest, and as his feet trod the hill-side he saw in each blade of grass, in each ear of corn, fresh proof of God's love, and his kind care of man. Not a thing did he lose sight of, for all would be of use to him in the days to come.

He did not lie round and dream, and fret, or wish that he had wealth and could go out in-to the world. He knew that where God had put him was the place where he ought to be, and he made the best of it, and was the light and joy of his home. He worked with his hands, as he grew in size and strength, and made ploughs or yokes for those who had need of them. He did not make those feel who lived near him that he was bet-ter than they, and not one of them guessed that the youth who grew up in their midst was to be crowned as king, and reign on high.

THE ROLL-ER BIRD.

Ah, how strange it is to think of Je-sus as a boy! and what a sweet boy he must have been! not cross, or rude, or self-willed, but quick to see where he could be of use; prompt to do as he was bid, and at all times full of kind thoughts and good deeds. And what a home of peace that must have been where Je-sus lived! How bright the light that shone a-round! How near to the land where God lives, and all good an-gels dwell!

While Je-sus was at Naz-a-reth, the world out-side grew rank with sin, and good men were in great fear of the wrath to come. The Jews were hard pushed, and it seemed as if their race was to die out, crime was ripe in the land.

JOHN THE BAP-TIST.

Men had grown hard of heart, and seemed not to care to do right, or to feel the least shame if they did wrong. Some change must come soon to break up this sort of life, and to bring in the pure fresh air where all was foul and rank, and not fit to breathe.

FORDS OF THE JOR-DAN.

All the years that Je-sus was at Naz-a-reth, John, who was near his own age, had led an out-door life, and learned the lore of the woods. The men who taught in school or in church, were smooth in their speech, and wore long robes, and spoke in such a mild way, that those who did not care to hear might go to sleep if they chose.

WIL-DER-NESS OF JU-DE-A.

But when John spoke, his voice rang through the woods, and men came from far and near to hear him, and then went home to talk a-bout him. The hour had come for him to teach men the way of life, and the force of the man soon made it-self felt through that part of the land of Ju-de-a.

Who was he? Where had he come from? Who had taught him all these things? He had been at God's school. He had lived on plain food, and drank from the pure streams that flowed down from the hills. His clothes were coarse and plain, and there were no signs of wealth by which he might hope to win friends for him-self or his cause. But it was soon noised a-bout that in the wild lands of Ju-de-a there lived a man whose words it was worth while to hear. Rich and poor, scribes and priests, Jews and Gen-tiles, all flocked to the fords of the Jor-dan, where the stream ran low, as this was the place where he preached.

They were moved by the charm of his voice. His words struck hard blows on their hearts of flint, and then burnt their way in like coals of fire. They could not get rid of them. They had read in the Book of the Proph-ets that one should cry out, Pre-pare ye the way of the Lord, make his paths straight. That which is low shall be raised up, and that which is high shall be brought down, the crook-ed shall be straight, and the rough ways shall be smooth, and all flesh shall see the glo-ry of the Lord.

But John said more than this. He used plain words, and called them hard names. He told those who were proud of their birth, proud that A-bra-ham was their fa-ther, that as God made Ad-am out of the dust of the earth, out of the stones in the road, he could raise up chil-dren to A-bra-ham. They were to look up to God, and to trust in him to save them from their sins. For now, he said, is the axe laid to the root of the trees, and each tree that brings not forth good fruit is hewn down and cast in-to the fire.

Those who stood near asked, What then shall we do? John said to them, He that hath two coats, let him give to him that hath none; and he that hath meat, let him give to those who have no food. Then the tax-men came to be bap-tized, and asked John what they should do to be saved. He told them to take no more from men than was their due, for he knew that they were fond of wealth, and were not just and fair at all times.

When those came who had learned the art of war, and asked John what they ought to do, he told them not to use their strength to vex and to harm those they were set o-ver, nor to play the spy, and tell false tales, but to do the work they had to do, and find no fault with the pay.

Those who came to hear John preach, thought that he might be the Christ whom they had long looked for. But he said to them all, I in-deed bap-tize you with wa-ter, but he that is to come—whose shoe-strings I am not worth-y to un-loose—He shall bap-tize you not with wa-ter, but with the Ho-ly Ghost and fire. His fan is in his hand, and he will cleanse his floor, and save the wheat, but the chaff he will burn up.

Those who heard, knew what this meant. They did not thresh grain in those days as we do now. The floor was a round space on the farm, where the ground was made hard, or paved with stones, and the grain was trodden out by hor-ses or ox-en. Then the chaff was blown off with a sort of fan, and the good wheat was saved, and the rest burned. So a-bout the axe that was laid to the root of the trees. Well they knew that this meant that those who did not do right and please God, would be cut down in their sins and feel the force of God's wrath.

BANKS OF THE JOR-DAN.

The fame of John had reached the small town of Naz-a-reth, and Je-sus went out to hear him preach. And when he came to the banks of the Jor-dan John knew him not for it was the first time the two had met. Yet there must have been some-thing in his look which awed the soul of John, for when Je-sus came to him to be bap-tized he said, Why dost thou come to me? I have need to be bap-tized by thee.

Je-sus said, Let it be so now, that we may both do what is right for us. And John bap-tized him. And as Je-sus went up out of the wa-ter, a great light shone out of the sky, that took the form of a dove, and spread its wings of flame o-ver his head. And a voice out of the sky said, so that all who stood by could hear it, This is my be-loved Son, in whom I am well pleased.

ONE OF THE FORDS OF THE JOR-DAN.

The next day, as John stood on the bank of the Jor-dan with two of his dis-ci-ples—or those whom he taught—he saw Je-sus, and said, Be-hold the lamb of God! And the two men, when they heard him, left John and went af-ter Je-sus. And Je-sus turned and saw them be-hind him, and said to them, What seek ye? They said to him, Mas-ter, where dost thou live? He said to them, Come and see. They came and saw where he dwelt, and staid with him for the rest of the day, for it was near the hour of noon. One of these, named An-drew, went to his broth-er Pe-ter, and said to him, We have found the Christ, and he brought him to Je-sus.

THE RIV-ER JAB-BOK.

The Jor-dan has its rise in the high hills of the north, and flows down in-to the Dead Sea, which the A-rabs called the SEA OF LOT be-cause it was in the vale of Sod-om where Lot chose to dwell. The springs, ponds, lakes,

ON THE DEAD SEA.

and streams that feed the Dead Sea are all fresh, and the grass grows on their banks, and the birds sing in the trees near by. But the Dead Sea it-self is so salt that noth-ing can live in it, and no trees or plants can take root on its shores save on the east side, where here and there is a deep gorge, and fresh wa-ter springs.

DEAD SEA.

The north shore of this sea, or lake, is a great mud flat, where lie the black trunks and boughs of trees with the thick coat of salt on them, that all things have in the reach of the spray from the Dead Sea. High cliffs are on the west side, but the south shore is low, flat, and like a great marsh, or swamp, and the air not fit to breathe. It was for some time thought that the air of the Dead Sea would be sure death to all who went near it, and it may have been this that gave the sea its name. But the old tale has been proved false, for birds fly there and sing their songs,

DEAD SEA BY MOON-LIGHT.

and men have gone there, and bathed in the Dead Sea that they might find out for them-selves if all that was said of it was true.

Je-sus left the banks of the Jor-dan to seek a place where he could fast and pray, and be a-lone with God.

The Home at Naz-a-reth.

And he went in-to the lands where wild beasts roam at will, and was there for for-ty days and for-ty nights, by

TEMP-TA-TION IN THE DES-ERT.

which time he was quite weak and in need of food. Then the dev-il came and said to him—for he is sure to come when we have the least strength—If thou art the Son of

God, speak the word, and change these stones to loaves of bread. Je-sus said, It is writ-ten, Man shall not live by bread a-lone, but by the words that come out of the mouth of God.

TEMP-TA-TION ON THE MOUN-TAIN.

Then the dev-il took him up to Je-ru-sa-lem and led him to a high place in the Tem-ple, and said to him, If thou art the Son of God cast thy-self down, for it is writ-ten, He shall give his an-gels charge o-ver thee, and in their hands they shall bear thee up, so that no harm shall come to thee. Je-sus said to him, a-gain it is writ-ten, Thou shalt not tempt the Lord thy God.

Then the dev-il took him up to the top of a high mount, and showed him all the broad realms of the earth, and the wealth that was there out-spread. And he said to him, All these things will I give thee, if thou wilt bow down to me and serve me. Then said Je-sus to him, Get thee hence, Sa-tan be-gone—for it is writ-ten, Thou shalt bow down be-fore the Lord thy God, and Him a-lone shalt thou serve. Then the dev-il left him, and lo, an-gels came and brought him the food of which he stood in need.

Sa-tan comes to tempt us to do wrong, to make gods of our-selves, and to lean up-on our own strength. He brings us books that he says will do us as much good to read as will God's Word, and when we are weak we can feed up-on them. He gives us stones for bread.

Then he comes and says, Why should you lead a pure life, and keep your-self so far from the world and its joys? There is no sense in it. Plunge in-to the depths of sin; stain your-self as black as you choose; go with the bad, and with those who do dark deeds, and no harm shall come to you. Do not lean so much on God. Learn to take care of your-self, for in that way shall a man gain strength, and be of some good in the world. In this way does Sa-tan tempt men out of the straight path.

When he finds that he can-not win them in this way, he leads them to a high place and shows them all the wealth of the world. He says to them, Do you see that house there?

It is the home of a rich man; and all those barns and fields are his, and he owns a great deal of land. You may have as much wealth as he has, ay, and much more, if you will lie and steal. He knows how hard men try to get rich, and how much they will do to add to their store of wealth, and he does his best to make them think that all they need in this life is Gold—Gold—and more Gold.

But that is not so. There is some-thing we need more than gold, and with-out which we are poor in-deed. And when Sa-tan comes to tempt us, to tell us what good times we will have if we make him our king and let him rule us, we must drive him a-way, and let him know that God shall be first in our hearts. And though we may be weak and prone to do wrong, as soon as we turn our backs on Sa-tan, and vow that we will serve him no more, God sends his an-gels down to give us the strength we need to help us fight this foe.

He meets us at all points, and if we yield to him we are lost. He spreads nets for our feet. We must take care how and where we walk. He has soft words for the ear. We must be deaf to them. He charms the eye with gems that flash and blaze; but they are not real gems as we find out to our cost, when we have lost the one pearl that was worth them all. A pure heart is the pearl of great price.

CHAPTER III.

JE-SUS AND JOHN PREACH AND TEACH.

Je-sus and his friends came to the land of Ju-de-a, and he staid there with them, and bap-tized. And John was at a place near Sa-lim, where there were fine clear streams of wa-ter, and crowds came to him and were bap-tized. Now wa-ter will cleanse the out-side skin, but it will not make clean the heart. Bap-tism does not mean that one is thus made free from sin, but it is a sign that as wa-ter will cleanse the flesh, so will Christ make white and clean the soul that trusts in him.

Now at this time there was quite a stir on the part of John's friends, be-cause Je-sus drew more men to hear him preach. And they came to John and said, Mas-ter, he that was with thee on the banks of the Jor-dan, and whose fame thou didst spread, now bap-ti-zes, and all men flock to him and not to thee.

John said, A man can have nought but what God gives him. You know your-selves that I said, I am not the Christ, but I am sent be-fore him. He that hath the bride is the bride-groom, but the friend of the bride-groom who stands and hears him, has joy at the sound of the bride-groom's voice. This my joy is filled to the full. My course is run. He must rise, but I must fall. This was a form of speech much used in the East. The

THE JORDAN VALLEY.

Church, or one who gave him-self to Christ, was called the bride. Christ was the bride-groom. Friends could share in his joy, and be glad that a soul was saved. This was the way John felt. And he went on to say that Je-sus came from a-bove, and was a-bove all, and to doubt his words was to doubt that God was true. For he had been sent to speak the words of God. God gave all things in-to his hands, and he that be-lieves in him, and trusts in him, has a share in God's love; and he who will not heed the words of Christ, or do His will, is sure to feel and know the wrath of God.

As soon as Je-sus found out that the Jews thought ill of him, he made up his mind to leave the place and go in-to Gal-i-lee, lest there should be strife in their midst, and John be made to feel that he had been wronged. And as he passed by the Jor-dan he saw two men, named Si-mon and An-drew, cast their nets in-to the sea, for their trade was to catch fish. Je-sus said unto them, Come with me, and I will make you fish-ers of men. And at once they left their nets and went with him. Was not this strange? They did not know who he was, they scarce knew what he meant, but some-thing in their hearts said Go, and they could not stay. That is the way to heed the call of Christ. When he says Come, we are to leave the nets in which we hope to gain the wealth of the world, and go with him, and do his work. The fish these men were to catch were the souls of those who led lives of sin, and would be lost if some one did not try to save them.

Then Je-sus went on and came to a place where he saw two men in a boat. Their names were James and John, and they were at work mend-ing their nets.

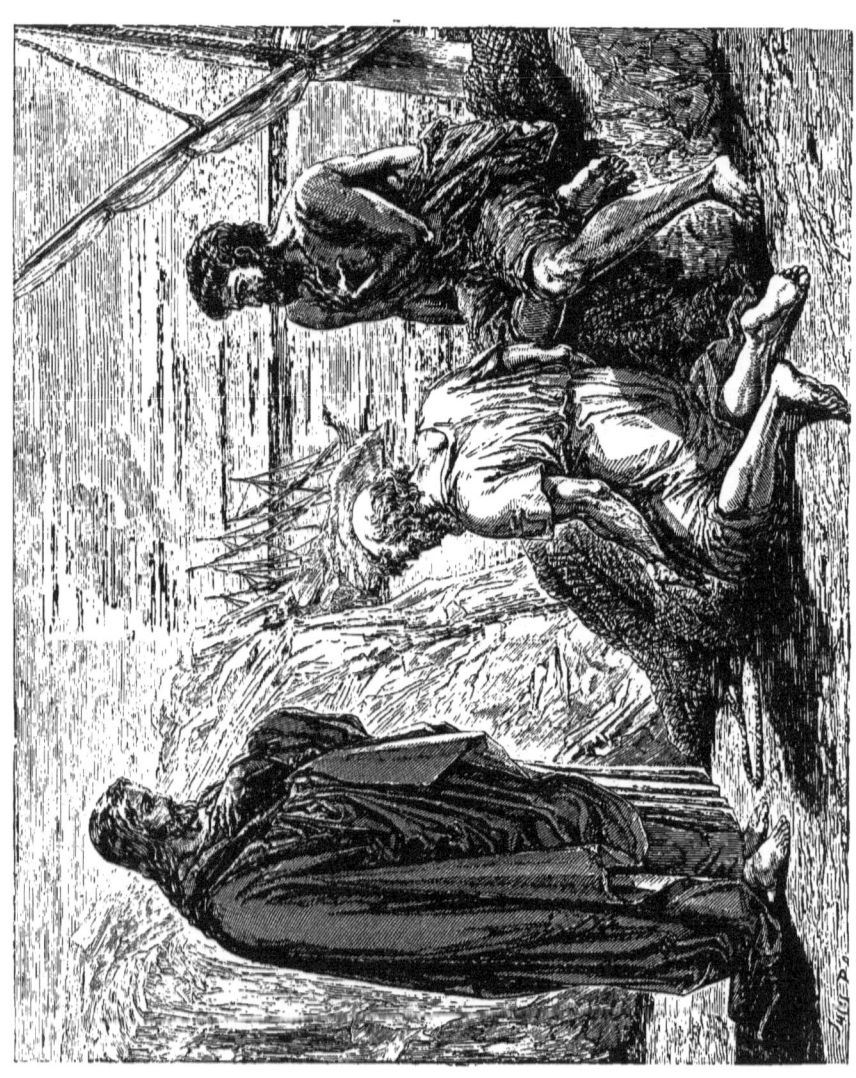

Je-sus called to them, and they left their fath-er, Zeb-e-dee, in the boat with the hired men, and went with him whom they knew to be their Lord. For he bore himself like a king, and the light that shone in his face made him seem more like God than man.

BOAT IN SEA OF GAL-I-LEE.

The next day when he was on his way to Gal-i-lee he found Phil-ip, and said to him, Come with me. And Phil-ip did so. And he had a friend Na-than-a-el to whom he said, We have found Him of whom Mo-ses in the law and the proph-ets did write—Je-sus of Naz-a-reth. Now Na-than-a-el knew Phil-ip, but did not know Christ, and he said, Can a good thing come out of Naz-a-reth? Phil-ip said to him, Come and see. When Je-sus saw Na-than-

CA-NA IN GAL.-I-LEE.

a-el draw near he said to him, Be-hold, a Jew in whom there is no guile! He meant that he was a good man, who thought not of self, but led a pure life and wished to do what was right. And on the way he had stopped 'neath a fig tree to think and to pray, for his heart was moved by the thought that Christ was so near, and that he was to see him face to face.

Na-than-a-el heard the words that Je-sus spoke, and he said to him, What canst thou have heard of me? Je-sus said un-to him, Be-fore Phil-ip called thee, when thou wast un-der the fig tree, I saw thee. Na-than-a-el said, Mas-ter, Thou art the Son of God, Thou art King of the Jews.

Je-sus said un-to him, Be-cause I said un-to thee, I saw thee un-der the fig tree, dost thou believe in me? thou shalt see great-er things than these. Tru-ly, tru-ly I say unto you, ye shall see heav-en o-pen and the an-gels of God that wait up-on the Son of man. These things he was to see with the eye of faith, and the thought that Je-sus had searched him and knew his thoughts brought Na-than-a-el at once to his knees with the cry, Thou art the Son of God!

On the third day there was a wed-ding at Ca-na, a small town in Gal-i-lee, and the moth-er of Je-sus was there. And they bade Je-sus come al-so, and bring his new friends with him. So great was the crowd of guests that the wine gave out, and the moth-er of Je-sus said to him, They have no wine. Je-sus said to her, Wom-an, what is that to thee and me? mine hour is not yet come.

His moth-er said to the ser-vants, What he tells you to do, that do. Now there were in the court-yard six great stone pots, or jars, each one of which would hold a great deal of wa-ter. Je-sus said un-to the ser-vants, Fill the wa-ter pots with wa-ter. And they filled them up to the brim. And he said to them, Draw now, and bear to the ru-ler of the feast. And they bare it. The ru-ler of the feast—the one who had charge of all things—took a taste of the wa-ter that was made wine, and knew not where it had come from—though the ser-vants who had drawn the wa-ter knew. And he called to the bride-groom, and said to him, As a rule men first set forth the good wine,

FILL THE WA-TER-POTS.

and when their guests have drunk so much that their taste is not keen, they bring on that which is worse. But thou hast kept the good wine un-til now.

This, the first sign of his pow-er, was wrought in Ca-na, of Gal-i-lee, and it showed forth his glo-ry, and his dis-ci-ples be-lieved that he was the Son of God.

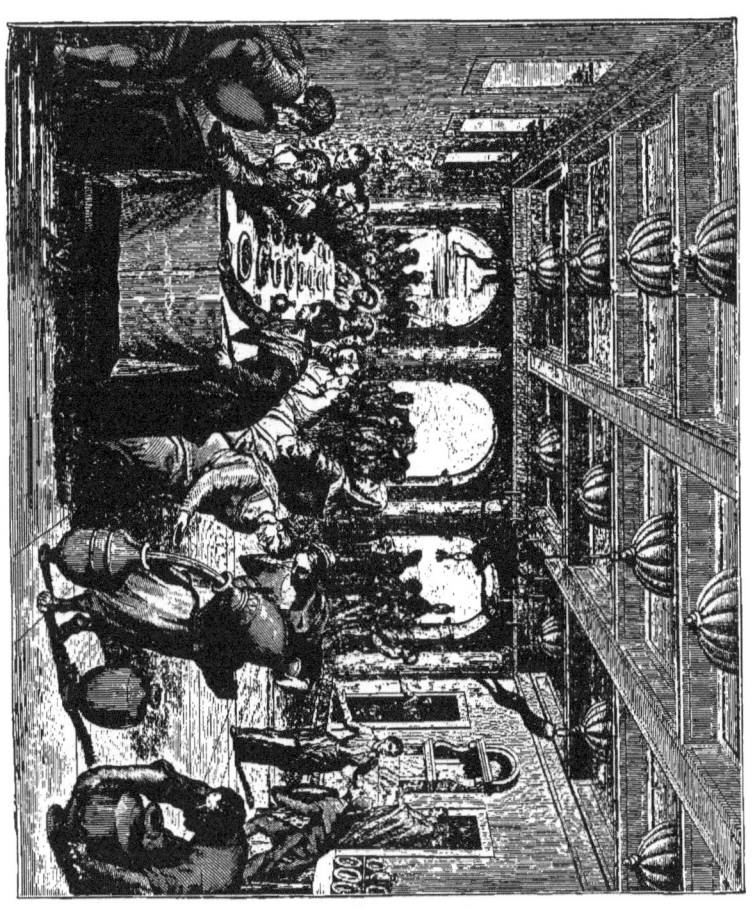

JE-SUS TURNS WA-TER IN-TO WINE.

From Ca-na Je-sus went to Ca-per-na-um, and his moth-er, his breth-ren, and his dis-ci-ples went with him, and they staid there for a few days. And the pass-o-ver of the Jews was at hand, and Je-sus went up with the rest of them and to the great feast at Je-ru-sa-lem. So vast was the crowd that it filled all the space in front of the church and flowed out in-to the streets that led up to it. On both sides of the great gate on the east, and as far as Sol-o-mon's porch, there were shops where knick-knacks could be bought, as well as ox-en, sheep, and doves to of-fer up on the al-tar. Here, too, were banks, where those who had not the right kind of coin,

RUINS OF CA-NA OF GAL-I-LEE.

might change their brass and cop-per for the small sil-ver piece they would have to give to the priest.

But such was the greed of gain, that men grew bold and pushed their way in-to the sa-cred parts of the Tem-ple, and sold their wares to all who would come and buy. Here were pens filled with sheep and ox-en, the stench and filth from which must have made its way in-to the church. All a-round were ca-ges filled with doves, and the loud talk of those who bought and sold, and the clink, clink of the coin broke in oft up-on the chants and the prayers of the priests, so that they could scarce be heard.

It was not strange that Je-sus should be wroth at such a scene as this. A well-brought-up Jew was made to feel that the church of God was a sa-cred place, from which the world, and the thoughts of the world, should be shut out. It was a great sin for them to buy and sell in this place, and they knew it, but so great was their haste to be rich, that they paid no heed to the Word of God, or the laws laid down for them. The clink of gold was far more sweet to their ears than the prayers of the saints, or their sweet-toned psalms. Christ can-not be where such things are. He must drive them out, or they will drive him out. He made a scourge, or whip of small cords and first drove out the sheep and ox-en and the low crowd that had charge of them. And he threw down the heaps of coin that had been piled up, and up-set the ta-bles that had served as banks. And he said to those that sold doves, Take these things hence; make not God's house a place to buy and sell goods.

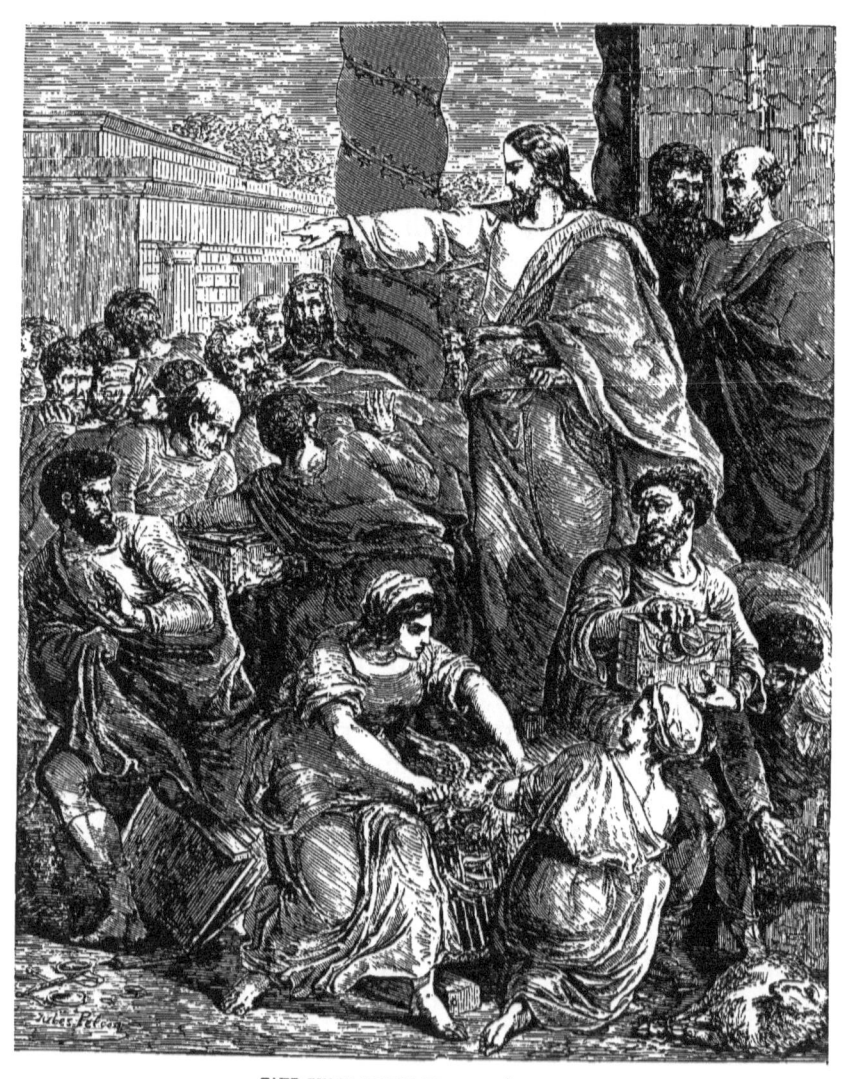

TAKE THESE THINGS FROM GOD'S HOUSE.

All did as they were told. Not one dared to turn and face his wrath and scorn. But the Jews said, By what sign wilt thou show us that thou hast a right to do this thing? Je-sus said to them, Pull down this tem-ple, and in three days I will raise it up. The Jews said, It took for-ty six years to build this temple, and wilt thou raise it up in three days? But Je-sus spoke of him-self as the tem-ple—the place where God dwelt—and when he was raised from the dead his dis-ci-ples brought to mind these words that he spoke to them, and they had faith in the Word of God, and in what Je-sus had said.

Now there were in Je-ru-sa-lem, as there are in all large towns, men of strange views, who formed them-selves in-to bands, or sects. Those who were well versed in the law, and taught it to those who were not, were known as Scribes. Those who thought they were bet-ter than the rest of folks, be-cause they went to all the fasts and feasts, and spent most of their time in church, and made long pray-ers so that men could see how good they were, were known as Phar-i-sees. Then there were three score and ten Jews who formed a sort of court, where men were judged by strict rules. This court was called the San-he-drim.

And rich and poor, scribes and priests, were there at the time of the feast, and had faith in Je-sus when they saw the won-ders that he did. But Je-sus put no trust in their faith, and did not need to be told of their good works, for he read the hearts of all men.

There was a man of the Phar-i-sees named Nic-o-de-mus, a ru-ler of the Jews. He came to Je-sus by night,

JE-SUS AND NIC-O-DE-MUS.

and said un-to him, Mas-ter, we know that thou art a teach-er come from God; for no one can do these signs that thou do-est if God be not with him.

Je-sus said, If a man be not born a-new he can-not see the king-dom of God. Nic-o-de-mus said to him, How can a man be born when he is old? Je-sus said, I say to thee, If a man be not born of wa-ter and spir-it he can-not en-ter the king-dom of God. That which is born of flesh, is flesh; and that which is born of the spir-it is spir-it. Think it not strange that I said to thee, Ye must be born a-new. The wind blows as it will, and thou dost hear the sound; but canst not tell whence it comes not where it goes. So is he that is born of the spir-it. Je-sus meant by this that when God breathed up-on the heart of man, the change was so great that he was like one new-born, for the things he once loved he loved no more, and his whole aim was to serve God and to live with him.

Nic-o-de-mus asked, How can these things be? Je-sus said to him, Thou art a teach-er of the Jews, and hast thou not seen these things? I say un-to thee, We speak that we do know, and bear wit-ness of that which we have seen, and ye be-lieve not. If I have told you of the things of earth and ye be-lieve not, how shall ye be-lieve if I tell you of the things of heav-en. No one hath gone up to heav-en but he that came out of heav-en, the Son of man. And as Mo-ses raised up the ser-pent, e-ven so must the Son of man be raised up on high, that all those who be-lieve in him shall live for-ev-er.

For God so loved the world that he gave his own Son, that all who be-lieved in him should be saved from death to live with God in his home on high. For God sent not his Son in-to the world to judge the world, but that the world through him might be saved. He that be-lieves in him is not judged; but he that be-lieves not has been judged be-cause he has not had faith in the Son of God. And this is the judg-ment, that light is come in-to the world, and men loved dark-ness more than they did the light be-cause their deeds were wick-ed. For he that is wick-ed hates the light, and comes not near it lest his deeds be found out. But he that does right and has the truth in his heart, comes to the light that his deeds may be made known, that men may see the work of God has been wrought in him.

How true this is! How well Je-sus knew the hearts of men! Those who love sin, hide them-selves in the day-time, and steal out at night like beasts of prey, to do the dark deeds they love so well. Those who have done wrong fear the Judge and dread to meet him. But those who love Christ, and put their trust in him, and try to do as he would have them, need have no fear of death, or of Him who will judge the world on the last day.

CHAPTER IV.

JE-SUS AT THE WELL.

It was the hour of noon. The heat was great. Je-sus had been long on the road, and was quite worn out when he came near the town of Sy-char (*si-kar*). And there was a well close at hand, or a fount, which was known as Ja-cob's well, and as he was tired Je-sus sat down to rest on the low wall that was built round it. Those who came with him, had gone in-to the town to buy food, and while he sat there all a-lone, a wom-an came out of the town to draw wa-ter from the well.

Je-sus said to her, Give me to drink. The wom-an said to him, How is it that thou, a Jew, can ask drink of of me, a Sa-mar-i-tan wom-an? for thou must know that the Jews have nought to do with our race.

Je-sus said to her, If thou didst know me, and who it is that saith, Give me to drink, thou wouldst have asked of him, and he would have given thee liv-ing wa-ter.

A fresh spring, or a clear stream that ran a-long by the banks of trees, was called liv-ing wa-ter. There was life and health in it, for those who came to quaff at the brink. And this was in her mind when Je-sus spoke of a gift of liv-ing wa-ter. How was it to be dug? Where was it to come from?

SY-CHAR.

Je-sus meant that those who come to him, and be-lieve in him, should have in them a fount of strength and joy. He is the source and spring of all life's joys. He is the

AN OLD WELL.

gift of God, a well set in a dry place to quench the thirst of all man-kind.

But the wom-an did not know this, and she said to him, Sir, thou hast noth-ing to draw with, and the well is deep; from whence then hast thou that liv-ing wa-ter? Art thou as great as Ja-cob who gave us this well, and who drank of it him-self, and his sons, and his flocks and herds?

Je-sus said to her, He who drinks of this wa-ter shall thirst a-gain, but he who drinks of the wa-ter that I shall give him shall thirst no more; but the wa-ter that I shall

RUINS OF THE TEM-PLE OF MA-NAS-SEH.

give him shall be like a fount whose springs fail not, but give life for-ev-er and ev-er.

The wom-an said to him, Sir, give me this wa-ter, that I thirst not, nor have to come all the way here to draw from this well. Je-sus said to her, Go, call thy hus-band, and come here. The wom-an said, I have no hus-band.

Je-sus saith to her, Thou hast well said I have no hus-band; for thou hast had five hus-bands, and he whom thou now hast is not thy hus-band. In this thou hast told the truth.

The Jews said that Je-ru-sa-lem was the place in which to meet and give praise and thanks to God, for there had

MOUNT GER-I-ZIM.

Sol-o-mon built his tem-ple. But those of her race thought that Mount Ger-i-zim was the true place, for there did Josh-u-a bless God, and there did A-bra-ham bring his son I-saac, to put him to death if such had been God's will.

Here was a good chance to set this old-time doubt at rest. With her hand raised, and her gaze fixed on the high mount near them on which could be seen the ru-ins of the old tem-ple of Ma-nas-seh, the wom-an said to Je-sus, Sir, I see that thou art a proph-et. All my race have been

FOOT OF MOUNT GER-I-ZIM.

wont to wor-ship on this mount; but ye say that Je-ru-sa-lem is the place where men ought to wor-ship.

Je-sus said to her, Be-lieve me, wom-an, that the time will come when ye shall not wor-ship God here nor in Je-ru-sa-lem. Ye wor-ship that which ye know not, but we wor-ship that which we know, be-cause the Jews have been taught of God. But the time will come when all those who wor-ship God will wor-ship in spir-it and in truth. They will give their whole hearts to him, for God seeks such to wor-ship him. God is spir-it—some-thing that is felt though not seen—and they that wor-ship him, must wor-ship in spir-it and truth.

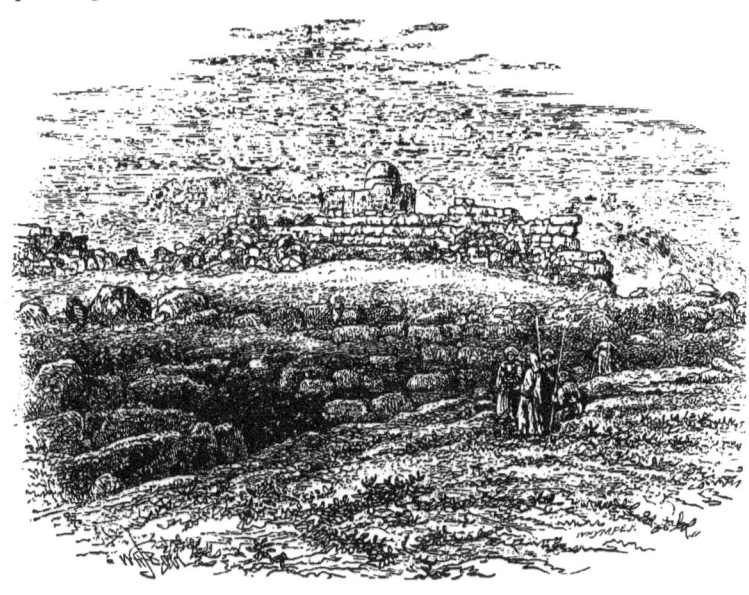

TOP OF MOUNT GER-I-ZIM.

The wom-an moved by his words said to him, I know that he who is called Christ is to come, and when he is come he will tell us all things. Je-sus said to here, I that speak un-to thee am he.

As he spoke these words his friends came back from the town, and were shocked to find that Je-sus had talked with a wom-an. For the Jews held it to be a sin for a Teach-er to speak to a wom-an on the street. Yet none of them dared ask him what he sought, or why he talked with her.

The wom-an, with her mind full of what she had heard, left her jar by the well and went back to the town, and said to those she met on the roads and streets, Come, see a man who told me all things that ev-er I did. Can this be the Christ? And they left the town at once, and went out to meet him.

In the mean-while the dis-ciples beg-ged him to rest, and to eat the food they had brought. But he said to them, I have meat to eat that ye know not. They looked at each oth-er and said, Can some one have brought him food? Je-sus said to them, My meat is to do the will of him that sent me, and fin-ish his work. Say not ye, There are yet four months, and then comes the har-vest? So, I say to you, Lift up your eyes, and look on the fields, for they are now white for the har-vest.

He that reaps is paid for his toil for he brings fruit, that is souls, to God; that both he that sows and he that reaps may share in the joy of the new life. For that which is said is true, One sows, and some one else reaps. I sent you to reap where you have not toiled. The work has been done, and you are to reap the fruits of their toil. These words were meant for all those who came af-ter Je-sus to do his work.

Some of those who came out from the town to see Je-sus, had faith in him be-cause of what the wom-an told. But there were still more who be-lieved when they heard him preach, and they said to the wom-an, Now we be-lieve, not be-cause of what thou told us, but we have heard

GAL-I-LEE.

him for our-selves, and know that he is the One who has come to save the world. And they urged Je-sus to make his home with them, and he staid there for two days.

At the end of two days he set out once more and came in-to Gal-i-lee, and taught from place to place as he went

GAL-I-LEE.

Je-sus at the Well.

on his way. His fame had gone out be-cause of the great things he had done at Ca-na, and at Je-ru-sa-lem at the time of the feast, and crowds thronged to see and to hear him.

He came to the town of Naz-a-reth where he had been brought up, and on the Sab-bath day went in-to the

STREET IN NAZ-A-RETH.

church where he used to wor-ship in the days of his youth, and stood up to read. On one side of the church sat the men; on the oth-er sat the wom-en, with long veils from their head to their feet.

106   Je-sus at the Well.

The Books of the Law, the Books of the Proph-ets, the Psalms and the rest of the Word of God, were on

A JEW-ISH SYN-A-GOGUE,

rolls of parch-ment, and in charge of the head man of the church, who was called the ru-ler. The ru-ler gave to our

Lord a roll, or book, of one of the chief proph-ets. And when he un-rolled the book his eye fell upon these words: and as he read all those in the church stood up to hear him:

The spir-it of the Lord is upon me, be-cause he sent me to bring good news to the poor, to heal the sick, to loose the chains of those who are bound, to give sight to the blind, to set free those that are bruised, and to tell them that Christ has come.

And he closed the book and gave it back to the ru-ler and sat down. And the eyes of all in the church were fixed on him, and he said, This day have these words come true that ye have heard. He spoke with so much grace that for some time they were held spell-bound; but it was not long be-fore their looks changed, and they be-gan to show signs of hate.

And they said, Is not this Jo-seph's son? Did he not live here with us, and grow up in our midst? What does he know? How can he teach us? Je-sus said to them, No doubt ye will say to me this prov-erb, If thou canst heal oth-ers, heal thy-self; and what thou hast done in Ca-per-na-um do here in thine own land. And he said, I say to you, No proph-et has fame in his own land.—He meant that he could not work here as he could at Ca-per-na-um. —But of a truth I say to you that scores of wid-ows were in Is-ra-el in the days of E-li-jah, when there was a great drought in the land and food was scarce for three years and six months. But to none of these was he sent, save to the one that dwelt in the land of Si-don.

And there were hosts of lep-ers in the time of E-li-sha, the prophet, and yet none of them was cleansed but Naa-man, from the land of Syr-i-a (*seer-e-ah*). All those in the church, when they heard these things, were filled with wrath; and they rose up and cast him forth out of the town, and led him to the top of the hill on which Naz-a-reth is built, that they might throw him down head-long. But his hour had not yet come, and he passed through their midst and went on his way.

HILLS AROUND NAZ-A-RETH.

Je-sus came to Ca-na where he had changed the wa-ter in-to wine. And there was a rich man, at Her-od's court, whose son was sick at Ca-per-na-um. When he heard that Je-sus had come out of Ju-de-a in-to Gal-i-lee, he went to him and beg-ged him to come down and heal his son.

Je-sus said to him, If ye do not see signs and won-ders ye will not be-lieve. The rich man said to him, Lord, come down ere my child die. Je-sus said to him, Go thy way; thy son lives. The man be-lieved the word that Je-sus spoke to him, and went on his way. And as he was on the road to his own home, his slaves met him, and told him that his son lived. Then he asked of them the hour that he showed signs that he was on the mend. They told him the hour that the fe-ver left him, and the fath-er knew it was the same hour in which Je-sus said to him, Thy son lives. And he and all his house had faith in Je-sus, and felt in their hearts that he must be the Son of God.

From Ca-na, Je-sus went on to Ca-per-na-um, and on the Sab-bath day went in-to the church and taught there. And those that heard him were held spell-bound by the charm of his voice, for he taught them as one who had strength from on high, and not in the dull way that the scribes were wont to speak.

All at once, in the midst of the hush that filled the church, there rose a wild shriek that made each one start and shake with fear. A poor man, who had a de-mon in him that made him do strange things, had crept in-to the church with the throng. And he cried out, Let us a-lone! What have we to do with thee, thou Je-sus of Naz-a-reth? Art thou come to put us to death? I know thee who thou art; the Son of God!

Je-sus turned, and said to the de-mon in the man, Hold thy peace, and come out from him. Then the man fell to the ground and writhed and screamed in the grasp of the de-mon. But soon he rose up and was cured; and all who saw him were struck with awe, and they said, What is this word? For with strange pow-er he bids the dev-ils come out and they do his will. And his fame spread through all the land.

When Je-sus left the church he went to the house of Si-mon. And the moth-er of Si-mon's wife was ill, and she had a high fe-ver, and the friends beg-ged him to give her ease. Je-sus stood by her bed-side, and touched her hand, and the fe-ver left her. And at once she rose up well and strong, and made haste to serve the Lord.

As soon as the sun went down, all they that had sick folks brought them to Je-sus, and he laid his hands on each one of them and made them well. And de-mons came out from those they had held in a strong grip, and they cried out, Thou art the Son of God! And he made them dumb, be-cause they knew that he was the Son of God.

Worn out with his toil, for they gave him no rest night or day, Je-sus rose at dawn, and went out of the town to a place where he could rest and pray. But it was not long ere the crowd went out in search of him; and Si-mon and those that were with him were in great fear lest some harm had come to him. They searched high and low, and when they found him, they beg-ged him not to leave the place, but to spend the rest of his days there.

Je-sus said to Si-mon and his friends, Come, let us go else-where in-to the next towns, that I may preach there. For to this end have I come forth. Still the crowd pressed on and Je-sus bent his steps to the sea-shore, and while he stop-ped to speak to them, Si-mon, An-drew, James and John went out in boats to catch some fish.

As Je-sus spoke, the throng pressed up-on him so that there was scarce room for him to stand; and he made a sign to Si-mon to push his boat to shore, that he might step

CHRIST HEALING THE SICK.

on board of it and preach to the crowd from that safe place.

When his talk was at an end, he said to Si-mon, Put out where it is deep, and let down your nets for a draught of fish. Si-mon said, Mas-ter, we have toiled all night, and took no fish, but at thy word I will let down the nets. And when they had done this, they caught such a haul of fish that their nets broke. And they called to James and John to come and help them.

FISH FROM LAKE OF GAL-I-LEE.

And they came, and both boats were filled with the load so that they be-gan to sink.

When Pe-ter saw it he fell down at the feet of Je-sus, and cried out, Leave my boat, for I am a man of sin, O Lord. For he was awe-struck, as were all those with him, at the vast haul of fish. And Pe-ter loathed him-self, and was in great fear.

Je-sus said to him, Fear not; from this time forth thou shalt catch men. And when they had brought their boats to land, they left all their spoils—the fish that lay in heaps, and shone in the light of the sun—and went with Je-sus, to help him in his work, and to share in his lot.

Now in all the large towns there was a place where the tax was to be paid. The Jews did not like to pay this tax, for it made them seem like slaves, and hurt their pride. The men who took the tax were called pub-li-cans, and oh, how the Jews did hate them! At or near Ca-per-na-um Je-sus found a man named Matthew, of the tribe of Le-vi, to whom all in that part of the land had to pay their tax. Je-sus knew how the Jews felt to such men, and more than all to one who was him-self a Jew, and wished to let them know that he called all un-to him and looked down on none. So he went to the place of toll and said to Mat-

THE DRAFT OF FISH-ES.

thew, Come with me. And he left all, and rose up and went with Je-sus. There is no doubt but that he had heard Je-sus preach. His words may have touched his heart. He had made up his mind to give up his sins and to lead a pure life, and when Je-sus said to him, Come, he could not hold back. Some-thing with-in him forced him to go, and do the Lord's work.

Je-sus at the Well.

We are not told of what he did, or where he went, but we know that he must have kept near to Je-sus and seen all that he did, and heard all that he said. All thoughts of self are cast out of his mind. He had been paid well

A MAN NAMED MAT-THEW.

by the Ro-mans, but he gave up wealth, and rank, for the sake of Je-sus. And great is the debt the world ows to him for the way in which he tells the good news, from the birth of Je-sus till his death up-on the cross.

CHAPTER V.

THE SER-MON ON THE MOUNT.

At the close of a day of toil, Je-sus, as was his wont, went up in-to the mount to pray, and spent the whole night there—a-lone with God. At dawn of day he called to him those who had kept with him and shown them-selves to be true friends. And from these he chose twelve, to whom he gave the name of A-pos-tles (A-pos-sels). Their names were Simon, (whom he named Pe-ter), and An-drew, and James, and John, and Phil-ip, Bar-thol-o-mew, and Mat-thew, and Thom-as, and James, Si-mon and Ju-das, and Ju-das Is-car-i-ot. These were to be a band of Christ-like men, to train them-selves to do his work, and to be sent out to do good in the world. And he came down with them, and stood on the low ground, and by this time a vast crowd had come up to hear him, and to be brought back to health. From the shores of the Sea of Gal-i-lee, from Ju-de-a and Je-ru-sa-lem, and from the far off coasts of Tyre and Si-don, they had come to touch him. For strength went out from him, and the sick were all made well.

At this time and place Christ gave his well-known Sermon on the mount, and the crowd sat down on the grass to hear what he had to say. And he taught them thus:

Bles-sed are the poor—those who are meek, and not puffed up with pride—for they have wealth that the world

TI-BE-RI-AS.

can-not give. Bles-sed are they that mourn—that weep for
their sins—for they shall be cheered and saved. Bles-sed
are the meek—the mild—for they shall have joy in this
world and the next. Bles-sed are they that hun-ger and
thirst for the Word of God, for they shall be filled. Bles-
sed are the kind and good, for God will be kind and good
to them. Bles-sed are the pure in heart, for they shall see
God. Je-sus meant by this that those who were free from
sin would live near to God here, and see Him face to face
when they left this world. Bles-sed are the peace-mak-ers
—those who are at peace with the world, and lead oth-ers
to make their peace with God—for they shall be called
Sons of God. Bles-sed are they that are ill used, and set
up-on when they strive to preach the good news, and to lead
men to do right, for they shall be well paid for all this in
the next world. Bles-sed are ye when men shall speak ill
of you, and vex you, and tell all kinds of lies a-bout you,
for my sake. Be glad with great joy, he said, for in heav-
en you will have your re-ward; for so did the Jews of old
brow-beat and back-bite the proph-ets who were be-fore
you.

Ye are the salt of the earth; but if the salt has lost its
taste, how can it be brought back a-gain? It is then
good for nought, but to be thrown out, and crushed un-der
foot. As salt is used to keep food, and to make it taste
less flat and stale, so those who love Christ and are called
by his name, are to keep the world free from sin, and from
that which spoils and drags men down.

Ye are the light of the world, Christ went on to say.
A cit-y set on a hill can-not be hid. Nor do men light a

THE SER-MON ON THE MOUNT.

lamp and set it where it can-not be seen, but put it on a stand where it gives light to all that are in the house. So let your light shine be-fore men that they may see your good works and praise God, whose sons you are. He told them that he had not come to do a-way with the Law, but to prove that the old Law was but an out-ward sign of the new Law of Love, which was to be in their hearts and in their thoughts.

GOLD-EN CAN-DLE-STICKS.

Ye have heard that it was said to them of old time, Thou shalt not kill. But I say un-to you, That he who hates with-out a cause, shall be in dan-ger of the fire of hell. They were not to call names, or to be in a rage, but must make friends with those near them, be-fore they could hope to make friends with God.

Je-sus told them that they were to sin not with the eye, nor to long for things they had no right to. For it was far bet-ter for them to give up all the good things of this life, than to lose their souls, and be cast out of the joys of heav-en.

The Jews thought that there was no harm in an oath, and that they need not keep their word with men, if they did not use the name of God. Je-sus said to them, Swear not at all. Not by heav-en, for it is the throne of God, nor by the earth for it is his foot-stool; nor by Je-ru-sa-lem for it is the cit-y of the great King. Nor shalt thou swear by thy head, for thou canst not make one hair white or black. But let your speech be pure and true, for more than this is proof of the sin that is in the world.

The old Law said, An eye for an eye, and a tooth for a tooth—what a man does to me must be done to him—but the new Law says, Strike not back, nor seek to harm those who have harmed thee; and give up more than the law has a right to seize, if by that means you can be at peace with all the world. Give to him that is in need, and from him that asks of thee a loan turn not thou a-way.

Ye have heard that it was said, Love your friends and hate your foes. But I say un-to you, Love your foes, bless them that curse you, do good to them that hate you, and pray for those who ill use you. That ye may be Sons of God; for He makes the sun to rise on the bad and the good, and sends rain on the just and the un-just. For it is no great thing to love those who love you, for the worst of men do that. And if you bow to none but your friends and those of your own race, or rank, can you call this a great thing, when e-ven those who know not Christ do the same? Be ye there-fore full of love, since God is love and ye are Sons of God.

Take heed that ye do not your alms be-fore men, to be seen of them, for those who do good to win the praise of men, do not in this way please God. When, there-fore, thou hast aught to give, do not make a noise a-bout it, in the church or on the street, as some folks do, that they may have the praise of men. This they have in full, but will get no more. But when thou hast aught to give, let not thy left hand know what thy right hand does. Let not those who are near and dear to thee know of all thy good deeds. Do them in such a way that they shall not be talked a-bout, or get in-to print. Some folks like to make a great show when they give to the poor, or to help the church. But this is not right. Je-sus says, Let not thy left hand know what thy right hand does—give with-out noise, or show. Do not hire the work done, but go out and do it thy-self, and God, who sees all things, will give thee the prize thou hast won at the last day.

When ye pray, do not be as those who court the praise of men, and have no real love of God in their hearts; for they love to stand and pray in the church, or in the street, that they may be seen of men. But thou, when thou pray-est, go in-to thy room, and when thou hast shut the door, pray to God, who is there with thee, and He will hear thee and be pleased with thee. And when ye pray use not words that have no sense, and say them as those do who bow down to gods of wood and stone. For they think there is a charm in the words, and the more times they say them the more chance there is that they will be heard. Be not like them, for God knows what ye have need of, be-fore ye ask him. We are not to tell God our needs, but to ask him to help us, and to show that we trust in him and know that he can do all things.

THE PART-RIDGE THAT FEEDS ON POOR SOIL.

Je-sus taught them how to serve God in all the acts of their lives. They were not to lay up stores of wealth on earth, where thieves break through and steal, but were to fix their thoughts on things a-bove, and seek to lead souls to Christ. No man can serve two mas-ters —one good and the oth-er bad. For if he loved the one he must hate the oth-er; and ye can-not serve God and the world at the same time. He told them not to be weighed down with the cares of life, nor to think too much of what they were to eat, and what they were to wear. For He who takes care of the birds of the air and gives them their food, and clothes, the flow-ers of the field so that their dress is far more rich than kings can wear, will feed and clothe all those who put their trust in Him. For are not ye more to Him than birds and flow-ers, and the grass of the field? Do not fret, then; for God knows what ye have need of. Seek first a pure heart. Live each day near to God, and do not show your want of trust in Him by doubts and fears. "God reigns, and all is right with the world."

They were not to be too harsh or strict when they judged men, and make them out worse than they were. But they were first to get rid of their own faults, and then they could see clear, and help men to get rid of their faults. He said they were to ask, that is, to pray for what they had need of, and God would hear and give them in his own right way.

If we ask for that which is not for our good, he will keep it back from us.

Some-times they might think that God's gifts were not the right kind, but if they knew how to give good gifts to their own chil-dren, how much more would God give good gifts to those who ask Him? They were to do to men as they would have men do to them.

THE PAR-TRIDGE THAT FEEDS ON RICH LANDS.

Je-sus said to them, Go ye in through the strait gate: for wide is the gate and broad the way that leads to death, and strait or nar-row, the way that leads to life.

All the towns of the East were built with a wall round them to keep out the foes. In these walls were gates which were kept shut at night, and no one could go in or out with-out be-ing seen by the sharp eyes of the watch-men who were placed on guard.

But in the day-time the gates stood wide, and the crowds poured in or out from dawn till dark. Je-sus meant to teach that the way the crowd went was not the right way to go. They are gay, and seek to please them-selves, more than they do to please God. It seems to them as if

STORK.

QUAIL.

the broad road was the right one to take, for there they have more room, and can lead a life of ease. And if they do wrong, no one will blame them, for all the rest do the same. But this broad road leads down hill. We start out all right. Then a small sin turns us from the right path, and we are caught in the flood-tide that bears us on to death.

These Jews, and all those to whom Christ spoke, thought that they were on the right road, and that all these forms, and out-side shows, would be sure to please God, and they would gain much good from His hands. But the wealth they sought was not the kind that makes men rich, and that out-lasts the things of time.

Je-sus meant by the strait gate, a hard rough road, where sharp stones bruised the feet, and thornes tore the flesh. No one can go through this gate with a load on his back. Is it a load of sin? Cast it off. Is it love of

THE GAL-LI-NULE.

dress? There is no chance to show off fine clothes. All the way is up-hill; and at first you may say, Why did I leave the broad smooth road? and Sa-tan may tempt you to turn back. But do not, I beg of you. The first steps are hard; but when strength gives out, or the path seems hedged in, pray, as those pray who are in great fear of their lives. Then the way will be made clear, and light will shine in where all was dark. Je-sus is near you at all

FLOWERS OF THE FIELD.

times. If he seems far off, it is be-cause you have turned from him. He has not turned from you, and will lead you, and guide you all through this life, and bring you home at last. We must lean on him, and trust in him, and feel that he knows what we need, and will help us in all our straits, if we but call on him.

WALL OF JE-RU-SA-LEM.

This is the course that all must take who love Christ. Not all those who call on the name of the Lord would be saved, but they must show by their lives which was false and which were true, and God would judge them at the Last Day.

The Ser-mon on the Mount.

Then he warned them that he who heard his words and did them, was like a man who built his house up-on a rock. And the rain fell, and the floods came, and the winds blew and beat up-on that house, and it fell not, for it was built up-on a rock. And he who hears my words and does them not, is like a man with no sense who built

DA-MAS-CUS GATE, JE-RU-SA-LEM.

his house up-on the sand. And the rain fell, and the floods came, and the winds blew, and smote up-on that house and it fell; and great was the fall of it.

And when Je-sus had brought his talk to a close, all those who heard him were in a state of awe, for he taught them as one who had come from God, and not as the scribes were wont to speak. He knew their lives, all their small faults and their great sins, and each word that he spoke, like a dart shot from a bow—went straight to its mark.

When he came down from the mount great crowds kept near him. And there came to him a lep-er, whose flesh was full of white sores so that he was shut out of the town, and a-way from all his friends! And this poor man fell on his knees at the feet of Je-sus, and cried out, Lord, if thou wilt, thou canst make me clean. At once Je-sus stretched forth his hand and touched the lep-er, and he was made clean. Je-sus said to him, See that thou tell no man, but go thy way, show thy-self to the priest, and bring thy gift of thanks to the al-tar as Mo-ses bade thee. But the man was so glad to be well once more that he spread the good news a-broad, and great crowds came to hear Je-sus,

RO-MAN CEN-TU-RI-ON.

and to be healed. Je-sus did not wish men to be drawn to him be-cause of the cures he made. It was his aim to teach them how to get rid of the plague spots on their souls, and how to lead good and pure lives. He wished them to take his words home to their hearts, and to show from day to day that they had done them good, and cleansed them through and through.

When a Jew had the plague he was shut out from the town, and a-way from the sight of men. No one went near him, to speak to him, or give him food, lest he should take the plague him-self or bear it to his home. Je-sus said that sin was like this plague. At first it was a small spot in the flesh—a small sin—a slight fault—but soon it spread and spread un-til there was not a sound place in him. There was no known cure for the plague. The poor lep-er had to be shut out from home and friends, and to die a slow sad death.

Till Christ came there was no known cure for sin. He brought the good news that those who had this worst kind of plague might come to him and be saved. Je-sus did not go to them, and cleanse them, and cure them. No. They must first feel their need of Him, and then show their faith in him. This they did when they cried out, Lord, if thou wilt thou canst make me clean.

One of the wise men of old, of whom the Jews thought a great deal, had fore-told these things that now took place. And his words, and dreams were traced out on a scroll, and are kept to this day as part of the Word of God. And in that book he says, Hear the word of the Lord. Cease to do wrong; learn to do well. Though your sins be as bright as a flame of fire, they shall be as white as snow; though they be red as blood they shall be as wool.

Je-sus next set out for Ca-per-na-um, but scarce had he reached the town when he was met by some of the chief men in the church. They had been sent by a Ro-man

SPEAK BUT THE WORD.

cen-tu-ri-on—or cap-tain of a hund-red men—to beg Je-sus to heal his slave of whom he was fond, for he was sick, and like to die. The Jews spoke well of the cap-tain, and said that he had been kind to their race, and had built them a church. And Je-sus said, I will go and heal him. And when he was not far from the house, the cap-tain sent friends out to him to tell him not to put him-self out to come to his home, For I am not good e-nough, he said, to have thee come un-der my roof, nor did I think my-self good e-nough to come un-to thee. But speak the word, and the sick one shall be healed. For I am a man in pow-er my-self, and have troops un-der me; and I say to that one, Go, and he goes; and to this one, Come, and he comes; and to my slave, Do this, and he does it. It was as if he said, If I can do so much, can-not Christ, the Son of God, do more? Je-sus was struck with these words, and turned to those who were with him and said, I have not found e-ven a-mong the Jews, such great faith as this. And when those that were sent out went back to the house, they found the slave who was sick had been made well.

CHAPTER VI.

JE-SUS AT NAIN.

In a few days Je-sus came to the town of Nain, which lies south-east of Naz-a-reth, and a great crowd went with him. And as they drew near the gate of the town they met a sad train—the friends of a dead youth whom they

NAIN.

were to lay in a grave out-side the walls. The moth-er wept as though here heart would break, for this boy who lay dead, was all in all to her. He was her pride and her joy. She had hoped to lean up-on him in her old age, but now this prop was gone. And what made it worse was that she was a wid-ow; her hus-band had died, and left her

THE WID-OW'S SON.

with this one son. And quite a crowd went out from the town with her and shared in her grief.

When the Lord saw her his heart was moved, and he said to her, Weep not. And he drew near, and touched the bier—or cof-fin—in which the dead youth lay. And as if they were spell-bound, those who bore the bier stood still in the road. Then Je-sus said in a calm voice, Young man, I say to thee, A-rise. And the dead man sat up,

PLAINS OF GAL-I-LEE.

and spoke; life, health, and strength came back, and joy took the place of grief. And great fear fell up-on all who saw what had been done, and they gave praise to God. And the fame of this great deed went out through all the lands, near and far.

In the mean-time John had said things that did not please Her-od, and the king had shut him up in jail, and would have put him to death, but that he feared the Jews, some of whom thought that John was a great proph-et.

While in jail John heard of the great deeds that Je-sus had done, how he cured those who were sick, and brought

HOUSE OF A RICH MAN.

the dead to life, and strange thoughts came in-to his mind. And he sent for two of his friends, and bade them go to

Je-sus, and told them what to say. And they came to Je-sus and said, Art thou in-deed the Son of God—He that is to come—or are we still to look for him? And in that hour he cured the sick, and those that had plagues, or were vexed by de-mons, and to those that were blind he gave sight.

Then Je-sus said to the men whom John had sent, Go your way, and tell John what things ye have seen and heard; how the blind see, the lame walk, the lep-ers are

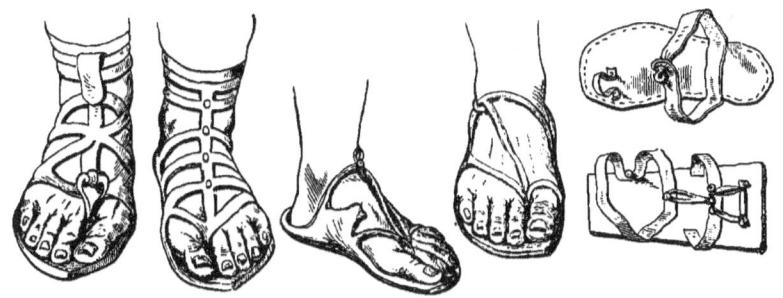

EAST-ERN SAN-DALS.

cleansed, the deaf hear, the dead are raised, and the poor have the good news preached to them.

When the men had gone, Je-sus talked to the crowd and told them of him-self and of John. John was like the light that sprang up in the east to tell of the dawn of a new Day; like the voice of one sent on a-head, to make it known that the king was on his way, and would come by that same road. God had sent both of them, and they that were wise would hear the truth from each, and take their words to heart.

As yet all had gone well, and there had been no strife be-tween the sects of Jews, some of whom had strict views, and held to the old laws and would have nought to do with new schools of thought.

At this time one of these Jews named Si-mon, a rich man, asked Je-sus to come to his house and eat with him. And Je-sus went.

COUCH USED AT MEALS.

Now it was the rule that when a guest of high rank came to a house, he was met by slaves, who brushed the dust from his clothes and poured oil on his hair and beard —rare oil that had a sweet smell—and he was then led in state to his seat at the board. But none of these things were done to our Lord, and he went in with the rest of the guests; but first left his san-dals, or low shoes, at the door, and took the place that was left for him.

SHE BOWED HER HEAD WITH SHAME.

In the East, in the time of our Lord, they did not sit in chairs when they took their meals, but lay on a long couch placed round the ta-bles. As they lay on their side, one hand would be free, and their feet would be on the out-side of the couch, or bed. As it was warm in these lands the doors were not shut, and while the feast went on a poor wom-an, who had led a life of sin, stole in-to the house, for she had heard that Je-sus was there. Oils were much used in the East, both on the hair, and on the skin to keep them smooth and soft. Some could be poured from flasks; but some was made more firm, like an oint-ment, and the box that held it was oft a gem in it-self.

SPIKE-NARD.

This poor soul who came in search of Je-sus brought with her a box of rare oint-ment, rich with spike-nard. It was all she had. And when she found him whom she sought, she stood back of him, and bowed her head with shame at the thought of her sins. Tears drop-ped from her eyes and fell down on his feet, and she wiped them dry with the hair of her head, and kissed his feet, and put some of the oint-ment on them.

Si-mon, when he saw this, said to him-self, If this man were a true proph-et, he would know what kind a wom-an this is that has touched him. For her sins have been great. Je-sus, who knew his thoughts, said, Si-mon, I have some-thing to say to thee. And he said, Mas-ter, say on. Je-sus said, There was once a man who had lent mon-ey to two men, and they were still in debt to him. One owed much more than the oth-er, but when he found that they could not pay him he for-gave them both. Tell me, then, which one will love him the most?

Si-mon said, I sup-pose that he to whom he for-gave the most. Je-sus said to him, Thou art in the right. And he turned to the wom-an, and said to Si-mon, Look at her. I came in-to thine house and thou didst give me no wa-ter to wash my feet, but she has bathed my feet with tears, and wiped them with her hair. Thou didst not meet me and kiss me on the face, but since the time I came in-to thine house she has not ceased to kiss my feet.

Thou didst not pour oil on my head, as a sign that thou wert glad to have me for thy guest, but she has poured out her high-priced oil up-on my feet. So I say un-to thee, Her sins, great though they be, are all wiped out. The debt is paid with love—for she loved much. One who does not feel his sins—the debt that he owes—has not much love in his heart. And he said to the wom-an, Thy faith has saved thee; go in peace. And those who sat at meat with him, said to them-selves, Who is this, that takes up-on him-self the right to for-give sins?

CHAPTER VII.

JE-SUS BY THE SEA SIDE.

We are told that Je-sus taught in par-a-bles; and as no one had taught in that way be-fore, it was not strange that crowds should flock to hear him. What is a par-a-ble? It is a tale told of real life, in which there is some-thing that each one who hears can take to heart. There is more meant by the words than one would think who does not read them with care, or hear them as they ought to hear.

Je-sus knew how to use words to paint scenes that stand out as bright as those that hang on walls in frames of gold. He took his texts from things that were close at hand, and as they stood out in the fields one day, when the crowd pressed close to him to hear his voice, he spoke thus:

A man went forth to sow seeds. And as he sowed, some fell by the way-side, and those who passed by trod up-on them and the birds came and ate them up. And some fell on a rock, where they had not much earth, and the heat of the sun scorched them; and as they had no roots they soon dried up. Some fell in the midst of thorns, and the thorns grew up with them, and choked the good seed so that they came to nought. But some fell on good ground, and sprang up, and bore rich fruit. And when he had said these words, he cried out, He that hath ears to hear, let him hear; which meant, Take heed how ye hear.

JESUS TEACHING BY THE SEA SIDE.

Some drew near and asked Je-sus to tell them what he meant; and to make it more plain, he said, The seed is the Word of God. Those that fall by the way-side are those that hear the word of God, but pay no heed to it. They do not care for such things, but love the gay world, and mix with those who are in the broad road that leads to

AN EAST-ERN SOW-ER.

death. Here all good thoughts are crushed out of them, and at last they give them-selves up to the world, and are not found with those who love God and strive to do His will.

Those on the rock, are those who at first hear the word with joy, and go to church, and for a while give them-selves up to good works. But as they have no roots—as the love of the truth does not sink deep in their hearts—false friends come and tempt them to join in with those who love the world and the things that please the flesh, and soon they lose all care for their souls, and they dry up and bring forth no bloom nor fruit to please Him who made them.

The seed which fell a-mong thorns are those who, when they have heard the Word of God, go forth in-to the world and mean to lead right kind of lives. But their cares, and their wealth, the gay scenes and gay sounds that charm the ear and the eye, take up so much of their time and thoughts, that they have no chance to do God's work, or to lead souls out of the mire of sin. They have no time to go to church, scarce time to pray, and the thorns of this life—small cares, the love of wealth, the joys that please, yet leave a sting—soon choke them so that they bring forth poor fruit, and do not much to please God.

But the seed which falls on good ground, is a type of the Word of God that falls in-to a good and true heart, and takes root there. It is much prized, and is dwelt up-on night and day, warmed with the fires of love, wet with the dew of tears. Such an one hears the word, as if God said, Do thou this! and he goes and does it and asks God to help him. In this way, in God's good time, he brings forth fruit; that is, he shows by his life that he lives near to God, and that God is first in his thoughts.

Take heed how ye hear; for he that hath shall have more giv-en to him; and he that hath not, from him shall be ta-ken a-way e-ven that which he seems to have. Christ meant by this that those who had the least chance to do good, and the least to do with, would be helped, and made rich in gifts that do good to the soul. When we are weak, and think not much of our-selves, then are we made strong,

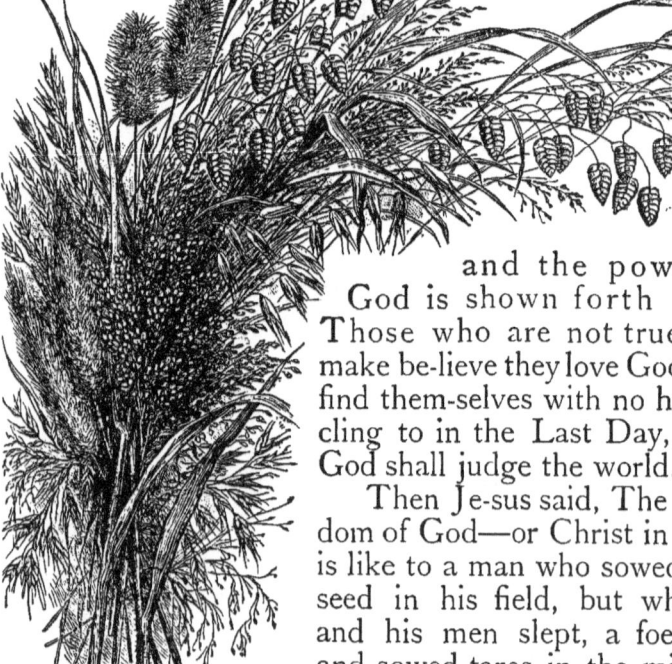

THE WHEAT AND THE TARES.

and the pow-er of God is shown forth in us. Those who are not true, who make be-lieve they love God, shall find them-selves with no hope to cling to in the Last Day, when God shall judge the world.

Then Je-sus said, The King-dom of God—or Christ in you—is like to a man who sowed good seed in his field, but while he and his men slept, a foe came and sowed tares in the midst of the wheat, and then went his way. Now tares are weeds that grow up and look so much like wheat, that it is hard to tell them a-part. But there is no good grain in them. And when the wheat sprang up and was ripe, then came the tares up with them. The work-men come to the farm-er and say to him, Sir, didst thou not sow good seed in thy field? from whence then come these tares? He saith to them, A foe hath done this. The men say to him, Shall we go then and pull them up? He saith to them, No; lest while ye pull up the tares, ye should pull up the wheat that is with them. Let both grow side by side un-til the har-vest, and in the time of the har-vest I will say to those who reap, Take up first the tares and bind them in sheaves to burn; but put the wheat in-to my barn.

Then Je-sus told what was meant by the par-a-ble of the tares of the field. He that sows the good seed is the Son of man. The field is the world, and the good seed are the Sons of God; but the tares are the Sons of the wick-ed one. The foe that sowed them is the dev-il; the har-vest is the end of the world, and the reap-ers are the an-gels. As there-fore the tares are all picked up and burned in the fire, so shall it be at the end of the world. The Son of man shall send forth his an-gels, and they shall cast out of heav-en all those who have kept oth-ers from Christ, or walked in the ways of sin, and they will be with the lost ones, who weep and mourn when it is too late. He said that men were not the ones to judge, for they might call the wheat, tares, and the tares, wheat: they might call those bad who were good; and might think those were good, whom God knew were as bad as they could be. But all would be known at the Last Day, and men would be judged by God who knows all hearts.

Then Je-sus said, The king-dom of God—or Christ in you—is like to a grain of mus-tard seed, which a man took and sowed is his field. It is the least of all seeds, but when grown it is the size of a tree, so that the birds come and make their nests in it. Je-sus meant by this that though one's faith was small—like to the least of seeds—it must not be looked down on with scorn, for if put in the

GREAT SPOT-TED CUCK-OO.

right soil, it would grow like a tree, and spread it-self, and do great good in the world, and bring souls to Christ, and add strength to his cause.

Je-sus said the King-dom of God was like to leav-en, or yeast, which a wom-an took and hid in three quarts of meal, till the whole was made light. The good we do in Christ's name may seem lost for a while—all our work seems in vain—but in time it will break through the mass of sin by which it is held, and spread out, and be like the bread of life to souls that starve for this kind of food.

Je-sus saith, the King-dom of God is like gold or sil-ver, or rich gems that are hid in a field, which when a man finds he is filled with joy. It is worth more than he can pay, but he goes and sells all he has, and buys that field, and is rich for all time. Then Je-sus said, The King-dom of God is like to a man who bought and sold pearls. We are to think that he was a good judge of pearls, and went far and near to add them to his stock. One day he found a pearl of great price, worth more than all the rest that he had on hand. It was a great prize, and he must have it. What did he do? Why, he sold off all the pearls and gems he had in his store, all the land he owned and the house he lived in, and bought this one pearl, and was glad all the rest of his days.

The pearl of price is, Je-sus in our hearts. With him there we are rich for all time, though we own not house nor lands, and are poor in this world's goods.

Then Je-sus told them that the King-dom of God was like to a drag-net cast in-to the sea, which takes in all kinds of fish. When it is full, and drawn up on the beach, the men sit down and pick out the good and throw the bad a-way. So shall it be at the end of the world.

When night came on Je-sus longed for rest, and to be free from the crowd which would not leave him. That he might be where it was calm, he said to those with him in the boat, Let us cross the lake; and they set out to do so. But ere they could push off one who was a Scribe came to Je-sus and said, Mas-ter where thou go-est I will go. Je-sus said to him, The fox-es have holes, and the birds of the air have nests, but the Son of man hath not where to lay his head. Je-sus meant that those who went with him must give up wealth and pride, and all hope of gain, such as men think much of in this world. And the Scribe did not go with Je-sus.

Next came one of the Twelve and said to him, Lord, let me first go home and see my fath-er laid in his grave, then I will go with thee. But Je-sus said to him, No, let the dead be; but go thou and preach the good news.

Then one came who said, Lord I will go with thee, but first let me go and bid good-by to those that are at my house. Je-sus said to him, No man that puts his hand to the plough, and then looks back, is fit to work with me in my field. The plough used in the East was apt to up-set, and the man who set out to guide it must use both hands and eyes. It was as if Je-sus said, If your heart is not with me you can-not do my work.

At last the sails were spread, and the boat was off; and ere they were far from shore Je-sus had lain down in the stern of the boat and was soon in a deep sleep. When they set out the lake was calm, but all at once a fierce storm of wind swept down and drove the waves in-to the boat. Those on board were in great fear, lest they should drown. And they came to Je-sus, and found that he had slept through all the noise. And they woke him; and cried out Lord! Lord! Save us, or we sink! Then he rose and gazed out up-on the waves, and said in calm clear tones, as one might hush a child to rest, Peace, be still! And at once the wind went down, the waves ceased to toss, and

LORD, SAVE US.

there was a great calm. And he said to them, as he says to all of us who are in the midst of the storms of life, Where is your faith? Am I not with you? And the men in the boat, as they saw the stars break through the clouds, were filled with awe and said in low tones, Who then is this? for he makes the wind and the sea do as he bids them.

At dawn they came to the west side of the lake, and as soon as Je-sus step-ped out of the boat there met him a mad-man who came out from the tombs, or caves, where

TOMBS.

the dead were placed. There he made his home. More than once he had been bound with chains, but he broke them a-part, and was so wild that no man could tame him. Night and day he was on the hills and in the caves, and he cried out and cut him-self with stones. But when he saw Je-sus—while he was still a long way off—he ran and threw him-self at his feet, and cried with a loud voice, What have I to do with thee, thou Son of the most high God? Let me a-lone!

Je-sus said to the man, What is thy name? But he could not tell it. He did not know who he was when in his right mind. And he beg-ged Je-sus not to let the de-mons with-in him throw him down the steep cliff. And there was a herd of swine that fed on the mount, and the de-mons beg-ged Je-sus to give them leave to go in-to them. So Je-sus gave them leave, and the de-mons went out of the man and in-to the swine, and they rushed down the steep place in-to the lake, and were drowned. When those that fed them saw what had been done, they fled, and told it to all near and far. And crowds flocked out to see him from whom the de-mons had gone out, and they found him who had once been a mad-man now clothed and in his right mind; and he sat at the feet of Je-sus like a child. And they were awe-struck. And those who had seen what Je-sus had done, told them by what means the mad-man had been cured. Then all who dwelt in that part of the land beg-ged Je-sus to leave their coasts, for they were in great fear of him. They thought more of their swine—their sins and the base things of this world—than they did of Je-sus, whom they wished to get rid of. And he turned and left them. He will not force him-self up-on those who do not want him. In vain had he sought rest at Gad-a-ra; and he went back to the boat with a sad heart.

These Jews were no worse than men in our day who are sunk so low in vice and crime that they have no thought or care for Je-sus. They fear that if He should come in

BE-HOLD I STAND AT THE DOOR.

their midst they would lose some of the wealth they have gained. For they have grown rich, not in the right kind of a way; they have not soiled their hands with work, but have learned to cheat and to rob those who put their trust in them, and are as low-lived as the swine that eat all that comes in their way. They have no wish to be fed with such food as Christ brings; they care not for a well taught mind, a well trained heart, or for aught that will help them out of the mire and filth in which they dwell.

Je-sus may knock at their door, and they rise not to let him in.

He may speak to them, but they hear not his voice.

He may weep be-cause they are so dead in their sins, but they care not. They are in-deed worse than mad-men. For a mad-man is sick, when he is not in his right mind. He knows not what he does. But these men know, and must take the blame to them-selves if Je-sus leaves them to their fate. They drive him from their homes, and their haunts, and treat him with scorn, and by their speech and their acts prove that they are not with him, and will have none of him.

How sad Je-sus must feel when he has to turn from those he fain would save.

The man whom Je-sus had cured—the one whom he had saved—begged to go with him. But Je-sus sent him a-way, and said to him, Go home to thy friends, and tell them what great things the Lord hath done for thee. And he went his way and spread the news through all the town, and told how he had been freed from his sins.

CHAPTER VIII.

JE-SUS AT CA-PER-NA-UM.

Je-sus crossed the Lake, and when the boat came on shore he went at once to the house where he stayed when at Ca-per-na-um. And as soon as it was known that he was in the place, crowds flocked there and filled the house and the court-yard, so that the way to the door was blocked up.

And there was a man, who had been sick for some time, and could not move without help. Four friends brought him on a bed, and when they found they could not get near the door, nor reach Je-sus through the crowd, they went up on the house-top, and took the tiles from the roof, and let him down on his bed in front of Je-sus.

Je-sus was pleased at this sign of faith, and he said to the sick man, Son, be of good cheer—fear not—thy sins are wiped out. To for-give sins, is to wipe them out so that they leave no mark, nor stain, and to think no more of them.

Some of the Scribes, who thought more of old forms than new ones, and were on the watch to find fault with Je-sus, when they heard his words, said to them-selves, Who is he that dares speak thus, when none but God can for-give sins?

Je-sus, who knew their thoughts, said to them, What

think ye in your hearts? Is it more ea-sy to say, Thy sins are for-giv-en thee; or to say, A-rise and walk? But that ye may know that I am the One who has pow-er on earth to for-give sins, he said to the sick man who could not move with-out help, A-rise, take up thy bed, and walk. And the man rose to his feet, took up the light bed on which he had lain, and as the crowd made way for him he went to his own house, and praised God as he went. And the crowd when they broke up to leave the place, said in tones of fear and awe, We have seen strange things to-day.

The house where Je-sus was at this time, was built low like most of the hous-es in the East. The rooms were all on the ground floor, and each one led out in-to a large hall or court, where Je-sus stood. Steps on the out-side of the house led up to the roof, for in the East the house-tops are made much use of. For men sit there to cool off at the close of the day, and at times sleep there for the whole of the night. It was not a hard task for strong men to tear up the roof to let their friend down at the feet of Je-sus. But that they thought of this thing, and cared to do it, shows how much they thought of their friend, and how great was their faith in Je-sus. It was some-thing to push their way through the crowd. But they did more than that. They bore the sick man up the stairs, and on to the roof. They might have left him there. Je-sus might have said the words he did, might have bid the man get up and walk then and there. For he knew all that took place, and naught was hid from him. But he wished the crowd to see with their own eyes what these men did, and to know how great was the cure. And it was to teach them and us more than can be learned at the first view.

There are two ways—three ways I should say—in which to read a book. In the first place we read it with our eyes. There are the words in plain print, and we fix our gaze on the page, and read on from line to line.

The next way is to read with the mind; that is, to think of what we have read. As the cow chews her cud, so that the milk she gives may be rich and sweet, we must chew the thoughts that are brought to the mind, so that we may grow by them our-selves, and teach young and old the truths that have been made plain to us.

There is still a third way to read, and that is with the heart: to be so in love with the book and the truths it may teach, that a light is thrown on the page and words and scenes stand out far more clear and plain than they do to those who just read with their eyes and their brain.

We are to learn from this scene that some men are so bound to their sins that they can-not get a-way from them. They have lost all the strength of will they once had, and can-not move hand or foot to get them out of the slough in which they have been cast. If left to them-selves they would not be saved at all. Some one must go out to seek him. Friends must bring him to Je-sus. They may coax in vain. May plead in vain. He may want to be saved, but will say, I have sin-ned too long. There is no hope for me. I can-not turn my hand to do good deeds, nor can I walk in the right way. Let me die on the bed where I have lain so long.

Do his friends leave him there? Not if they are true friends. They take hold of him, sins and all, and bring him to Je-sus. They pray with and for him. Crowds may push them back. The way to Je-sus may be blocked up; his face may be hid from us for a-while; we fail to hear the sound of his voice. But if we stop there, or turn back we are lost.

These friends push on. They lead the man of sin up heights that bring him a-way from the crowd, and in-to pure fresh air. They care not what the world may say or do. It can-not keep them back from Christ. They have fought their way through, but there is still more to do. Great faith shows it-self by great works. They must break down all that keeps this soul from Je-sus. They have brought the man to the house-top but they can-not leave him there. He is still sick, though in a high place.

This man was a Jew and could not give up the old time laws which had come down to him from Mo-ses, and hung like a veil be-tween him and Je-sus.

But friends who knew that these old laws must give way to new ones, broke through the wall, or veil, and let the man down at the feet of Je-sus. We must take a low place if we wish to get near him.

We are led to think that this poor man, bound as he was by his sins, must have longed to be free. For when Je-sus bade him get up and walk, he stood on his feet at once, and took up the bed on which he had lain for years. This showed that he had strength now to break loose from the ties that had held him, and to be a new man in Christ Je-sus. And as he went on his way he gave thanks to God.

From Pe-ter's house Je-sus went down to the sea shore, and taught there for a-while, and then went to the house of

Mat-thew, who had made a great feast for his friends. And as he had been a sin-ner him-self, his friends would, of course, be of the same stamp. Yet Je-sus and the Twelve, with no thought of scorn or hate, sat down with them at the feast. And the strict Jews and their Scribes found fault with them, and said, Why do ye eat and drink with tax-ta-kers and vile men?

Je-sus said to them, They that are well need no doc-tor; but they that are sick do. I am not come to call the good to turn from their ways, but to urge the bad to give up their sins and to lead new lives.

He said that God thought more of kind deeds than he did of the blood of beasts, or the oil that was poured out for him. And some of those who had been taught by John, came to Je-sus and said, We fast twice a week; but none of those whom thou hast taught, and who are with thee, keep the fasts as we do.

Je-sus said there was no need for the friends of the bride-groom to mourn when the bride-groom was with them. This was a form of speech, which meant that a fast was a sign of grief, but those who are with Christ—whose hearts are joined to his as is the bride's to the bride-groom's have no need of tears. But the days will come, he said, when the bride-groom shall be ta-ken from them, and then will they fast.

This was the first time that he gave out a hint of his death; but the truth was veiled in such a way that it was not clear to their minds. Je-sus said, No man puts a patch of new cloth on to an old robe, for the piece of new cloth tears a-way the old, so that the rent is made worse. Nor do men put new wine in-to old wine-skins, lest the new wine, which has not ceased to swell, should burst the old wine-skins and be lost. But they put the new wine in-to fresh wine-skins, and both are saved. Je-sus meant by this that it would not do to put the new life in with the old forms. But the man must be freed from these forms which hold him in, and spoil the good work he might do, and must give his whole heart to the new truths, and by his acts and his thoughts must show that he is filled with the wine, "which makes glad the heart of man." There is but one kind of wine that does this, and that is the love of Je-sus.

While Je-sus yet spoke in these strange words; there came to him a man named Jai-rus, one of the chief men of the church, and much thought of by the Jews. And he threw him-self at the feet of Je-sus, and, in a burst of grief, cried out, My child—the dear girl whom I love so well— lies at the point of death! I pray thee, that thou come and lay thy hands on her that she may live!

Je-sus rose at once and went with him, and the Twelve kept near him, and were hard pushed by the dense crowd that was close at their heels.

In this throng was a wom-an who had been sick for twelve years. In vain had she sought help from doc-tors of great fame and great skill. But now she had spent all she had, and was worse off than she was be-fore. She had heard of Je-sus, and tried to push her way through the crowd that she might touch his robe. For she said to her-self, If I but touch his robe, I shall be made well.

It is as if some of us said, I want to be good. I am sick of my sins. I have been to this one and that one—and heard them all preach—but all they have said has done me no good. I lose strength each day, and if I am not helped soon I shall die.

We have spent all our gold, and poor, and with no pride in our-selves, we kneel down and pray God to for-give our sins, and save us at last, for Christ's sake. This is what is meant by the hem of his robe. The wom-an must kneel to touch it, or at least stretch out her hand, and this act would show that she had faith in Je-sus, and a heart warm with love.

With her to will, was to do. If the crowd kept her back so that Je-sus could not touch her, she would touch him. How oft we miss some great good, be-cause we are loath to go out of our way to get it. We wait to do some great deed, to have some-thing come to us, and so lose the chance to win the prize that may be ours if we will but stretch out our hand to take it.

This wom-an touched the robe Je-sus wore, for she had heard of him, and knew that he could cure her.

At once—while this thought was in her mind—she felt a new sense of health. She was cured of that which had caused her so much grief and shame for the past twelve years of her life.

Je-sus, who felt that strength from him had gone forth, turned round and faced the crowd, and said, Who touched my robe? Those near him said it was scarce worth while to ask such a thing in the midst of so great a throng. But Je-sus knew that the touch he felt was the touch of faith—as

WHERE THE JEWS WENT TO WEEP AND WAIL.

though one said, Help me, Lord!—and he looked round to see who had done this thing.

The wom-an, filled with shame and fear, flung her-self at his feet and told him all the truth. She feared his wrath; it might be that her touch had done him harm, and if she owned her guilt he might not be harsh with her. But if she had dared to look up she would not have meet the face of a stern judge; and how sweet and soft must have been the sound of his voice, when he said, My child, thy faith hath saved thee; go in peace!

In the mean-time the poor ru-ler whose child was sick un-to death was in a sad state of mind, but did naught to urge his claim. And there came those from his house who said, The child is dead. It is of no use to both-er the Mas-ter.

Je-sus heard their words, and said to Jai-rus, Fear not; trust in me. When they came to the house, they found it filled with those who in the East were hired to weep and mourn o-ver the dead. And they made a great noise. Je-sus stop-ped at the door, and brought the crowd out-side to a stand-still. Then he called Pe-ter, James, and John to his side, and the four went in-to the house.

His first care was to still the noise; and he said to those who wept and wailed, and played on the flute, Why do ye make such a din? and why do ye weep? The child is not dead, but is a-sleep. And they laughed him to scorn. But when he had sent the crowd out of the house, he took the fath-er of the child and her moth-er, and those that were with him, and went in-to the room where she lay.

THE DAUGH-TER OF JAI-RUS.

He took the cold dead hand in his and said, Rise, my child. And at once the child got up and walked, and was just as well and strong as she had been. For she was then twelve years of age. And her fa-ther and moth-er when they saw her were awe-struck, and knew not what to say. Je-sus told them not to talk much a-bout what had been done, but to give the child some-thing to eat, for she was weak yet, and in need of food.

As Je-sus went on his way, two blind men—who sat by the road-side and beg-ged for alms, as they were wont to do in the East—heard the crowd, and knew what it meant. And they went with the throng and cried out, Have mer-cy on us, thou Son of Da-vid. Je-sus let them cry thus, till they came to the house where he stayed. And as they went in, he said to the blind men, Do you be-lieve that I can make you well? They say un-to him, Yes, Lord. Then he touched their eyes, and said, Let the cure be as great as your faith. And their sight came back to them, and Je-sus charged them not to boast of what had been done. But when they left, they spread the news in all that part of the land.

This did more harm than good to Je-sus, as it roused the hate of his foes, and made them lay plans to put a stop to his work, and to make more haste to put him to death. Je-sus meant that those who were cured, or saved, should be glad in their own hearts, and full of thanks to God.

There are times when the cause of Christ is hurt by too much noise; when it is well for those who love Je-sus to lead calm lives, and do his work in their own homes, where, though hid from the sight of men, it is not hid from

RISE, MY CHILD!

the sight of God. But it is right at all time to give thanks, and to pray; and this we can do in our own homes. If we have been blind so that we did not see our own faults, we can show that we have gained our sight, and are with those who walk in the foot-steps of Je-sus.

One day there was brought to Je-sus a man who was both mad and dumb. And Je-sus cured him so that he spoke, and was in his right mind. And the Jews who saw this were a-mazed, and said, Nev-er were such strange things done in this land. And they said that he could cast out dev-ils be-cause he was in league with the dev-il.

And Je-sus went a-bout through all the large and small towns, and taught and preached the good news, and healed the sick, and all those who came to him for help.

When Je-sus saw the crowds, his heart was touched, for he felt that they were as sheep that had no shep-herd. And he spoke to the Twelve, and told them that the world was like a great field of grain, which had grown quite ripe. It was time to reap it, but there were, as yet, too few to do the work. And he gave them power to heal the sick, and to do such works as he did, and then sent them out two by two to teach and preach as he had taught them.

As yet they were to preach to no one but the Jews. They were to take no purse with them, no scrip—or bag—for food, no change of coats, nor shoes, nor staff; for it was but right that those for whom they worked should feed and clothe them.

They must find out where good folks lived, and stay with them till they left the place. And when they came to a house they were to bow—as men were wont to do

BROUGHT HIM THE DUMB.

in the East—and say, Peace be to you. And if no one came to ask them in or to make them guests of the house, they were not to be hurt. The peace would not go to those in the house, but would come back to them. And

VIEW IN DA-MAS-CUS.

if they went to a house or town, and could find no one to take them in, no one who cared to hear their words, they were to shake the dust off their feet, to leave the place with-out hard words, for God would judge that town at the Last Day, and it would go hard with those who lived there.

Je-sus said, Ye must be wise as ser-pents—who watch

and keep out of harm's way and as meek and mild as doves; for I send you out as sheep in the midst of wolves. He told them that men were more to be feared than wolves, for they would bring them up to the church courts and scourge them; and they would be charged with crimes, and be brought be-fore the judge, or the king.

When they thus bring you up, take no thought how or what ye shall speak, for the words will be put in-to your mouth. All men would hate them for his sake, but those who held out to the end should be saved.

Je-sus said, If they ill use you in this town, flee to the next one. There is some-where a place to preach Christ, and to tell of the love of Je-sus. If we can-not do it where we are, we may be sure we are not in the right place for us, and it is well to move on. These men were not to think they could lead a life of ease. Their task was a hard one, but Je-sus would be with them all the way. They were not to think that men would be more kind to them than they were to Je-sus.

They had called him hard names, and how much worse names would they call these whom he sent out. But they were to be bold, and fear not, for his truth should be made known and he would set things in the right light. If they held back the truth it would be found out. They had been to school to Je-sus, and now they were to go out and teach. He said to them, what I tell you in the dark, that speak ye in the light; and what ye hear in the ear, that preach from the house-tops. They were to speak in a loud voice, so that all could hear. They were not to fear for their lives, for God who cared for the birds that are so small that they are sold in pairs, would be sure to care for them.

He said that each one who would serve Christ with a true heart, must give up the world and all the things that held him back, and bear his own cross with a firm and child-like trust. Each one has a cross to bear in this life. My cross may not be the same as yours. One may be poor, or sick, or may have to live with those who are not kind, or who have no fear of God, and take his name in vain, and spend their days in sin. Those who are near and dear to us may not think as we do, and this would be a hard cross to bear.

Je-sus said, Think not that I came to send peace on earth; I came not to send peace, but a sword. The sword of Christ brings true peace. It puts to death the worst of foes. Je-sus and Sa-tan can-not live in the same place. The two are at strife, and will be till the end of time. Peace on earth, the an-gels sang, and they meant peace with God which all may have, if with the sword of the Lord they keep sin out of their hearts. I came, said Je-sus, to set men at sword's point with those near and dear to them. A man's foes shall be those of his own house-hold. Je-sus meant that we must not let the ties of earth keep us back from him. We are to love Je-sus more than we love those of our house-hold; to give them up if need be, but to cling to Christ till the last hour of life. As I shall bear my cross, said Je-sus, you must bear yours.

He said to the Twelve, Those who give their hearts to you, give their hearts to me. Those who lose their lives for my sake, shall live when this world is no more. And those who do a kind act out of love to Christ, if it be but to give a drink to a child, shall not miss the crown that God will give them.

CHAPTER IX.

THE POOL OF BE-THES-DA.—JE-SUS IN JE-RU-SA-LEM.—
DEATH OF JOHN THE BAP-TIST.

As Je-sus had sent off the Twelve, he had now to do his work a-lone. It was near the spring of the year when he set out for Je-ru-sa-lem, and a feast was held there at that time which brought a great throng of Jews to the place.

Now there was in Je-ru-sa-lem, near the well-known sheep-pool, a twin pool, which was called Be-thes-da, or The House of Grace. It had five arch-ways from which were steps that led down to the pool, and here in the shade a great crowd of sick folks lay in wait—for what? Why it was said that from time to time an an-gel came and stirred up this spring, or pool, and those who first step-ped in-to it when it was moved in this way, would be cured of all their aches and pains.

We know how it is in these days. There are springs in all parts of the world, to which men go to be cured of the ills that flesh is heir to. Some are salt; some have lime in them, or i-ron, or some-thing else that is good for the health. They start from some place deep down in the earth, and find their way up to the day-light, and form a spring, or pool. Some of these springs have tides, and ebb and flow, like the waves of the sea. But most of them

POOL OF BE-THES-DA.

gush forth, as free as God's love, and seem to say, Come ye to the fount that flows for you. Drink of it! Bathe in it! It will give you life and health! The pool that is calm and still year in and year out, is not a pure fount. It needs to be stirred up. The pool at Be-thes-da was one of those that gushed forth from time to time, and so it was said that an an-gel stirred it, for all good deeds were laid to the an-gels. And, of course, the sick ones, who were rich, were the first to get there, and to crowd back those who were poor, and could not hire men to wait on them.

And there was one poor man there who had had no use of his limbs for nigh un-to two-score years. When Je-sus saw him there, and knew that he had been a long time in that state, he said un-to him, Wilt thou be made whole? Which was the same as if he had asked him, Do you wish to be made well?

The lame man said, Sir, I have no friend, when the wa-ter is stirred up, to put me in-to the pool: but while I am on the way, some one else steps down be-fore me. He was poor, he could not hire help, and may have felt a hope that Je-sus would prove a friend in need. Though he might be dip-ped in the spring it would be some time be-fore he was made quite well.

Je-sus felt sorry for the poor man, and said to him, Rise, take up thy bed, and walk. And at once the man rose, and took up his bed, and walked, for that voice had thrilled him through and through, and he was both strong and glad.

There was no need for him to bathe in the pool. No need for him to wait for a chance, and to lose heart from

AN AN-GEL STIR-RED THE POOL.

day to day. Je-sus says to him, Do you wish to be well? He does, and the cure is made at once. Je-sus does not lay hands on him, or touch him. He speaks, the man hears, and takes Je-sus at his word. He might have said when Je-sus told him to rise, I can-not get up. I am too lame to walk a step. If you can-not help me in my way you are not a true friend. He wished to be well. He did not know Je-sus, but looked on him as a friend, and when he said, Rise, the man got up at once, and was strong and well.

What are we to learn from this? Why, that we need not wait for some one to lead us to Christ, or to put us in the way of good things. We can-not help our-selves or make much head-way, be-cause we lean on our own strength. We must give up our own wills. When he asks us if we wish to be freed from our sins—when first we hear him speak to us—we must say, Yes, Lord, I do. Make me clean; and give me strength to walk in thy foot-steps. And when he says, Rise, we must not think we can-not give up the life we have so long been used to. He will give us strength to lift our-selves up from low things if we but put our trust in him.

This lame man felt at once that he had done the right thing. The voice of Je-sus was like a draught from a fresh pure spring, that sent new life through his veins. To hear was to o-bey—to do as he was told—and he went forth strong and glad.

Now this was done on the Day of Rest, and the Jews were so strict they would let no work at all be done on that day. They built no fires in the house, and cooked no food, and when they met a man with a load on his back they could scarce be-lieve their eyes. What Jew would dare to break the law of Mo-ses in this way?

So they went up to the man, and asked him if he did not know it was wrong to take up his bed on the Day of

POOL OF SOL-O-MON.

Rest. The man said to them, He that cured me, said to me, Take up thy bed and walk.

Then they asked, Who is it that cured thee, and told thee to take up thy bed and walk? But the man did not know, for he had lost sight of Je-sus in the crowd. In a few days, when Je-sus was in the Tem-ple-courts, he saw

POOL OF HEZ-E-KIAH.

this same man whom he had cured; and he said to him, Be-hold, thou hast been made well: Sin no more that some worse thing come not un-to thee. And the man went and told the Jews that it was Je-sus who had made him a well man.

The Jews were up in arms at once, and for this cause did they hate Je-sus; for he had no right, they said, to do such things on the Day of Rest. And he was brought be-fore the Chief Priests that they might warn him; for if he did not cease to break the law he would be scourged, or put to death. These priests thought to strike fear in-to the heart of this strange man who claimed to be the Son of God. And for this were they more fierce to kill him, for each word that he spoke made the fires of hate burn fierce in their hearts.

He said that he could do naught but what his Fath-er told him to do. God did not rest on the Sab-bath, nor did he rest. The sun, moon, and stars kept on their course. The earth did not stand still, and the rain fell, the grass grew, and the trees gave forth their fruits. The sick had need of care on that day; and God did not mean to make the Day of Rest a hard, dull day, but to so fill it with joy that it would stand out far more bright than the six days that make up the rest of the week.

Af-ter six days of toil, in which the mind is more or less filled with the cares of the world, we need at least one day of rest. We need it to keep our-selves in health, to let off the strain on brain and nerves. But more than all we need time to think—to give up the greed of gain—and to give our souls a chance to grow. Why, the man who toils day in and day out, and thinks of naught but how he can earn more gold, will pinch and starve his soul till it dries up with-in him. For the soul needs to be fed, and each Day of Rest ought to find us in the House of God, and glad to be there. We are to think of it as God's Day, and to do all we can to make it a bright day in our homes and in our hearts. Je-sus said, There were good deeds that must be done on that day. He told them that he had raised up those who were dead in their sins; and that an hour should come when those who were dead and in their graves should hear his voice and come forth. Those that have done good shall rise to live with God; and those who have spent their lives in sin shall go down where the lost ones dwell. God has made me the judge. I can do naught of my-self. As I hear, I judge, and am just to all. For I seek not to do my own will, but the will of him that sent me.

If I should claim to stand a-lone, my words would not be true. There is One who is with me, and He will prove that my claims are not false. In Him I trust. Ye have sent to John, and he told what was true of me. But great though John was, he was but a man, and could not do the works that I do. And these things I say to you that ye may be saved. John was like a lamp that burns and shines, and for a while ye were glad in that light.

The lamp was to guide men to Je-sus, to point out the right way for them to live. Da-vid says of the Word of God, in one of his Psalms, Thy word is a lamp un-to my feet, and a light un-to my path, and Je-sus made use of this, so that the Jews would know what he meant.

They liked to hear what John had to say, but the words that he spoke took no root in their hearts. If they had done so these men who heard John would have been on the look-out for Je-sus, and would have known him when he came. It was not John's fault; he had done good work, but the light he bore had failed to reach their hearts. As a lamp can be put out, so was John put out, when the sun shone, for there was no more need of him. The light of which he told, had come in to the world.

Je-sus said, I do not come from John, but I come from God, and the works that I do show that he sent me. But though I have talked to you, and done these works in the midst of you, ye have not heard the voice of God nor seen his form. This is proof that ye have no love for Him in your hearts, for ye have turned from him whom He hath sent.

Ye are well read in the Word of God, for ye think that he who knows all the Law is fit for the life of the world to come. And yet the Word of God speaks of me, and tells that I am to come. And yet ye will not come to me that ye may have life. I seek not fame from men. But I know you, that ye have not the love of God in you. I am come to do the will of God, and ye will not be-lieve in me; but if one should come in his own name, and to seek his own ends, ye would give your whole hearts to his cause. How can ye be-lieve, and seek to know the truth, when ye care more for the praise of men than for the praise of God? Do not think that I will charge you with these sins in the sight of God; there is no need, for it has been done by Mo-ses, in whom is your hope and trust. For if ye had faith in

Mo-ses ye would be-lieve in me. But if ye be-lieve not in the words that he wrote, how can ye be-lieve in the words that I speak, or the works that I do?

The Jews had not a word to say. They had set themselves up to judge Je-sus, and he was their judge. They could but gnash their teeth with rage, and lay plans in their hearts to get rid of this strange man who claimed to be One with God.

Ju-sus knew that his end was near, that the Jews would vent their spite up-on him, and that it would not be safe for him to stay in Je-ru-sa-lem. So, sad at heart, he went back to Gal-i-lee, and was met with the news of what Her-od had done to John.

This was not the Her-od who was on the throne when Je-sus was borne, but his son, a weak man, and not fit to rule.

Now Her-od had a wife of his own but he had put her a-way that he might wed the wife of his broth-er, whose name was He-ro-di-as. This was a crime and both of them knew it, yet who would dare to charge them with sin?

John the Bap-tist. Such crowds went to hear him that it was feared some harm would be done, and Her-od sent for him to hear what he had to say. He spoke plain truths to Her-od, and told him that he had no right to live with her whom he called his wife. Her-od was pleased with John's words, he liked to hear him talk, but he would not give up his wife; and to please her—for she was in a rage at what John had said—he had John shut up in jail. His wife wished him to be put to death, but the king would not do that, for he liked John, and thought he was a good man.

But what she could not gain in a fair way she set out to gain by fraud. Now when Her-od's birth-day came he made a feast, and the chief men of the land sat at the board with him. His wife had one child—his own niece—a fair young girl, named Sa-lo-me. When the feast was at its height and the men were filled with wine, the young girl came in and danced to the sound of the flute and harp, and pleased Her-od and those that sat at meat with him.

EAST-ERN FLUTE PLAY-ER.

Those who drink wine, or strong drink, are led to do strange things, that they would not do if in their right minds. The drink goes to the brain, and is the worst thing that we can put in our mouths. We can-not trust it. It does not serve all in the same way, and is the cause of most of the great crimes that are done in the world. It turns men in-to beasts. Some are like wolves that wish to rend and tear, and sad are the homes where these go in and out. Some, like swine, grow dull by the day, and spend the best years of their lives in sleep, their breath strong with the fumes of rum and beer. They can-not think as they ought. They can-not work as they ought. Men of fine minds have made wrecks of them-selves by their love of strong drink, which has been well called the curse of the land. It is a curse. What woe has it brought to our homes and hearts! Much wine was drunk at these feasts in days of old, and as Her-od wished to make a fine show at this time, there had been no lack of food or drink. The new queen was shrewd. She knew how men were when full of wine, and with-out a word to Her-od planned out this scheme, and made her own child share with her in the great crime. The girl was fair, and full of grace, and the king said to her, Ask what thou wilt and I will give it to thee. And he swore that he would keep his word though she might ask for the half of his realm. The girl went out, and said to her moth-er, What shall I ask for? And her moth-er told her to ask for the head of John the Bap-tist. So the girl came back at once to the king, and said to him, My wish is that you have brought to me here, on a large dish, the head of John the Bap-tist.

The king was grieved at this, for he had not thought that a young girl would ask for so strange a gift, and he had no wish to put John to death. But for the sake of his oath, and be-cause those who sat with him had heard him swear that he would give her what she might ask for, he would not say, No. Weak man that he was, he had more fear of men than of God! And he sent a man to cut off John's head, and it was brought in on a large dish. And the girl took it, and gave it to her moth-er.

When what had been done to John came to the ears of his friends, they at once took up his corpse and laid it in a tomb, and went and told Je-sus that he was dead.

At the same time the Twelve, whom Je-sus had sent out, came back and told him all that they had done and taught. Their work, and the cures they had made, had caused more or less talk, and men sought in vain to make it clear to their minds who Je-sus could be.

Some thought he was one of the old proph-ets, or seers, come back to earth. But Her-od did not think so. When he heard of him, and of the strange things that had been done in his name, he feared that John, whose head he had struck off, had come back to haunt him. And for this cause did he wish to see Je-sus.

CHAPTER X.

FIVE THOU-SAND FED.—JE-SUS WALKS ON THE SEA.—HE WARNS JU-DAS.

Since the Twelve came back, they had had no chance to rest night or day. So great were the crowds that flocked to see and to hear them, and Je-sus, that they scarce had time to eat. And Je-sus felt that they must slip off to some place far from the throng, where they could rest and pray, and gain fresh strength for the work there was yet to be done. So they took a boat and sailed to the north-east end of the lake, to a place called Beth-sai-da, or "Fish-house." When the crowd found it out, they set off on foot, and ran a great part of the way, and were there to meet Je-sus and the Twelve as soon as the prow of their boat touched the shore.

When Je-sus saw this his heart was touched, for he felt that they had need of him, and he healed the sick, and

Five Thou-sand Fed. 187

taught them till the day was far spent. Then the Twelve came to him, and said, Send these a-way that they may go out in-to the towns near at hand, and find them-selves food,

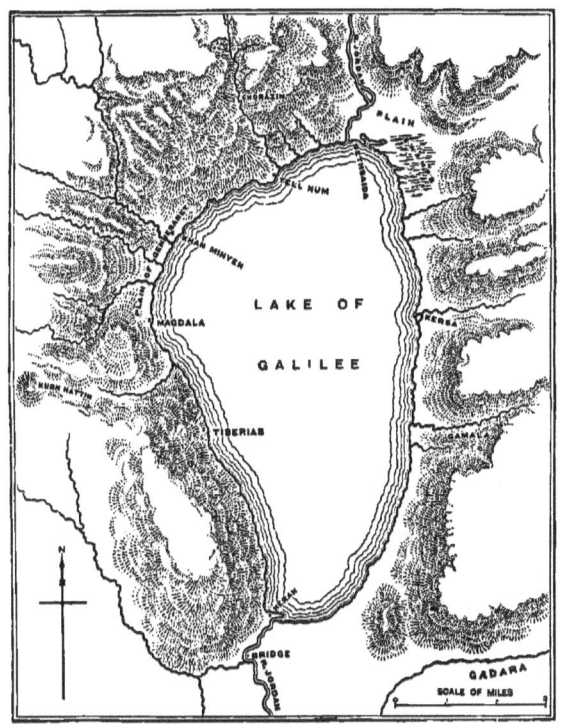

MAP OF THE LAKE, OR SEA OF GAL-I-LEE.

and a place to sleep. Je-sus said, They need not go. Give ye them some-thing to eat. They said, Shall we go and buy as much bread as it would take to feed them? For there were at least five thousand there.

Je-sus said, How much bread have ye? Go and see. They brought back word that they had but five loaves and two small fish. He told the Twelve to bid the crowd sit down on the green grass. And Je-sus took the bread and the fish, and blest them, and gave them to the Twelve that they might feed the crowd. And when all had their fill, there were left twelve bas-kets full of bits of bread and fish.

We are to learn from this that if our store is scant, if we have on hand but a small stock of faith our-selves, we have but to pray to Je-sus and he will give us all and more than we ask for. His flock must be fed; and though it may not be clear to us how they can be cared for, the Lord will show us the ways and means we are to use. The Word of God is a small book, but what a great host have been fed from it! and there is still no lack! The Twelve had first to bring the bread and the fish to Je-sus, that he might bless them in their use. And we must go to him with all our needs and our cares, and he will bless us and help us, and we will have strength to do a great and a good work.

Such a great thing drew the crowd more and more to Je-sus, and the Twelve shared in the awe that was felt. Je-sus read their hearts; and feared that they might break off the chains that bound them to Rome, and seek to make him their king. This would not do, for he would at once be put to death by those who sought to kill him. His time had not yet come; there was still more work for him to do in the world, and he must check those who thought to gain wealth if they placed him on a throne.

CHRIST FEED-ING THE MUL-TI-TUDE.

So Je-sus told the Twelve to take the boat and cross the Lake to Ca-per-na-um and he would join them there. As dusk came on he coaxed the crowd to leave him, and when most of them had gone he went up to the hill-top to pray and rest. Not a friend was near him but God.

Je-sus taught men how to pray. God is near us at all times, and knows the thoughts of our hearts. But though he is near us, we may not be near him, and it does us good to go off by our-selves that we may speak with God, and hear the sound of His voice in our hearts. At times we are cast down and walk, as it were, through a vale of tears. We are on low ground; we may be sick, or poor, or in grief of some sort, and the whole world seems dark and drear.

But what a lift it gives the soul to go up on some hill-top! We seem to shake off the dust of earth. The air is pure and clear. And all is calm. We look down on the road by which we came, and what seemed great rocks in our way we see now are the steps by which we rose to high ground. The griefs, and toils, and cares, which we have to bear, are not to cast us down, but to lift us up; to make us feel our need of Jesus. When we feel weak and sad, and the way seems dark, then we must look up, and pray. Though you may stand in a low place—though you may be sick, or poor—you can still have a mount of prayer. When we seek to rise—when we want to be good and to do good—Je-sus is there to help us. A lift from him is worth all the help that men can give; for when the soul is on high ground, we can be brave and bold, for the Lord is with us.

Da-vid says, I will lift up mine eyes un-to the hills from whence comes my help. My help comes from the Lord, which made heav-en and earth. The Lord will care for thee and keep thee. The Lord is thy shade up-on thy right hand. The sun shall not smite thee by day, nor the moon by night. In this song he shows how great was his trust in God, and we, too, should have the same trust, for he is our Rock and our Strength. If Je-sus had need to pray, how much more do we need to seek him, and to pray to him. And how calm and still was the place on the hill-top, where our Lord went to talk with God at the close of a hard day's work.

The night grew dark. Now and then the moon broke through a rift in the clouds, and Je-sus saw the boat in the midst of the sea. The wind beat her out of her course, and she could make no head-way, and Je-sus grieved that those he loved were so tossed by winds and waves, with no one near to calm them.

How oft we hear it said, "the dark-est hour is just be-fore the dawn!" And how true it is! Just when we give up hope; when we feel as if we were lost, and there seems naught to do but to lie down and die, then help comes. God leaves us in this way to test, or try, our faith. If he chose, he could keep all those who love him, free from fear, or ills of all kinds. But then they might trust in their own strength, and not look up to him, or lean on him as they ought. With a word Je-sus could have hushed the storm that dashed the waves to foam. But the men had first to try to save them-selves. If they had had real faith in Je-sus they would have called on him. But this they did not do. They thought he must be near them or he could not hear them. Their boat was in the trough of the sea, and so were they. They did not lift up their hearts as they should have done, but spent most of the night at their vain tasks. With sad hearts they plied the oars, and feared their boat would soon be a wreck. But while Je-sus prayed for them they could not be lost. It was the fourth watch of the night—near dawn of the next day—when the men, worn out with their toils, saw a strange shape on the sea. On, on it came, and trod the waves with ease, and seemed as if it meant to pass them by. They thought it was a ghost, and cried out with fear. But the voice they well knew spoke to them and said, It is I; be not a-fraid.

So when we are in the midst of the storms of life, when the sea is rough, and we are borne down with a weight of woe, when all is dark, and we lose hope, then Je-sus comes, and we hear his voice say, I am near; have no fear. And strength comes, and light shines in, and joy fills our souls once more.

When Je-sus spoke to the Twelve, and they knew who he was, they beg-ged him to come in-to the ship. But ere he could reach there, Pe-ter, who knew not how to wait, said, Lord, if it be thou, bid me come to thee up-on the waves. Je-sus said, Come. Pe-ter at once got down from the boat, and set out to walk to Je-sus. With his gaze fixed on the Lord all went well; but as soon as he looked at the waves, and felt the force of the winds, he lost faith, and began to sink. Then he cried out, Lord save me! And Je-sus stretched forth his hand, and caught hold of him, and said, O thou of lit-tle faith, why didst thou doubt?

JE-SUS WALKS ON THE SEA.

Then both of them climbed in-to the boat, and the wind ceased to blow. And all those in the boat—the crew and all the rest—bowed down at his feet, and said, Of a truth thou art the Son of God.

We are all right—safe from winds and storms—if Je-sus is in the boat with us. For we are all like sea-men. The world is our sea. All goes well when the skies are clear, and the waves are calm. But when the storms come— when the harsh winds blow, and grief and pain are to be borne—what then? Shall we trust Je-sus in the day-time and not in the night? If Je-sus is with us in the boat, we are safe; we shall be sure to reach the port for which we steer.

The next day, when those whom Jes-sus had fed, found that he, as well as the Twelve, had left the place, they took boats and came to Ca-per-na-um to seek for them. And when they found Je-sus on the west shore of the lake, they asked him how he got there, for they knew that he had no boat.

Je-sus did not tell them, for there was no need that they should know. He said that they did not seek him be-cause of the words that he spoke, but be-cause of the signs they had seen, and be-cause they did eat of the loaves and were filled. Toil not for the food which does not last, but for that which is a feast for all time. The Son of man will give this food to you, for this did God send him in-to the world.

They said to him then, What must we do, that we may work the works of God? It was as if they said, What works must we do to please God? The works of the law were such as the law bade them do, and the works of God would be the things that God bade them do. Je-sus said to them, This is the work of God, that ye be-lieve on him whom he hath sent. This was the one thing they were to do, to have faith in Je-sus. They were to toil, as the men did in the boat, to come to Je-sus, and while they were yet on the way he would go out to meet them.

They had thought more of works and deeds, than they did of faith, but the words of Je-sus made things more plain to them. It was clear that he meant to turn their thoughts from the works they had in view, and fix them on him-self. No one else had put forth such a claim, and he must prove that by this act of faith men would do God's will.

So they said to Je-sus, What sign dost thou give us, that we may see, and be-lieve thee? What deeds dost thou do? Our fath-ers, they said, Were fed with man-na, or bread, which rained down on them out of heav-en. This was a hint that the bread Je-sus gave them was made on earth, and as though they said, Canst thou do more than this, so that thy laws will take the place of the laws of Mo-ses?

Je-sus said to them, I say to you, Mo-ses gave you not bread out of heav-en; but my Fath-er gives you the true bread out of heav-en. For the bread of God is that which comes down out of heav-en and gives life to all the world. The man-na which fell from the skies, when Mo-ses led the Jews out of the land of E-gypt, was food to last them from day to day. It served them in place of bread for that time of need. It kept the breath of life in them. So did these loaves, with which Je-sus had fed the crowd by the sea-shore. The food they took in-to their mouths, was not the kind that Je-sus meant, when he said, The bread of God comes out of heav-en, and gives life to all the world.

They said to him, Lord, give us this bread that we may want no more.

Je-sus said to them, I am the bread of life; he that comes to me shall hun-ger no more; and he that be-lieves in me shall thirst no more.

If we give our hearts to Je-sus, he will come in, and dwell with us, and feed us with food that shall give us strength and joy.

He said to the Jews, But I would have you know that ye have seen me, and be-lieve not in me. All that which God gives me shall come to me; and him that comes to me I will in no wise cast out.

God's gift to us was His Son, Je-sus Christ. God's gift to Je-sus was the souls of those who had faith in him. These were to be the stars in his crown: the fish in his net. He had spread wide his net of love, and those caught in it —young or old, great or small—would not be thrown out. For I have come down from heaven, said Je-sus, not to do mine own will, but the will of him that sent me. And this is the will of God, that all those who come to me should live with me in the next world, and that I should raise them up on the Last Day.

The Jews did not dwell up-on the hope he held out to them of a new life, but found fault with him be-cause he said, I am the bread, which was sent down to you as a gift from God. And they said, Is not this Je-sus, the son of the car-pen-ter at Naz-a-reth? How then can he say that he came down from heav-en? How can he claim to be more than mere man?

Je-sus said to them, Do not find fault with my words. No one can come to me till God who hath sent me draw him, and I will raise him up at the Last Day. For it was said of old, And they shall all be taught of God. He that hath heard and learned of God comes un-to me. We must first have faith in God and his word be-fore we can have faith in Je-sus, and give our hearts to him.

No one has seen God, save he which is from God, he has seen him. And what I say to you is true, he that has faith in me shall live for-ev-er. I am the bread of life. Your fath-ers did eat the man-na, in the wild lands where no food was, and they died.

This was to bring to their minds the speech that Mo-ses made, when the Jews found fault with him. They came to him and said, We will send men out to seek for the land, and to bring us word by what way we must go up, and in-to what towns we shall come. And Mo-ses was pleased, and said, I took twelve men of you, one of a tribe; and they left us, and went up in-to the mount, and came to the vale of Esh-col, and searched through it. And they took of the fruit of the land in their hands, and brought it down to us, and brought word back, It is a good land which the Lord our God doth give us. But ye found fault, and held back, and said that for hate, and not for love, had the Lord brought you out of the land of E-gypt.

Mo-ses told them to dread nought, and to fear nought that might come in their way, for the Lord their God would go be-fore them, and would fight for them. He was their fire by night and their cloud by day, to show them the way they were to go. But they would not be-lieve in Him, or give their hearts to God, and so He said, Not one of these men shall see that good land. This is what Je-sus meant when he said, They did eat man-na, and died. And the Jews that stood round Je-sus knew of this if they had read the Books which made up the Word of God.

Je-sus said, This is the bread which comes down out of heav-en, and those who eat of it shall not die. I am the bread of life, which came down from God; he that eats this bread shall live for-ev-er. The bread is my flesh which I will give for the life of the world.

The Jews then took hold of his words, and were so loud in their talk it was feared there would be a fight. They said, How can this man give us his flesh to eat? They did not take what he said in the right sense.

Je-sus said to them, If ye do not eat my flesh and drink my blood ye have no life in you. He that eats my flesh and drinks my blood, shall not die; and I will raise him up at the Last Day. For my flesh is meat in-deed, and my blood is drink in-deed. He that eats my flesh and drinks my blood, dwells in me and I in him. Je-sus meant by this that he was to be to men what food and drink were. All those who come to him and be-lieve in him, are said to feed on him. They have no fear of death, for they know that when this life ends, Je-sus will bear them to his home on high.

These words seemed strange to most of those who heard Je-sus speak them in the church at Ca-per-na-um. They did not know just what he meant. Some of them sought to find fault with Je-sus, and when we set out to pick flaws we are quite sure to find them. They thought more of his words, than of what the words meant.

Bread is oft-times called, "the staff of life." That means, that as we lean on a staff to help us when we are weak, so do we feel the need of bread to keep up our strength.

Je-sus is to us the bread of life. We are to feed on him in our hearts by faith. If the hearts of the Jews had been touched, if they had felt the least shame for their sins, they would have paid heed to the words that Je-sus spoke.

Some of those who had been drawn to Je-sus had their doubts, for their faith was not yet strong and free from the taint of the world. Je-sus knew this, and ere they left the church he spoke to them and said, Does this cause you to doubt and fear? What will ye say then if ye see me go back to the place from whence I came, and be no more on earth?

It is the soul that makes us live, the flesh in it-self is of no use. The words that I speak are the life of the soul. But there are some of you, he said, who still have no faith in me. For this cause have I said un-to you, that no one can come to me if God has not drawn him. For faith is the gift of God, which all can have who will. If you do not have it—if self comes be-tween you and Je-sus—if pride keeps you back—if the gold you have shuts out your view—if you hate the good and love that which is bad—it is your own fault.

From this time some of those who had left all to be with Christ, went back to their homes, and walked with him no more. His words had not brought life to them.

Sad at heart, Je-sus spoke to the Twelve, and said, Will ye, too, leave me? Pe-ter spoke up, and said, Lord, to whom shall we go? Thy words give life to the soul. And we have faith in thee, and know that thou art the Son of God.

Je-sus said, Did I not choose the Twelve, and one of you is a dev-il? Now he spoke of Ju-das; for he it was who would prove a false friend, and would give him up to the Jews to be put to death. None knew this but Je-sus; but if Ju-das had had a good heart he would have felt that these words were to warn him. For he was one of the Twelve.

Je-sus felt more and more a-lone. He had some friends; but he had more foes; and the Jews were so wroth with him that they sent out spies to watch him, and to dog his steps, and to bring back word of all that he said and did.

No one could be quite so much alone as Je-sus was. These men he went with were rough in their speech and their ways. It was hard to talk to them, and to make things plain to them. Most of them were quite poor, and lived, as we say, from hand to mouth. That is, they had to work hard each day for the food they had need of. For they must eat to live. Je-sus had no home, no near ties. It was God's will that he should roam the earth, to seek and to save those who are lost. He was to go, as men go out for the lambs and the sheep that have strayed from the flock. And he was to bring them back to the fold: that is, to the home on high. And he will take the lambs in his arms, and they shall be safe with Him.

Je-sus had not a friend on earth to whom he could tell his woes, and who would share in his griefs and joys. He

RU-INS OF A SYN-A-GOGUE.

was born as we are, and felt all our needs. He must have longed for the love of wife and child, and the sweet joys of home. When we have to bear a cross, we have him to help us. But he had no one; no one but God.

As Je-sus was on his way through Gal-i-lee he passed by a large field of corn. It was God's day, but as those with Je-sus were faint for want of food, they thought it no harm to pick and eat the ears of corn that grew by the way-side. But when the Jews, who lay in wait to find

IN THE CORN-FIELD.

fault, saw what was done, they cried out that these men broke God's law. They held it was a sin to reap or to thresh on God's day, and to pluck the corn was to reap it, and to rub it in the hands and to blow off the chaff was the same as if they had threshed it. So strict were these

WOMEN GRINDING CORN.

Jews that no one must walk on the grass, or pluck fruit from the trees on this day that was set a-part as a Day of Rest.

Je-sus said to them, Have ye not read what Da-vid did, when he and those with him were in need of food? How he went in-to the house of God, and did eat the shew-bread, which the law said none but the priests should

TA-BLE OF SHEW-BREAD.

eat? Or have ye not read in the law, how that the priests broke the Sab-bath and are not held up to blame? I say un-to you that here is One who is the real tem-ple of God. For the Son of Man is Lord of the Sab-bath. Since Je-sus came on earth the first day of the week has been called the Lord's Day. If we do good works and lead souls to Christ we keep the Lord's Day, but if we do things that lead souls from Christ, and if we turn our-selves from good works, and fill our minds with thoughts of sin, and waste our time, we do not keep the Lord's Day as we ought.

One day when Je-sus went in-to the church, or syn-a-

WILD WITH RAGE.

gogue, to teach as was his wont, there was a man there who had no use of his right hand, for it had been hurt so that the flesh shrank a-way. It may be that he prayed Christ to heal him that he might not be forced to beg.

The Scribes and the rest of the Jews kept a close watch on Je-sus, to see if he would dare to heal the man on the Day of Rest; for then they would charge him with the crime, and bring him be-fore the San-he-drin, the great court of the Jews.

Je-sus knew their thoughts, and did not keep them long in doubt. He bade the man whose hand was of no use, to stand out were he could be seen by all. Then said Je-sus to them, I ask if it is the law to do good or to do harm on the Day of Rest? to save life, or to take life? And he looked round on them all, that they might speak if they chose, for he read their hearts and knew what they meant to do. But they held their peace. They did not speak.

Then he said to the man, Stretch forth thine hand. And he stretched it out, and his hand was made whole.

The Jews left the church, wild with rage, and laid plans to put Je-sus to death, for it was not safe to have such a man teach and preach in their midst.

CHAPTER XI.

THE LORD'S PRAYER.—THE LAW-YER.—THE RICH FOOL.—JE-SUS TALKS TO THE CROWD, AND BIDS THEM WATCH.

Je-sus was wont to pray on the hill-tops, where he could be far from men, and where none but God could hear him. And one day, when the Twelve were with him, they asked Je-sus to teach them how to pray as John was wont to teach those who were with him. Je-sus said, When ye pray, use these words, Our Fath-er who art in heav-en, hallow-ed be thy name. Thy king-dom come. Thy will be done on earth as it is in heaven. Give us this day our dai-ly bread. For-give us our debts as we for-give our debt-ors. Lead us not in-to temp-ta-tion, but de-liv-er us from e-vil, for thine is the king-dom the power and the glo-ry, for-ev-er. A-men.

In plain words they were to ask that God's name might be kept ho-ly, and his reign come soon up-on the earth. They were to pray that all the world might know God, and do His will as did the an-gels round His throne. They were to ask for bread, or strength, day by day. They were not to pray but once, and think that that would last them for the rest of the year, or the rest of their lives. As they would need bread from day to day so would they need strength from God. For-give us our sins as we for-give those who have done wrong to us. Lead us not in-to sin—let no one tempt us—but do thou save us—for thou art the King of kings, and thy strength and glo-ry is with-out end. The word A-men means, So let it be; or, may all this be done for the praise of thy great name. Then Je-sus spoke a par-a-ble and said, Which of you shall have a friend, and shall go to him at mid-night, and say to him, Friend, lend me three loaves; for a friend of mine has come to me from a long way off, and I have nought to give him to eat. And the man in the house vexed that he has been roused from his sleep, shall say to him, The door is now shut, and my chil-dren are in bed with me; I can-not rise and give thee the loaves.

I say to you, Though he will not rise and give him be-cause he is his friend, yet be-cause he pleads with him he will rise and give him all that he needs. I say un-to you, Ask, and it shall be giv-en you; seek, and ye shall find; knock—for he knows what we need, and will keep back no good gift. We think we know what we need, but if God should give us just the things we asked for, we would find out, some time, they were not the best things for us.

The Jews were still on the watch for Je-sus, and sought to trip him up in his words. One day a Jew asked Je-sus to dine with him, and he went in and sat down to meat. When the man of the house saw it, he thought it strange that Je-sus did not first wash his his hands. For the Jews were strict in all such things, and were apt to think more of clean hands than they did of clean hearts.

WASH-ING HANDS.

It was rude for this man to speak out so to his guest, and Je-sus had cause to chide him. And the time had come for him to speak to this sect of Jews, of this one great sin of theirs.

Je-sus said to the man whose guest he was, Now is this a proof of the way that ye do. For ye make clean the out-side of the cup and the plat-ter; but in-side you are vile and full of sin. Ye fools, did not he who made the out-side make the in-side as well? But give for alms those things that are with-in—the good gifts of the heart—and all things shall be clean un-to you. But all ye do is to be seen of men.

Now the Jews had to pay a tenth part of all they earned, or made off the land, as a tax to the church, and for the care of the priests. This tax part was called tithes, which means a tenth part, and is in use in some parts of the world to this day.

Je-sus said to these Jews, Woe un-to you, for ye pay tithes of mint, and rue, and all kinds of herbs, for these things cost you not much. But ye are not just to men, and show no love for God. And these things ye ought to have done, for they were worth more than what you did. Ye blind guides! ye strain out the gnat, and eat the cam-el.

Je-sus meant by this that they gave more thought to small things than they did to large ones. They did not see the right way them-selves, and so were not fit to act as guides. For "if the blind lead the blind, both will fall in-to the ditch."

Woe un-to you! said Je-sus, for ye cleanse the out-side of the cup and of the dish, but leave them foul with-in. He said they were blind, for they did wrong to gain wealth. And spent all they had on them-selves. Love of self makes us blind to all needs but our own.

Ye are like tombs said Je-sus, which are hid from sight. The ground seems fair and smooth, and those who walk there know not that with-in they are full of dead men's bones—Je-sus meant that these Jews were false friends; their hearts were not true,

There were some at this mid-day meal who were well versed in the law; and one of them said to Je-sus, Mas-ter, when you speak thus you find fault with us as well as the rest.

Je-sus said, Woe un-to you, ye men of law! for ye load men with more than they can bear, and ye your-selves do nought to ease them.

It was as if he said, Ye have not taught men what they ought to know; Ye have not sought the way of truth your-selves, and have kept out those who might have walked there-in.

Much more he said, and the Scribes and the rest of the Jews pressed up-on him and urged him to talk. For they lay in wait as wild beasts lie in wait for their prey, or as dogs watch for their game—that they might catch him in some of his words; and bring him up to the chief court where the high-priest sat.

In the mean-time the crowd was so great that Je-sus was forced to go out of the house and speak to them. And first of all, he spoke to the Twelve, and warned them to pay no heed to what these men taught, who seemed to be true, and yet were so false. All should be made clear in the end, for there is nought that is hid that shall not be known. And he said, What ye said in the dark, shall be heard in the light; and that which was told in the ear, shall be cried out from the house-tops. God will set all things right. Je-sus told them to have no fear of man, or what man could do; but to fear God, and to trust in Him. And when they bring you be-fore the priests, or those who are to judge you, take no thought of what ye shall say. For

God will put the right thoughts in your mind, and teach you the words ye ought to speak.

One of those in the crowd had heard Je-sus say that God would set all things right, and so he said to him, Mas-ter, speak to my broth-er so that he share with me the half of his wealth.

Je-sus said un-to him, Man, who made me a judge o-ver you, to give each one his share of such things? And he said to the crowd, Take heed, and keep your-selves from the love of greed; for a man's wealth in this life is not in the goods that he owns.

And he spake a par-a-ble to them, and said, The ground of a rich man brought forth much fruit and grain. And he said to him-self, What shall I do, for I have no room to stow a-way my fruits. He did not look up-on his crops as the gift of God, but claimed them as his own, to do with as he liked.

And he said, This will I do. I will pull down my small barns, and build large ones that will hold all my grain, and my goods. And I will say to my soul, Soul, thou hast much goods laid up that will last thee for years to come; take thine ease, eat, drink, and be mer-ry.

But God said un-to him, This night thou shalt die; and the things thou hast laid up, whose shall they be? So is it with him who lays up wealth for him-self, and has no love of God in his heart, and has done no good in the world.

Je-sus said they were not to give too much thought to what they were to eat, or where they were to get clothes. They were to trust in God, and not fret, and He would take care of them. He said, Look at the birds; they do not sow nor reap, nor have they store-room or barn; yet God gives them all the food they need from day to day. How much

YOUNG RA-VENS.

FISH HAWK.

more are ye worth than these birds of the air? And which of you can add to his height? If ye then can-not do that which is least, Why take ye thought for the rest? See the lil-ies how they grow; they toil not, they spin not, and yet I say un-to you that Sol-o-mon in all his glo-ry was not robed like one of these. If then God doth so clothe the grass of the field, which lives but one day, and is then thrown in-to the fire and burnt up, how much more will he clothe you, O ye of lit-tle faith? Give not all your thoughts to what ye shall eat and drink, nor be ye full of doubts and fears. Those who are in the world seek the things of the world, but your Fath-er knows what things ye need, and will take care of you. Trust in God. Seek first his king-

COR-MO-RANT.

dom, and all these things shall be yours. Fear not, lit-tle flock; for it is your Fath-er's good will to give you his king-dom. Then, as if he knew that in their hearts some in the crowd asked, What shall I do? How shall I get this king-dom? Je-sus said, Sell what ye have, and give alms. Get rid of the wealth that holds you down, and give some of it to the poor. Make for your-selves bags which wax not old, and lay up for your-selves wealth in heav-en—be

RA-VEN.

rich in love to God—and you need have no fear of thieves or of moths. And where your wealth is—where are the things you think the most of—there will your heart be.

The out-side robe worn in the East was so long that it had to be held up a-round the waist, or loins, by a belt or cord. If not thus girt up, those who wore this dress could not walk or run, or serve those who were in need. So Je-sus who wished to teach them to be on the watch to do good works, and not to sit down and wait for a chance to come, went on with his talk, and said:

Let your loins be girt a-bout, and your lamps be lit. And be ye like to men that wait for their Mas-ter to come back from the wed-ding feast; so that when he comes and knocks, they may rise at once and o-pen the door. Blest are those ser-vants whom the Lord when he comes shall find on the watch; for I say un-to you that he shall gird him-self and make them sit down to meat, and will come forth and serve them. Those who are on the watch for Christ, who keep the door of their hearts a-jar, are sure to have him for a guest. And while they seek to serve him, he serves them and fills them with joy and peace such as the world can-not give, nor take a-way.

Je-sus said, If the good-man of the house had known at what hour the thief would come, he would have watched, and not let him break in-to his house. Be ye on the watch, for the Son of Man comes at an hour when ye think not. They were to watch and pray and not lose heart. We are to be on the look-out for Je-sus, and not lose faith in him if he fails to come at the hour we have set. He is sure to come. The Son of Man comes as a thief in the night—so does death—with soft foot-fall, no one hears, no one knows. If we have led good lives, and are of those who wait on the Lord, then it is all right; but oh, how sad it is when those who have had no room for Christ in their hearts, are cut down in the midst of their sins!

Pe-ter said un-to Je-sus, Is this par-a-ble for us or for all? and Je-sus went on with his talk as if he had not heard what Pe-ter said: Who then is the faith-ful and wise stew-ard whom his lord shall set to rule o-ver his house-hold, and to give them their share of bread? A stew-ard is one who is left in charge. He sees that the rents are paid in, and pays all the bills that are due, and acts in all things as the mas-ter would do if he were there. Blest is that ser-vant, or stew-ard, whom his lord when he comes shall find so true to the trust that has been placed in him. Of a truth I say to you, that he will set him to rule o-ver all that he hath.

But if the ser-vant say in his heart, My lord does not come at the hour we looked for him, and shall be-gin to beat the men and maids, and to eat and drink, and to get him-self drunk: the mas-ter of that ser-vant shall come in a day when he looked not for him, and in an hour that he knows not, and shall judge him as he finds him.

The ser-vant, who knew the will of his lord, and yet did not do right him-self nor teach those in his charge to do as they should, shall bare his back to the lash and shall have at least two-score stripes for his fault.

But he that knew not, and yet did things he ought not to have done, and for which he ought to be flogged, shall have but few stripes. For of him to whom much is giv-en, much shall be asked; and of those who have much placed in their care, men will ask more than they do of those whom they do not trust.

I am come to send fire on the earth, said Je-sus. The good news was to spread like a blaze through the land. But ere this could be done, he must die; and he spoke of his death in words that were strange to those who heard, though he said with a sigh, What a weight is on me till this thing be done? Each step he took was in the shade of that dark cross, to which each day he drew more near.

Do ye think, he said, that I am come to give peace on the earth? I tell you, No. But there will be strife in each house-hold, and it will be made known who are my friends, and who are my foes.

He turned then and said to the crowd, When ye see a cloud rise out of the west, at once ye say, It will rain, and so it does. And when the south wind blows ye say, There will be great heat; and it comes to pass. Ye false prophets! Ye know how to read the signs on the face of the sky and of the earth, but ye know not how to tell the signs of this time. Plain as the signs were, they could not see them. Yes, and why e-ven of your-selves judge ye not what is right? For as thou art on the way with him whom thou hast wronged, thou dost give heed to him, that thou mayst be set free; lest he hale thee to the judge, and the judge shall give thee to an of-fi-cer, and thou be thrown in-to jail. I tell thee, thou shalt by no means come out till thou hast paid the last mite—Je-sus was the one they had wronged, and if they made their peace with him now, all would be well with them. But if they did not he would bring them to God, and God would cast them out in-to the dark, would turn His face from them, and there they would have to stay till they got rid of all their sins.

CHAPTER XII.

JE-SUS GOES TO TYRE AND SI-DON.—HEALS THE CHILD
OF THE GREEK WOM-AN.—COMES TO GAL-I-LEE.—
GIVES THE BLIND MAN SIGHT.—HIS
CHARGE TO PE-TER.

Je-sus left the Jews, and went to Tyre and Si-don,

RU-INS OF TYRE.

two large towns north of Gal-i-lee, on the west coast of this land, which is called The Ho-ly Land, be-cause Je-sus lived there. Sad at heart, he thought to hide him-self

SI-DON.

or a while, where he would not be known. But scarce
had he reached those parts when a wom-an, a Greek, came
out and cried un-to him, Help me, O Lord, for my child

SEND HER A-WAY.

is out of her mind, and it is a grief to see her. But Je-sus
spoke not one word.

She had been brought up to bow down to gods of
wood and stone, to cry out to them for help who had no
help in them. It may be that they had failed more than

once, and still her faith held out. But love for her child brought her to Je-sus. She must have heard of him in some way, or she would not have gone out to meet him Je-sus read her heart, but wished to prove to the Twelve that she had faith in him. Je-sus had been sent to the Jews, but the Twelve were to go out, and preach to all the world, and must plead for this poor wom-an, and not shut her out of the fold.

And the Twelve came and said to him, Tell her to go a-way, for she cries af-ter us. They feared she would draw a crowd a-round Je-sus, which they knew would not please him, since he had come there for rest.

Je-sus said to her, I was sent but un-to the Jews; whom he called the lost sheep of the house of Is-ra-el, the name that God gave to Ja-cob.

Still the woman cried Lord, help me, and threw her-self down at his feet. Je-sus said, It is not right to take the chil-dren's bread, and cast it to the dogs. In the East, the dogs, those, at least, that were kept in the house, had a place on the floor when their masters sat at the feast, and were free to pick up what fell from the edge of the ta-ble. The wom-an, quick to note what was meant, said at once, Yes, Lord, but the dogs eat the crumbs which fall from their mas-ters ta-ble. She meant that she would be glad of a small part of that which the Jews did not care for, and would not miss.

Je-sus said to her, O wom-an, great is thy faith; be it done to thee e-ven as thou wilt. And her child was well from that hour.

Je-sus went on till he came to the east shore of the Sea

of Gal-i-lee; and he went up on the hill-side, and sat down there. But he could not rest; for there came to him great crowds, and they brought with them the lame, the blind, the dumb, those who had lost hand or foot, or were sick in some way, and they cast them down at the feet of Je-sus

HE SAT DOWN TO REST AND PRAY.

that he might heal them. They had heard of Je-sus, but had seen none of the signs that he did, and when they heard the dumb speak, and saw the lame walk, the blind see, and the maimed—those who had lost some part of hand or foot—made well and sound, they gave praise to the One, true God. For these folks were Jews, but had dwelt with those who bowed down to false gods, and were half won to think as they did.

Then Je-sus called the Twelve to him, and said, My heart aches for this crowd, for they have been with me for three days and have had nought to eat. I will not send them home with-out food, af-ter such a long fast, lest they should faint on the road. The Twelve said to him, Where could we go to get the bread we should need to feed so great a crowd?

Je-sus asked them how much bread they had, and they said, Sev-en loaves and a few small fish. Je-sus bade the crowd stretch them-selves on the ground; and he took the sev-en loaves and the fish, and gave thanks and brake them. Then he gave them to the Twelve, and they gave the food to the crowd. And they did all eat till they could eat no more, and when the feast was at an end, there was still left sev-en bas-kets full of bread and meat. And those that were fed at this time, were four thous-and men, wom-en, and chil-dren. Then Je-sus sent the crowd a-way, and went with the Twelve in-to a boat, and came to a place called Mag-da-la on the west shore of the Lake.

Here the Jews came to him and asked him to show them some sign by which they might know that he came down from heav-en. Je-sus said to them, When the sun sets ye say, No storms are near, for the sky is red. And at sun-rise ye say, It will storm to-day, for the sky is red, and the clouds hang low. Ye know how to read the face of the sky, but are not quick to read the signs of the times. Those who were full of sin them-selves, and shut their eyes and their hearts to the truth, were fierce to have men prove their words. But Je-sus would give them no sign. The signs that told of him, were all in the Word of God. And with a deep sigh Je-sus turned and left them, and went back to the boat, which soon set sail.

MAG-DA-LA.

When Je-sus and the Twelve came to the east side of the Lake, it was found that they had but one loaf of bread with them. Je-sus said to the Twelve, Have nought to do with the leav-en of the Jews—those who were his foes. And they said in their hearts, He said that be-cause we brought no bread with us.

Je-sus, who knew their thoughts, said, O ye of lit-tle

faith, why be vexed be-cause ye have brought no bread? Ye have eyes that see not, and ears that hear not, and how hard your hearts are. Did I not feed great crowds with a few loaves of bread? and how is it that ye fail to see that I spoke not to you of bread to eat, but that ye should not

LAKE, OR SEA OF GAL-I-LEE.

touch the leav-en of the Jews. Then they knew that Je-sus meant that they should pay no heed to what the Jews taught, who had set them-selves up as his foes.

As they came to shore at Beth-sai-da, where no doubt they stop-ped to buy bread, a blind man was brought to

Je-sus, that he might be healed. Je-sus took hold of the blind man by the hand, and led him out of the town. And when he had spit on his eyes, he laid his hands on him, and asked him what he saw. The man looked up, and said, I see men, and they are like trees that walk from place to place. Then Je-sus put his hands once more up-on his eyes, and

RU-INS AT CÆS-A-RE-A PHIL-IP-PI.

made him look up, and his sight came back, and all things were plain and clear to him. And Je-sus sent him to his own home, and told him not to go in-to the town.

Now when Je-sus came near the town of Cæs-a-re-a Phil-ip-pi which was at the foot of Mount Her-mon, he asked the Twelve, Who do men say that I am? They said, Some say thou art John, some E-li-jah, and some Jer-e-mi-ah, or one of the proph-ets. He said un-to them, Who say ye that I am? Pe-ter spoke up for the rest as well as for him-self, and said, Thou art the Christ, the Son of God.

MOUNT HER-MON.

Je-sus said to him, Bles-ed art thou, Si-mon son of Jo-nah, for flesh and blood hath not made it known to thee, but my Fath-er who is in heav-en. And I say un-to thee, Thou art Pe-ter, and on this rock I will build my church, and the gates of hell shall have no hold up-on it. And I will give to thee the keys of my king-dom, and all that thou shalt bind on earth shall be bound in heav-en, and all that thou shalt loose on earth shall be loosed in heav-en. Then charged he the Twelve that they should tell no man that he was Je-sus, the Christ—the One who had come to save the world.

The word Pe-ter means a stone, or rock, and Je-sus, made use of this as his text when he spoke to Pe-ter at this time. He meant that all whom he sent were like stones on which his church—Christ's Church—were to be built. "The gates of hell" was a phrase much used in the East, when men spoke of death. Christ was to give life; and those who kept near him, need have no fear of death. He gave to Pe-ter, not the keys of a church on earth, but the keys of the king-dom of God; and told him that what he did for the cause of Christ on earth, God would not find fault with.

From that time Je-sus be-gan to make known to the Twelve that he must go to Je-ru-sa-lem, and be ill-used by the chief priests and scribes, and be killed, and on the third day be raised up. Pe-ter laid hold of him, and said, Be it far from thee, Lord; this shall not be done un-to thee.

But he turned round and said to Pe-ter, Get thee be-hind me, Sa-tan; thou art a stone in my path, for thou dost mind not the things that are of God, but those that are of men. Pe-ter had need to say, the will of God, not mine, be done.

Then said Je-sus to the crowd near at hand, He who will come af-ter me, let him give up all thoughts of self, take up his cross, and walk in the same path I tread. For he who would save his life shall lose it, and he who would lose his life for my sake shall find it. He who thinks too much of this life shall lose the next life; and he who shrinks not from death, if he can serve Christ, will have a life of joy be-yond the grave.

Je-sus said, For what good will it do a man if he gain the whole world, and lose his own soul? or what price will he have to give to buy back the life he has lost? For the Son of Man shall come in the glo-ry of God the Fath-er, and with his an-gles, and shall judge each man by the works that he has done. And I say un-to you, It is true that some of those that stand here shall in no wise taste of death till they see the Son of Man come in-to his king-dom.

CHAPTER XIII.

JE-SUS IS TRANS-FIG-URED.—THE LIT-TLE CHILD IN THEIR MIDST.—HOW TO FOR-GIVE DEBTS.

From time to time Je-sus had in his talks thrown out a hint that the time of his death was not far off. He and the Twelve were now on the east side of the sea of Gal-i-lee, near mount Her-mon. At the end of six days Je-sus went up-on the mount to pray and took Pe-ter, and James, and John with him. Night came on, and in the hush of that hour, as Je-sus spoke with God, those who were with him saw a great change take place. His face shone like the sun, and his clothes were so white that the eye could not gaze up-on them. And Mo-ses and E-li-jah came and talked with him.

THE TRANS-FIG-U-RA-TION.

Je-sus is Trans-fig-ured.

Pe-ter said to Je-sus, Lord, it is good for us to be here: if it is thy will, let us make here three tab-er-na-cles, or tents; one for thee, one for Mo-ses, and one for E-li-jah. While he yet spoke a bright cloud hid the three from

REST AND SHADE.

sight, and there came a voice out of the cloud which said, This is my be-loved Son, in whom I am well pleased; hear ye him. They were to hear what he said, to take his words to heart, and to do as he told them.

When Pe-ter, James, and John, heard the voice, they

MOUNT TA-BOR.

fell down with their face to the ground. And Je-sus came and touched them, and said, Rise, be not a-fraid. And when they looked up they saw no one but Je-sus.

Some think that this scene took place on Mount Ta-bor, but as our Lord was now on his way to the north, Her-mon was the mount most near at hand. It was more than a hill, for its top reached up to a great height, and was at this time of the year tipped with snow. All down its sides were tall trees, with leaves so white that they shone like sil-ver in the sun; and when Je-sus was changed, when light shone all a-round, it is not strange that Pe-ter and John hid their eyes, and were dazed by what they saw and heard.

As they came down from the high mount, Je-sus bade them tell no one what they had seen, till the Son of Man had been raised from the dead. One of them said to Je-sus, Why then do the Scribes say that E-li-jah must first come? Je-sus said to them, E-li-jah shall first come, and make straight the paths of the Lord. But I say un-to you that E-li-jah has come, and they knew him not, but have done un-to him that which they chose. In the same way will they treat the Son of Man. Then they knew that he spake to them of John the Bap-tist.

The next day, when it was known that they had come down from the mount, a great crowd were there to meet Je-sus; and when they saw him they were struck with awe, and bowed down at his feet. And one of them said, Mas-ter, I brought un-to thee my son, who has a dumb dev-il. And he takes him, and tears him, so that he froths at the mouth, and grinds his teeth, and grows thin by the day.

The boy was dumb, and from time to time had fits which made him act in this way.

And the man said, I asked thy dis-ci-ples to cast out this de-mon, and they could not do it. Je-sus said, Bring him to me; and as soon as the boy came near Je-sus he fell down on the ground, and rolled back and forth, and frothed at the mouth.

Je-sus said to the fath-er, How long is it since this came up-on him? The man said, From the time he was a child. And oft-times it has thrown him in-to the fire and in-to the wa-ter, to burn him or drown him; but if thou canst do aught, help us, I pray thee. Je-sus said, The case rests with thee. If thou canst have faith, all things can be done.

Straight-way the fath-er of the boy cried out, Lord I be-lieve; help me to have more faith in thee. Then Je-sus said to the deaf and dumb de-mon, Come out of him, and go in-to him no more. With a cry the boy fell down to the ground, and lay as if there was no life in him. Some of the crowd thought he was dead. But Je-sus took him by the hand, and raised him, and he stood up and was cured.

When Je-sus was come in-to the house, some of the nine, who were not with him on the mount, said to him, Why could not we cast out the de-mon? Je-sus said to them, Be-cause your faith is weak. For I say un-to you, If ye have faith as a grain of mus-tard seed, ye shall say to this mount, Move from this place to that place, and it shall move. Je-sus did not mean that the mount would, in truth, change its place, but that those whose faith was great might see as great things done.

They went from this place, and passed through Gal-i-lee by lanes and by-ways; and he taught the Twelve, and said to them, The Son of Man shall be giv-en in-to the hands of men, and they shall kill him, and he shall rise from the grave on the third day. And those who heard him say this were sad and grieved, but dared not ask him what he meant.

And they came at last to Ca-per-na-um, and when they were in the house, Je-sus said to the Twelve, What was it that ye talked of while on the way here? And their shame was so great that they could not speak; for on the way they had quite a strife as to what rank they should hold in the king-dom that Je-sus was to set up. They knew what it meant to be on good terms with the Prince —the heir to the throne—for when he was made King he would do well by them. This was the way of the world, and all their thoughts were of self.

Je-sus sat down and called the Twelve to him, and said: If a man plans to be first of all he shall be last of all, and the slave of all. And he called a child to him, and took him in his arms, and said, If ye do not turn from your sins, and be as chil-dren, ye shall in no wise have part in the king-dom of God. He who shall be as meek as this child, shall be great in the king-dom of God. And he who puts down pride, and tries to teach a child and to do him good, in my name, I will be with both of them. He who takes me in-to his heart, takes not me a-lone but Him who sent me.

John said, Mas-ter we saw one cast out de-mons in thy name, and he was not one of us, and for this cause we told him to do so no more. But Je-sus said, For-bid him not; for no man who will do great works in my name, can speak ill of me. For he that is not a-gainst us is with us. He who shall give you a drink in my name, or be-cause ye are Christ's, shall in no wise lose his re-ward. God takes note of these good deeds, but they must be done in the right way, to please God, and with no thought of gain.

Je-sus said, He who shall cause a child to do wrong, or shall harm the weak ones who have faith in me, to turn them from me, it were as well for him that a great mill-stone were hung a-bout is neck, and that he were sunk in the depths of the sea. Je-sus meant by this that there was no hope that such a man would rise at the Last Day. Woe un-to the world be-cause of the sins of the world!—but woe to him who lays traps in the way of those who would seek Christ, so that their feet slip and they fall back in the ways of sin! The guilt is on those who lead men to do wrong. And he went on to warn them that it was bet-ter to put all things out of the way that led them in-to sin, or caused some one else to sin.

Men sin with their hands. They steal; they forge names to checks; they turn keys they have no right to touch; they strike, and fight, and raise the glass to their lips that lights with-in them the fires of hell. Je-sus said it were bet-ter to have both hands cut off, than that they should lead us in-to sin, and shut us out of heav-en.

Men sin with their feet. They go where they should not go. They make paths for them-selves, and say that they are right, and lead those to join them who look to them to be taught. They go not to church, or where good folks meet, but are found in the ways of sin. They walk not in the ways of the Lord. Je-sus said it would be bet-ter to have both feet cut off, and go through life thus maimed, than to lose our way to God's home, where all is light and love, and to be cast out of his sight at the Last Day. It

SOR-ROW FOR SIN.

is not thought that the lake of fire, means a real lake, or pit, in-to which the bad are thrown at the Last Day.

Each child knows how he feels when he has done wrong. He burns with shame. His fath-er knows it, and is not pleased. But he says not a word; for it is his wish to have the boy or girl come to him and ask him to forgive the sin. If the child does, it is all right, and all is joy and peace. But if he does not; and goes on and does worse things, can you blame the fath-er if he feels sad, and can-not own the boy, or girl, as his child?

Then, some day, there will come a great grief in the child's heart, though he may be a child no more, and shame, and woe, will burn, and burn, and burn, and tears that might once have put out the fire, fail to put it out now.

Je-sus went on to say, See that ye look not down up-on these who are young in years, or weak in faith, for I say un-to you that their an-gels in heav-en stand near the throne of God. For the Son of Man is come to save that which is lost. How think ye? If a man have a hun-dred sheep, and one of them is lost, does he not leave the nine-ty and nine, and go off on the hills to find that one which is lost?

And if so be that he find it, he will feel more joy o-ver that one sheep, than o-ver all the rest which have not gone a-stray. So it is not God's will that one of these lit-tle ones be lost. Je-sus will take them in his arms, and save them.

Then Je-sus told them how they were to deal with those who did wrong in the church. If one has done wrong go and tell him of his fault, and let no one else know of it. If he hear thee, thou hast gained his love, and brought him to see his sins, and to make his peace with God.

If he hear thee not, then take with thee two or three more that they may plead with him. If he will not hear them, tell it to the church; and if he will not hear the church, or those who make up the church, let him be to thee as one who loves not Christ, and has no right to bear his name. And he said to them what he had said to Peter, What things ye shall bind on earth shall be bound in heav-en; and what things ye shall loose on earth shall be loosed in heav-en. These men were to build up the Church of Christ on earth, and in all that they did they would have God's help. They might take in Jews, or Greeks, and it would be all right, and those they put out of the church on earth, God would have no place for in his home on high.

Then he said to them, If two of you shall be of the same mind, and ask for the same thing, God will hear you when you pray, and grant you what you ask. For where two or three meet to pray or praise, there am I in the midst of them.

Then came Pe-ter, and said to him, Lord how oft shall a man do wrong to me, and I for-give him? sev-en times? Je-sus saith un-to him, I say to thee, not sev-en times, but sev-en-ty times sev-en.

THE SHEEP THAT WAS LOST.

Love does not stop to count. If some one who is dear to us does wrong, we for-give and for-give for our hearts will not let us turn from them and cast them off. We hope from day to day that they will cease to do wrong, and learn to do well. If such is man's love, how strong is God's love, and how long it will hold out! Up to the last hour of our lives He waits for us to come to Him with love in our hearts. Just think of it! The sins of a whole life-time we may blot out, if we will come to God, and ask Him to for-give us, not for our own sakes, but for the sake of his dear Son, Je-sus Christ. We know not when we are to die. We may not live to be old. Let us then make our peace with God now, that we may walk with Him all the rest of our days, and be His child.

Je-sus said to the Twelve, and to those who drew near him, The king-dom of God is like to a King who called up his stew-ards, or ser-vants, that they might pay him what they owed him. The King gave a sum in-to the hands of these men which they were to put to the best use, and to add to from day to day. Not a cent of it was their own, but they were to buy and sell with it, so that there would be great gain for the King whose work they were to do.

And one man was brought to the King who owed him a vast sum. He had not done well with the wealth that had been placed in his hands, and was now deep in debt. And as he could not pay this large sum, his lord and mas-ter gave com-mand that he and his wife, and chil-dren, and all that he had, should be sold, that what they brought might at least pay part of the debt.

The poor man then fell down at the feet of the King,

and said to him, Lord, do not be hard up-on me, I pray thee, and I will pay thee all. And the lord of that ser-vant felt sor-ry for him, and let him go, and did not ask him to pay back what he owed him. He for-gave the debt.

He took it up-on him-self, in the same way that Je-sus, our Lord, takes up-on him-self our sins—our debts—and wipes them all out. We can-not pay them. He pays them all. All he asks is that we pray to him, and love him. This ought not to be a hard task. Think of all we owe to him. If we had a friend on earth who paid all our debts, and did for us what Je-sus has done, how we would love him, and how glad we would be to please him. Our hearts would go out to him with thanks and joy, and we would think of him day and night.

But that same ser-vant went out and found a man who owed him a small sum—not more than fif-teen dol-lars; and he laid hands on him and took him by the throat, and said, Pay what thou dost owe me. The man fell down at his feet, and begged him to be less harsh, and said, Bear with me for a while, and I will pay thee. But these words did not move him, and he cast the poor man in jail, to stay there till he had paid that which was due.

When the rest of the ser-vants saw what was done, they felt sad and sor-ry, and they came and told their lord, the King. Then his lord called the ser-vant un-to him, and said, Thou wick-ed ser-vant, I for-gave thee all that debt, be-cause thou didst ask me. Shouldst not thou for-give him who owed thee, e-ven as I for-gave thee? And the King was wroth, and gave him up to be vexed by the courts of law till he had paid all that was due. So shall God do to you, if ye from your hearts for-give not those who have sin-ned a-gainst you.

We owe to God more than we can pay. He is kind to us, and prompt to for-give when we turn from our sins

SHOULDST THOU NOT FOR-GIVE AS I FOR-GAVE THEE?

and ask Him to give us new and clean hearts. We should then be kind to those who are in debt to us, and not turn from them with harsh words and looks.

CHAPTER XIV.

THE TEM-PLE TAX.—THE GREAT FEAST OF THE JEWS.—
JE-SUS GOES NOT UP WITH HIS KINS-FOLK.—"I AM
THE LIGHT OF THE WORLD."—THE
MAN BORN BLIND.

While Je-sus and the Twelve were at Ca-per-na-um the men came to whom the tax was paid to keep the Tem-ple at Je-ru-sa-lem in good or-der. Each male Jew who was more than twen-ty years of age had to pay the small coin, which was worth less than fif-ty cents.

The men came to Pe-ter, and said, Doth not your master pay the tax? Pe-ter said, yes, and would have paid it. But when he came in-to the house, Je-sus stop-ped him, and said, From whom dost thou think the kings of the earth take toll? from their sons, or from those not of their house-hold?

Pe-ter said, From those not of their house-hold. Je-sus said, Then the sons are free. But lest we should cause them to do wrong, go thou to the sea, throw out thy hook and line, and take the first fish that comes up. Look in its mouth, and there thou shalt find a piece of mon-ey; take that, and give it to them for me and thee.

Pe-ter did as he was told, and went out and caught the fish, and in its mouth was the small coin which was to pay the tax called for. Pe-ter had shown that he felt it to be a just debt, and lest he should give the priests cause to find fault with him, Je-sus told Pe-ter how he could pay the small tax. Pe-ter must go back to his old trade to earn the sum he had need of, and the first fish he caught paid him for his work. So it is with us. God sets us to do some task—to toil for him, with-out a thought of pride—and if our hearts are right, if we love Je-sus, we will get our pay right straight a-long.

Je-sus had not been in Ju-de-a for some time, for he knew that the Jews there sought to kill him. But now the great feast was at hand, the third and last one of the year, when the Jews from all parts of the land went up to Je-ru-sa-lem, to give thanks to God for the good crops that were stored in their barns.

It is a good thing to give thanks to God, to praise His name for all that He has done for us!

It was a gay and glad time; friends met, and sat side by side in the House of God, and songs and hymns of praise filled all the place.

The kins-folk of Je-sus, those with whom he had been brought up, said to him, Go up to Je-ru-sa-lem, and make thy-self known. Be bold, and if thou canst do strange things let all men see thee. For his own folks did not have faith in him, or think that he was the Son of God. They thought that if his claim was a just one, if he was in truth the Son of God, he would not hide him-self as he did.

Je-sus said to them, My time has not yet come. The world can-not hate you—for they were of the world—but it hates me be-cause I prove that it is full of sin. Go ye up to the feast. I will not go up yet as my time has not come. And he staid on in Gal-i-lee.

His kins-folk went up to be there at the first part of the feast, and in two or three days Je-sus went up, but kept by him-self that he might not be known. The Jews there sought him and said, Where is he? And there was much talk a-bout him. Some said, He is a good man; but oth-ers said, No, he is not; for he leads men the wrong way. But no one dared to speak out loud for fear of the chief men of the Jews.

In the midst of the feast Je-sus went up to Je-ru-sa-lem and the Tem-ple-courts and taught there. And the Jews that heard him were awe-struck, and said, How is it that this man knows so much when he has not been to the schools?

Je-sus said, The truths I speak are not mine, but His that sent me. He who has the will to do God's will, shall hear in my voice, the voice of God.

The man who speaks from him-self seeks his own praise; but my words and works prove that I seek not to praise my-self, but Him that sent me. Did not Mo-ses give you the law, and yet not one of you keeps the law. Why seek ye to kill me? He had come to do God's will, and to make these laws plain to the Jews. They had no right to put him to death, and they knew it. Je-sus threw a light on their guilt they could not fail to see. But they would not look at their own sins. They turned their eyes a-way. And when he said, Why seek ye to kill me? they cried out, Thou hast a dev-il, and it is he that seeks to kill thee.

Je-sus said, I did one work, which has caused all this stir. Ye have rites which ye do in the church on the Day of Rest, and why should ye be in a rage with me be-cause I healed a man on that day? To break the law of Mo-ses was to them far worse than to break God's law of love. To bid a man rise, take up his bed and walk, on the Day of Rest, was a great sin. Je-sus said, Judge my work as you judge your own, and you will find no fault in it.

Some of those who heard him said, Is not this whom they seek to kill? And lo, he speaks in this bold way, and they say nought to him. Can it be that they know that this is the Christ? We know where this man came from; but where the Christ comes from no one can tell.

Je-sus, who knew how men thought of him, cried out with a loud voice so that all could hear him, Ye both know me, and ye know the place from whence I came. I have not come of my-self, but He that sent me is the true God, whom ye do not know. I know Him, for I am from Him, and He sent me.

Then they sought to take him, but did not lay hands on him, for it was not yet God's time. And some of those whom he taught had faith in him, and said, When Christ comes, will he do more signs than these which this man hath done?

The chief priests and the scribes heard what the crowd said, though they spoke in low tones; and they feared that more of the Jews might be led to think well of Je-sus, and to take his words to heart. So they sent armed men to seize Je-sus and to put a stop to his work at once, lest more harm should be done.

Je-sus said, But a short time shall I be with you, and then I go to Him that sent me. Ye shall seek me, and shall not find me: and where I am, there ye can-not come. The Scribes said, Where will this man go that we can-not find him? Can it be that he has cast off the Jews, and means to go out to the Greeks and teach them? What else can he mean, when he says, Ye shall seek me, and shall not find me; and where I am, there ye can-not come? This they said with hate and scorn, for they took pains to twist the words of Je-sus, and not to look at them or him in the true light.

When Je-sus said, I am the light of the world, they thought the world meant the Greeks, those who bowed down to false gods. They did not think that the Jews were in need of light; and as Je-sus up-set all the old ways and old forms they had kept up for so long a time, he was more fit to preach to the Greeks than to them.

On the last, and the great day of the feast, Je-sus stood up and cried out, If a man thirst, let him come to me and drink. The heart that be-lieves in me shall have in it-self the fount of life. And some said, Of a truth this is the Christ. Some of the crowd said, What! doth Christ come out of Gal-i-lee? Are we not told in the Word of God that Christ is to come from Beth-le-hem, where Da-vid used to live?

So there was much strife in the crowd, for they took sides as friends or foes of Je-sus. And some of them would have seized him, but no man laid hands on him. His hour had not yet come.

Je-sus spoke a great deal of thirst. Those who dwelt in the East knew what it meant, for they had had to march through great plains of sand, where not a well could be found. And oh, what joy it was when they came to a rock from whence the cool clear stream gushed forth! No draught so sweet to the lip! No sight so fair to the eye! No sound so sweet to the ear!

In times of drouth, when the wells, and springs, and streams are dry, men grow faint, and are like to die of thirst. This one dreams of the deep pure well from which he used to drink. That one, with his brain on fire, raves of the clear cool stream which ran near his boy-hood's home. All cry out for some-thing to cool their parched lips, and to quench their thirst. They drag them-selves on to the palm tree's shade, in hopes that there they shall find what they seek. They dig in the sand with their own hands, and their tongue cleaves to the roof of their mouth.

Through-out the Word of God Je-sus is called, A rock

in a dry land; a spring; a well of wa-ter; a Fount from which all may drink. The worst want that men can know is that of thirst, and Je-sus sought to teach these Jews, and all the tribes of the earth, their need of Him.

Mo-ses smote the rock and the wa-ter gushed forth. Je-sus smites the hard hearts of men, and love flows out for him and for all man-kind. We are to thirst for Je-sus; to feel that the world is a dry place, that our lives are hard and dry with-out him. The more we drink at this fount—the more we learn of Christ—the more strength have we for the march, and to do the things God means us to do. We must drink from the fount that flows so free, and then pass on the cup. Tell all we meet how good it is.

The men who had been sent to seize Je-sus were awed by his words, and they went back with-out him. And the chief priests, and the strict Jews, said, Why have ye not brought him? The men said, He is more than a man, for no one ev-er spake as he does.

The chief men of the Jews said to them, Have ye too been led a-way by this man? Do those who know the Law—the wise men of the Jews—do these yield to the claims of Je-sus? No, it is the crowds that run after him, those who know not the Law nor the curse that they will bring up-on them-selves.

Nic-o-de-mus—he that come to Je-sus by night—was one of this great court of law; and he said to the rest, Does our law judge a man be-fore it hears him, or knows what he has done? Ought we not first to try him?

They said to him, Art thou, too, led a-way by this man from Gal-i-lee? Search all the books and see that that

248   "*I am the Light of the World.*"

land can-not be the birth-place of Him who is to come, and be King of the Jews.

At the close of the day Je-sus went up to the Mount of Ol-ives, and there on the cool green slope he lay down to

MOUNT OF OL-IVES.

rest, and to be near to God.

The next day, at dawn, he went back to the Tem-ple, and the crowd drew round him, and he sat down and taught them there. As men lay snares for a bird, or some game they wish to catch, so did the base Jews lay snares to catch Je-sus, and to have some cause to find fault with him.

But he was calm in the midst of it all, he did not fear death, and from time to time put to shame the fore-most of his foes.

It was now the eighth day of the feast; and the great light, which was the pride of all the Jews, and which had cast so bright a glow up-on the scene, was put out. The feast was at an end, and the main part of the Temple was closed. But the out-side courts were not closed, and here it was that Je-sus taught.

He took his text from things near at hand. The great lamp they had lit them-selves was out, and they missed it. Je-sus said, I am the light of the world, and he that comes to me shall not walk in the dark, but shall have the light of life. Da-vid said in one of his Psalms, The Lord is my light; and spoke of Him as a Light that shines in the night.

The foes of Je-sus said, Thou dost speak these words of thy-self, and they are not true. Je-sus said, Though I speak of my-self my words are true; for I know whence I came and to what place I go, but this ye do not know, ye judge as men judge. I judge no one. But if I should judge, God is with me. It is laid down in your own law that the words of two men are true. In the courts of law a man would be set free if he could get some one else to speak a good word for him.

Je-sus said, I am here to prove who I am, and the Fath-er that sent me speaks for me. They said un-to him, Where is thy Fath-er? Je-sus said, Ye know not me nor my Fath-er. If ye knew me, ye would know my Fath-er. They would know in their hearts that he had been sent from God, or he could not do the things he had done. His foes were awed by his words, and though they longed to seize him, no one laid hands on him, for his hour was not yet come.

Then Je-sus spoke to them and said, I go my way, and ye shall seek me, and shall die in your sins. For where I go, ye can-not come.

Then said the Jews, Will he kill him-self? Is that what he means when he says, Where I go ye can-not come? Je-sus said to them, Ye are of this world. I am not of this world. Je-sus meant that they chose the things of this world, and by their own acts shut them-selves out of the light and joy that might have been theirs.

For this cause I said to you that ye shall die in your sins. For if ye will not see that I am the one sent to save you ye shall die in your sins.

They said un-to him, Who art thou? Je-sus said, The same that I said from the first. I could say more, but ye will not hear me. Ye turn a deaf ear to my words. But He that sent me is true, and the things which I heard from Him, those speak I un-to the world. When ye have raised up on high the Son of Man, then shall ye know who I am, and that I do nought of my-self, but as my Fath-er has taught me I speak these things. And he that sent me is with me, he hath not left me a-lone, for I do at all times those things that please him.

As he spoke these words not a few in the crowd had faith in Je-sus, and thought that what he said was true. But their hearts were as yet hard, and Je-sus spoke to them and said, If ye keep my words in your hearts and live by them, then shall ye prove that ye are true friends of mine. And ye shall know the truth, and the truth shall make you free. He meant that faith in him, would set them free from the bonds of sin and death.

Now the Jews called A-bra-ham their fath-er, and thought they should all be saved be-cause of his great faith. This, they had been taught, gave them the right to call them-selves the Sons of God. So they said to Je-sus, We have not yet been slaves, how then canst thou say, Ye shall be made free?

Je-sus told them they were not Sons of God, but slaves of sin, and had no more hold on the house of God, than the slave had in the house where he dwelt. But the Son could claim a place in the house, and had rights there the slave did not have. If then the Son shall make you free, ye shall be free in-deed. I know that ye are heirs of A-bra-ham, but ye seek to kill me be-cause my word is not found in you. I speak the things which I have seen with the Fath-er, ye do that which ye have seen with your fath-er.

They said, A-bra-ham is our fath-er. Je-sus said to them, If ye are A-bra-ham's chil-dren do as he taught you. But now ye seek to kill me, a man that hath told you the truth which I heard from God: this did not A-bra-ham. Ye do the works of your fath-er.

They said to him, We have one Fath-er, that is God. Je-sus said to them, If God were your Fath-er, ye would love me; for from God I came forth and am here; and I came not of my-self, but He sent me. If ye were Sons of God ye would know what my words mean.

These men were proud that they were Jews. They were not like those who bowed down to false gods, but were as chil-dren of one house-hold, who looked up to God as their Fath-er. But that they did not love God in their hearts was shown by their deeds. If a dear friend should send his son to us, from a far off land, we would want to be good and kind to him if not for his own sake, to show how great and how true is the love we bear his fath-er.

Je-sus said to them, The dev-il is your fath-er, and it is your will to do his works. It is not strange that you should want to put me to death, for since he came in-to the world his work has been to kill men. There is no truth in him. He is the fath-er of lies. But be-cause I speak the truth ye be-lieve me not. Which of you can charge me with sin? If I say what is true, why then do ye not be-lieve me?

Je-sus laid much stress on this word, truth, be-cause he knew that these men were false, and were fond of lies. Have you not met with those who seemed to lose no chance to tell a lie? who act as if it hurt them to speak the truth? Keep a-way from them. Go not near them, lest you, too, fall in-to the same sin. Speak the truth at all times—when it is right to speak. There are things that we ought not to tell. But if we can-not tell the truth, we need not tell a lie. We can keep still.

Je-sus said, He that is of God, hears the words of God; for this cause ye hear me not, be-cause ye are not of God.

Then said the Jews, Say we not well that thou hast a dev-il? Je-sus said, I have not a dev-il. I seek not praise for my-self, but my Fath-er seeks it for me. My cause is in His hands. And it is true, If a man have kept my word in his heart, he shall not die. Je-sus did not mean that such an one should not go in-to the grave. All must die. But those who have loved Je-sus, and lived as he has taught, shall find that death is but a sleep, from which they wake in the home on high.

Then said the Jews, Now we know thou art a mad-man;—for this is what they meant when they said he had a dev-il. A-bra-ham has died, and so have the proph-ets; and yet thou dost say, If a man keep my word he shall not die. Art thou great-er than A-bra-ham or the proph-ets? Whom dost thou make out thy-self to be?

Je-sus said, If I seek my own glo-ry to win praise for my-self, there is no glo-ry. Self-praise does not raise a man.

It is my Fath-er who gives me the glo-ry, whom ye say is your God. Yet ye have not known Him; but I know Him: and if I should say I know Him not, I should be like un-to you, who speak not the truth. But I know Him, and do His will. A-bra-ham, by faith, saw this day a-far off, and was glad.

God had made it clear to A-bra-ham that in His own good time, He would send some one in-to the world to save men from their sins, and to bring all the tribes of the earth in-to one great tribe, in the land of peace and love. This gave great joy to A-bra-ham. He longed to see the dawn of that blest day. It was the hope of his heart.

But these Jews were not like him. They did not make a right use of their ears. Their hearts were not in what they heard. They said to Je-sus, Thou art not yet fif-ty years old, and hast thou seen A-bra-ham? Je-sus said to them, Be-fore A-bra-ham was born, I am. I am He "which is, and was, and is to come." This claim to be One with God was more than the Jews could bear, and they took up stones to throw at him, for they were in a great rage. But Je-sus hid him-self in the crowd, and went out of the Tem-ple-courts.

Not long af-ter this, as Je-sus walked out on the Day of Rest, he saw a man who had been blind from his birth. It used to be thought that such things were sent up-on men for their sins; so some of the Twelve, who were with Je-sus, asked him the cause of this. Was he or his par-ents to blame?

Je-sus said, This man did no sin, nor did his par-ents; at least their sins did not cause him to be born blind, but he is as he is that the works of God should be made known in him.

The man did not ask for help. He was born blind, and had be-come used to the dark. Je-sus came to give sight to the blind, to let in the light to those who sit in the dark. We are blind when we do not see Je-sus as he is, and look on him with the clear eyes of faith. We are in the dark when we do not read the Word of God, and learn all that we can of Him, who came in-to the world to save us from our sins. But though men are blind, the good work must go on; the good news must be told through-out the length and breadth of the land. Je-sus says, I must do the works of Him that sent me, while it is day; for the night comes when no one can work. As long as I am in the world, I am the light of the world.

They were not to talk a-bout their work, or to stand

The Man Born Blind.   255

and wait for some-thing to turn up. Life is short, and much time is lost in this way. Those who love Je-sus should spring to their work, and strive to do all the good

VIL-LAGE OF SI-LO-AM.

they can while the day-light lasts. There comes a time in all our lives, when we can, if we will, do good work for Je-sus. It is our chance to save souls. It does not last.

POOL OF SI-LO-AM.

If we let it slip by, it is gone for good. Da-vid says, My tongue shall speak of thy praise all the day long. Show me thy ways, O Lord, teach me thy paths. Lead me in thy truth, and teach me. On thee do I wait all the day.

When Je-sus had said these words—I am the light of the world—he spat on the ground and made clay with the dust, and put this clay on the eyes of the blind man. And he said to him, Go wash in the pool of Si-lo-am. And the man went a-way, and washed, and came back cured.

Those who had seen him and knew that he was blind, said, Is not this he that sat and beg-ged by the road-side? Some said, Is it he; oth-ers said, No, but he looks like him; but the man said, I am he. Then they said to him, How did you get your sight? He said, The man called Je-sus made clay, and put it on my eyes, and said to me, Go to Si-lo-am and wash. And I went, and washed, and sight came to me. Then they said to him, Where is he? The man said, I know not.

Je-sus might have said but one word, and the blind man would have been cured. But means were used to test his faith. Did he care to be cured? Had he just as lief sit by the way-side as not, and beg from day to day? Did he long for the light? If so, he would do as Je-sus told him. The pool was not far off, and he could find his way there with-out help, for those born blind find their way a-bout with great ease. He knew what the name Je-sus meant, but he knew nought of him who bore it. God makes use of strange means to bring men to Je-sus. In an hour when they think not the scales drop from their eyes, and they see how vile they are, and from that time forth they walk in the light.

THE MAN BORN BLIND.

This deed was done on the Day of Rest, and some of the Jews were wroth, and said, This man does not come from God because he keeps not the Day of Rest. Others said, How can a man who sins do such strange things? And there was a strife a-mong them, a great war of words.

They asked the blind man what he thought of Je-sus. The man said, He is a proph-et. But the Jews would not be-lieve that he had been born blind till they had seen and talked with his par-ents. And they said to them, Is this your son, who ye say was born blind? how then doth he now see? They say, We know that this is our son, and that he was born blind, but by what means he has been made to see we know not or who gave him his sight. Ask him; he is of age, and can speak for him-self.

Then they said to the man born blind, Give God the praise, for we know that this man is a sin-ner. The man said, I know not if he be a sin-ner; but this one thing I do know, that once I was blind and now I see. Then they asked him once more, What did he do to thee? How did he give thee thy sight? The man said, I have told you, and ye did not hear, why do you wish me to tell it a-gain? Do ye wish to be his dis-ci-ples?

Then they mocked him, and said, Thou art taught by him, but we are taught by Mo-ses. We know that God spoke to Mo-ses, but as for this man, we do not know where he came from.

The man said to them, Well, it is a strange thing, that ye do not know where he comes from and yet he gave me sight. We know that God hears not those who sin; but if a man serves God, and does His will, him He hears. Since the world was made it has not been heard that a man gave sight to one born blind. If this man come not from God, he could not do these things.

The Jews said to the man, Thou wast born in sins thyself, and dost thou teach us? And they put him out of the place where they had met. Je-sus heard that they had put him out, and when he had found the man, he said to him, Dost thou be-lieve in the Son of God. The man asked, Who is he, that I may be-lieve in him. Je-sus said to him, Thou hast both seen him, and he that talks with thee is he. The man said, I be-lieve, Lord; and bowed down at his feet.

Je-sus said he had come in-to the world that those who are blind might come to him for sight, and that those who see might be-come blind. It was their own fault if they did not come to him, and for this they would be judged. Those who came to him like babes, who feared the dark, and kept hold of his hand all the way, should find a light on their path from day to day.

And those who come to the light would judge themselves and be vexed be-cause they were so blind as not to see the right way. Yet there are those who know the law, and have all the guides they need, and yet do not come to Christ. They shut their eyes to the true light, and pay no heed to those that point out the way. What will be their fate? Why, they will live in the dark. They may think them-selves wise, but they are not wise. For when they lose Je-sus they lose all the light that makes the joy of life.

Some of the Jews who were with Je-sus as spies, when they heard what he said to the man born blind, asked him if they too, were blind. Je-sus said to them, If ye were blind, ye would not have sin; but now ye say, We see, you are still in sin. If these Jews were in truth blind, and could not see the light that shone round them, they would not be to blame. But when they say, We see, and do not come to Je-sus, the Light of the world, the sin is theirs.

Then Je-sus spoke the par-a-ble of the sheep-fold. The fold, where the sheep were shut in at night, was a square space, with a fence or wall of no great height on its four sides. There was but one door for the flocks to go through, and here a man stood on guard to see that no sheep came in-to the fold that had no right there.

Each morn the shep-herds came to lead forth their flocks to the hill sides where the grass was green. Not one of those who heard Je-sus, but knew how a sheep-fold was made, and to what use it was put, for in the East there were men whose whole wealth was in flocks and herds.

Je-sus said, He that comes not through the door of the sheep-fold, but climbs up some oth-er way, the same is a thief and a rob-ber. But he that comes in by the door is a shep-herd of the sheep. The man who keeps the gate knows him, and will let him in. The sheep hear his voice, and he calls his own sheep by name, and leads them out. And when he has put out all his own sheep, and none is left, he goes be-fore his flock, and they keep near him, led by the sound of his voice. A strange man they will not fol-low, but will flee from him. The sheep do not know his voice; he can-not call them by their names.

Plain as these words were that Je-sus spoke, the Jews did not know what he meant. And he said to them as he

262   The Man Born Blind.

had said be-fore, I am the door of the sheep. The door through which the sheep are led out of the fold.

All those that came be-fore me are thieves and rob-bers; but the sheep did not hear them. There were some who had claimed to be the Christ, and tried to raise false hopes to gain some good for them-selves. But the Jews gave no heed to them. Their words fell on deaf ears.

THE GOOD SHEP-HERD.

Je-sus said, I am the door: by me if a man go in he shall be saved, and shall go in and out and find rich fields to feed in. The thief comes not but that he may steal, and kill, and make a reck of all things. I came that they may live in the midst of joys that have no end, and that shall please them more and more.

The Man Born Blind.

I am the good shep-herd. The good shep-herd gives his life for the sheep. He that is hired, and is not a true shep-herd, whose own the sheep are not, when he sees the wolf come, leaves the sheep and runs off to a safe place. And the wolf drives the sheep here and there, and breaks up the flock.

The man who takes the work of a shep-herd for hire, and has no love for the sheep, will leave them to their fate when the foe draws near, and save his own life at the cost of theirs. Such are those who teach and preach for pay, and yet fail to warn the flock they have charge of, and to stand by them in the time of need.

Je-sus says, I am the good shep-herd, and I know mine own sheep, and mine own know me. E-ven as the Fath-er knows me, do I know the Fath-er: and I lay down my life for the sheep. And oth-er sheep I have, which are not of this fold: those I must lead as well as these, and they shall hear my voice, and there shall be one flock and one shep-herd. My Fath-er loves me be-cause I lay down my life, that I may take it a-gain. No man takes it from me, but I lay it down of my-self. I have the right to lay it down and to take it a-gain. For in this I do the will of my Fath-er.

A BIRD OF PREY.

There was a great strife a-mong the Jews be-cause of these words. Not a few said, He has a dev-il, and is mad; why hear ye him? But some said, These are not the words of one that has a dev-il. Can a dev-il give sight to the blind?

CHAPTER XV.

JE-SUS LEAVES GAL-I-LEE.—SENDS OUT THE SEV-EN-TY.—HEALS TEN LEP-ERS.—THE WOM-AN BOWED DOWN.—PAR-A-BLE OF THE KING'S WED-DING FEAST.

Je-sus went out through the lands to teach and to preach, and a great crowd went out with him, of those who had faith in his words and wished to be taught by him. From these Je-sus chose out three-score-and-ten, and sent them two and two un-to all the large and small towns, where he meant to come. And he said to them, The har-vest is here, the grain is ripe, but there are few to work in the fields. Go your ways. I send you forth as lambs in the midst of wolves. Take no purse, no bag, no shoes, and speak to no man on the way. This would take up too much time, and there was need of haste.

When ye stop to go in-to a house, first say, Peace be to this house. And if it is the right kind of a house, your peace shall rest up-on it; but if not, it shall come back to you. In that house stay, and eat and drink such things as they give you. Go not from house to house in search of ease, and the good things of life. When ye come to a town, and find friends there, stay and share in their lot. Heal the sick, and say to them, The King-dom of God has come nigh un-to you. But when ye come to a town where they

RU-INS ON SITE OF CHO-RA-ZIN.

are not glad to see you, and will have nought to do with you, go out in-to the streets, and shake the dust of that town from your feet. But know this, that the king-dom of God has come nigh; and that town shall meet with a worse fate than came up-on Sod-om.

Then he told of the woes that should come up-on all

RU-INS AT CHO-RA-ZIN.

those towns from whence he had been cast out; or which would not let these through their gates, who had been sent out in His name. And it all came true as he said, for it was not long ere all those towns, once so full of wealth and pride, were just great heaps of stones.

Then Je-sus spoke those sweet words that have been like balm to worn-out, sin-sick ones, tired with the toils of life, and weighed down with a sense of their own guilt. He said, Come un-to me all ye that la-bor and are heav-y la-

RU-INS OF TEM-PLE AT GER-A-SA.

den, and I will give you rest. Take my yoke up-on you, and learn of me; for I am meek and low-ly in heart; and ye shall find rest un-to your souls. For my yoke is ea-sy, and my bur-den is light.

Je-sus Leaves Gal-i-lee.

Those to whom Christ spoke were Jews, and knew well what he meant by these words. The Jews were fond of forms, and were strict in the use of them. Those who came to Je-sus would have rest from these toils, which did no good to the soul. The Jews called the law a yoke. Je-sus says, Take my yoke up-on you and learn of me, for

RU-INS OF GER-A-SA.

I am meek and low-ly in heart. He did not teach as the Scribes taught. They were not meek and low-ly in heart, but proud and vain, and apt to look down on the poor.

The yoke of Je-sus is in the shape of a cross. We are not to be free from toil or care, and the yoke at times seems hard to bear. We must go to him and be taught how to bear it as we ought. If we try to bear it a-lone, it weighs us down. But as soon as we look up to him, He makes it light. He shares it with us.

TOW-ER OF AN-TO-NI-A.

While Je-sus was at Ca-per-na-um for a few days, word was brought him of an out-break at Je-ru-sa-lem, in which some of the men from Gal-i-lee had been killed. These

270   Je-sus Leaves Gal-i-lee.

RO-MAN SOL-DIERS.

deeds had been done by Pi-late, who was paid by the Ro-mans to rule in the land of Ju-de-a, and keep a watch o-ver the Jews there.

Of late there had been so much strife in and near the Tem-ple, that Her-od had built a tow-er close by, that led to it by a flight of steps. Here an armed guard was kept, so that if a fight took place the troops could rush down the steps at once, and put a stop to the noise, and strike down with their swords those who would not yield to the law.

Je-sus left Gal-i-lee and came to the land where Her-od ruled.

And some Jews came to him and said, Get thee out of this place, for Her-od has made up his mind to kill thee. Je-sus said to them, Go and say to that fox, that I

RO-MAN ARMS.

cast out de-mons, and heal the sick, and shall stay here for three days more when my work comes to an end. He would leave Pe-re-a, not from fear of Her-od, or be-cause of his threats. He was on his way to meet death, but not in this place should he die.

GROUP OF SA-MAR-I-TANS.

Then as he thought of what had been done at Je-ru-sa-lem, he spoke with grief and pain of the fate in store for that town, where the Jews thought their long-looked for King would live and reign.

Their way led through Sa-ma-ri-a, and as they drew near one of the small towns Je-sus sent some of the band a-head to find a house where they could stop and rest. But the folks there would not grant house-room to Je-sus and those with him. They would have nought to do with them. When John and James saw this they were in a fine rage, and said, Lord, wilt thou that we bring down

LEP-ERS OUT-SIDE THE GATE.

fire from heav-en to burn them up? But Je-sus told them that no such thing must be done, it was not Christ-like.

As Je-sus went on his way there met him ten lep-ers, who dwelt in this place far from the haunts of men, for it was a-gainst the law for them to live in or near the towns. They were sick, and there was no cure for them. At first one white spot came on their flesh; then it spread, and spread, till there was not a bit of sound flesh on their bones, and they were glad to die.

Sin is like this. At first it is but a small spot. But it spreads, and spreads, till soon the whole man is him-self a plague-spot and it is not safe to go near him.

But these lep-ers had heard of Je-sus, and may have seen some of the great works that he did. And they called him by name, and cried out, Je-sus, Mas-ter, have mer-cy on us. Help us we pray! And when he saw them, he said to them, Go and show your-selves to the priest. They had faith to rise and go. They did not hold back, and ask to be cured in some way that they thought best. But when Je-sus told them to go, they went, and on the way they were made well. And one of them, when he felt that he had been brought back to health, turned back, and with a loud voice gave praise to God. And he fell down on his face at the feet of Je-sus, and gave thanks to him, with a heart full of love. And he was from Sa-ma-ri-a, and had been brought up to hate the Jews.

Je-sus said, Were not the ten cleansed? but where are the nine? Were there none that came back to give thanks to God but this stran-ger? He called him this be-cause he and his kins-folk were not friends with the race of Jews. The nine were Jews, who thought more of what they owed to the priests than of what they owed to God, which showed that their hearts were not yet free from sin.

Je-sus said to the one who came back, Rise, and go on thy way; thy faith hath made thee whole.

Do we give thanks to God as we ought? We are sick, and He makes us well; and we go on our way, light of

JE-SUS PREACH-ING IN THE SYN-A-GOGUE.

heart once more, and yet with scarce a thought of what we owe to him.

RU-INS OF A SYN-A-COGUE.

We take care to thank our friends for what they do for us, but are slow to give thanks to God. We are in haste to get back to the world, as the lep-ers were. We take all we can get, and in our love of self, give noth-ing back. The Lord waits up-on us. He is good to us. Is it too much then for us to turn to Him, and say, Lord, I thank thee! and to lift up our hearts in praise to Him?

When the Day of Rest came round, Je-sus went to one of the syn-a-gogues and taught there. And there was a wom-an there, who for near a score of years had been so bowed down that she could not lift her-self up. It was as if she were tied down with cords she could not break.

When Je-sus saw her, he called her to him, and said, Wom-an, thou art loosed from thy bonds. And he laid his hands up-on her; and at once she was made straight, and gave praise to God. The ru-ler of the church was wroth that Je-sus had done this work on the Day of Rest. But he did not dare to find fault with him to his face, so spoke to those who were in the church in this wise: There are six days, he said, in which men ought to work; if there are those of you who wish to be cured, come then, and not on the Day of Rest.

There are some folks who dare not come out and strike a blow, but will say sharp things that hurt and sting. They will not say these sharp words to the face of the one they wish to hurt, or scold, but will speak as this man did. Well did those in church know whom he wished to hit, and their eyes and ears were fixed on him who stood in the midst of them, and taught as no one else did. What would he say? What would he do? They would have been cast down with shame, had they done aught to call down such a curt speech as that from the head man in the church: the one set to rule the rest.

But the Lord spoke to him, and said, Does not each one of you loose his ox or his ass from the stall, on the Day of Rest, and lead him to the place where he may drink? And ought not this poor wom-an who has been bound in sin for so long a time, be loosed from her chains on the Day of Rest? And when he had said this all his foes hung their heads with shame; and he was heard with joy by those in the crowd who were glad of the things he had done.

Now the Jews gave feasts on the Day of Rest, but none of the food was cooked on that day, and as Je-sus went in-to the house of one of the chief men of the Jews, to dine with him, a close watch was kept up-on all that he said and did. He was in the midst of foes, and he knew it. And there was there a man who had the drop-sy. He was not a guest, but had been brought there to see what Je-sus would do.

Je-sus, who knew their thoughts, said to these men of the law, Is it right to cure the sick on the Day of Rest, or not? But they held their peace. They had not a word to say. And Je-sus took hold of the man, and healed him, and sent him a-way. And he said to those who had been called to the feast, If one of you had an ass or an ox fall in-to a pit, would you not pull him out at once though it were on the Day of Rest? They knew that they would, and so had nought to say to these things.

The guests at this time filled the room, and there was more or less strife as to which should have the first place, or the best seat. It is so to this day. When great feasts are made, the choice seats are left for those of high rank. This is the cause of a great deal of pride, and of hard words and looks.

Je-sus took this for his text, and spoke to those who were bid to the feast when he saw how they chose the chief seats. He said to them, When thou art bid to a wed-ding feast sit not down in the chief place, lest some one of high rank should come, and the host should say to thee, Give this man thy place. Then thou shalt go with shame to a seat at the far end of the board. But when thou art bid to a feast, go and sit down in a low place; so that when he that has bid thee comes in-to the room, he may say to thee, Friend, go up to a high place. Then shalt thou be well thought of by all those who sit at meat with thee. For he who makes too much of him-self shall be put down; and he who keeps him-self in the back-ground, shall be raised up to a high place.

Then he said to them, as if he spoke to each one, When thou dost make a feast, call not thy friends nor kins-folk, nor those who are rich, lest they make a feast for thee, and so pay thee back. But call in the poor, the maimed, the lame, the blind, and thou shalt be blest, for they can-not pay thee back. But thou shalt have thy pay at the Last Day.

We are not to do good deeds in the hope of gain, nor to have our-selves talked a-bout. If we have a real love of God in our hearts we will seek to do good to all who are in need, with no thought of pay. We may give time, and thought, and care to some one who is sick, and the sick one may be cross and hard to please; but we must not give up, and think the work does not pay. It pays well, for it does us good to work for Je-sus, and the true heart is glad to be of use in the world. There is a place for us, and work to do, and if we find the work hard we must ask Je-sus to help us, and he will. And he pays us for all that we do for him. When one of those that sat at meat with Je-sus, heard these things, he said to him, Blest is he that shall eat bread in the King-dom of God. Je-sus said, A man once made a great sup-per, and bade a great crowd come to it. And he sent forth his ser-vant at sup-per time to say to those he wished to be his guests, Come, for things are now read-y. And they all be-gan to make some sort of ex-cuse.

The first said to him, I have bought a field, and I must needs go out and look at it. The next said, I have bought five yoke of ox-en, and am on my way to try them, and see if they are worth what I paid for them. A third said, I have just ta-ken a wife, so of course I can-not come. So the ser-vant went and told his mas-ter these things.

Then the mas-ter of the house was wroth to think that his friends would so slight his feast; and he said to his ser-vant, Go out with haste in-to the broad-ways and streets of the town, and bring in the poor, and maimed, the lame and the blind.

And the ser-vant did so. And he came back and said, Lord, what thou didst bid me do is done, and yet there is room. Then the lord said to the ser-vant, Go out in-to the high-ways and by the hedge-rows, and urge them to come in, that my house may be well filled with guests. For I say un-to you that none of those that did not come when I bade them shall sit down at my feast.

The man who made the feast is God. Those whom he bade come in were the Jews. The ser-vant sent out is

Christ. He speaks to the Jews, but they do not heed him.
They have plans of their own. Then he is sent out to call

THE WED-DING FEAST.

in the poor, and all those who will come. And yet there
is room! So he is sent out once more to urge those who

have no homes of their own, whose feet are bruised and sore, and who are faint for want of food, to come in, and find sweet rest and joy in the dear home on high.

These words were food for thought to the man who had said to Je-sus, Blest is he that shall eat bread in the King-dom of God. Love God. When he says, Come, come; and do not wait to be forced in to a feast which is spread for you.

CHAPTER XVI.

THE UN-JUST STEW-ARD.—THE RICH MAN AND LAZ-A-RUS. —THE GOOD SA-MAR-I-TAN—THE PROD-I-GAL SON.—THE LOST SHEEP.—THE LOST PIECE OF SIL-VER.

Je-sus spoke once more in a way to make the crowd think, and find out in their own minds what he meant. He said to them, There was a rich man who had word brought to him that one of his slaves, one who had charge of a great deal of his goods, was false to his trust. He lived on the fat of the land, and paid all his bills out of the lord's means. And the lord sent for him, and said, What is this that I hear of thee? Show me what thou hast done for me; for thou canst take charge of my goods no more.

Then the stew-ard said to him-self, What shall I do now I am to lose the place I filled? I have not strength to dig; and am too proud to beg. I know what I will do, so that when I lose my place I shall not be left quite out-of-doors.

So he sent for those who had bought goods of the rich

man and had not yet paid him; and he said to the first, How much dost thou owe my lord? He said, A hundred gal-lons of oil. He said to him, Take thy bill, and sit down at once, and write fif-ty. Then to the next one he said, How much dost thou owe? And he said, A hun-dred tubs of wheat. He saith to him, Take thy bill, and write four-score. And the mas-ter of the un-just stew-ard praised him be-cause he had been so shrewd; for the sons of this world are far more wise than the sons of the light. He told them to use their wealth to make friends, so that when their wealth was gone they might still have a home with the friends they had made. The friends that Je-sus means are the an-gels, who will be glad, to greet us, and to share their home with us when we have done with the things of this world.

The Jews who thought a great deal of wealth, sneered at Je-sus for these words. And he said to them, Ye are those who seem to men to be pure and good; but God knows your hearts, and that which calls forth the praise of men, does not please God in the least.

The sons of this world are those who live for self. The sons of the light are those who live for Christ. Bad men, who live for self, are more sharp and shrewd than good men, and are all the time on the look-out for what they call the main chance. We are to look up-on the wealth God gives us as not our own, but His. In this case of which Je-sus spoke, both mas-ter and ser-vant were sharp men, and the mas-ter praised the stew-ard for his tricks. But God is not pleased when men waste the wealth he has placed in their hands. They should make a wise use of it. For though they may cheat men, and play tricks on them, they can-not cheat God. He knows them, and knows whom they serve. They are slaves of the dev-il.

That he might teach them the right use of wealth, Je-sus said, There was a rich man who was clothed in fine robes, some of which were worth their weight in gold; and he lived well from day to day. And there was a poor man, named Laz-a-rus, who was brought each day and laid at his gate that he might beg from those who came out or went in. He would have been glad of some of the crumbs that fell from the rich man's board, but none of these were brought to him. He was full of sores, and the rich man might have sent out some salve to heal them. But this he did not do, nor did he feed the dogs, and so they came and licked the sores of the poor man, and made his woes far more hard to bear.

At last the poor man died, and was borne by an-gels to his home on high. And in time the rich man died, and was laid in his grave. The Jews, when they spoke of the dead, said that they had gone to A-bra-ham's bo-som. In hell—the place of lost souls—where he was in great pain, he raised his eyes and saw A-bra-ham a-far off, and Laz-a-rus with his head up-on his breast. And he cried out and said, Fath-er A-bra-ham, have mercy on me, and send Laz-a-rus, that he may dip the tip of his fin-ger in wa-ter, and cool my tongue, for I am sore vexed in this flame.

But A-bra-ham said, Son, in thy life-time thou didst have thy share of good things, and Laz-a-rus had none; now here he is rich, and thou art poor. And this is not all, for be-tween us and you there is a great gulf fixed; so that

THE BEG-GAR AT THE RICH MAN'S GATE.

those who wish to go from here to you can-not; nor can those cross who wish to come to us from where you are.

Then the rich man said, I pray thee then that thou wouldst send him to my fath-er's house, that he may speak to my five broth-ers, lest they come to this dread place that I am in.

A-bra-ham said to him, They have Mo-ses and the proph-ets, let them hear them. He said, Nay, fath-er A-bra-ham, but if one went to them from the dead, they will be led to give up their sins. And he said to him, If they hear not Mo-ses and the proph-ets—if the Word of God does not find its way to their hearts—they will not hear the truth though one should rise from the dead.

The rich man had made the wealth of earth his chief good. He lived in sin, and did not try in the least to please God. The scene that Je-sus drew was to teach these Jews, that af-ter death would be too late to say they were sor-ry for their sins.

We teach more by our lives than we do by our words. This rich man might have thought of his kins-folk, and tried to lead a good life for their sakes, as well as his own. If they were lost, it was his fault. Hosts of those who lead lives of sin, think they will make it all right with God on their death-bed. They pass the eighth hour, the ninth, the tenth. They have but two hours more, but they will be long ones. There will be time e-nough. They will be old then, and will not care so much for the things of this world. But self has ruled too long to be put a-side. And what if there is no death-bed? If you are cut off in your sins, with-out time to think, to speak, or to pray, what then? You may drop down dead, and have no time to warn those you love not to do as you have done. The sick-bed is no place to make your peace with God. See to that when you are well and strong. Learn to love Je-sus while you are young. Give your heart to him in the first fresh glow of youth, when you have strength to work for him. It is not safe to put it off. You may put it off too late.

Then there stood up a Scribe, who taught the law of Mo-ses; and that he might find out if Je-sus taught in the same way, or try to get him to say some-thing new, he asked him, What shall I do to be saved?

He was full of pride, and self-love. He was well-read in the law, which he taught; and might be seen at all times with book in hand, and the marks of deep thought on his brow. He spoke to Je-sus in a way that said, What canst thou teach me that I do not know? He thought he should hear of some new or great thing, that was not laid down in the law of Mo-ses. He did not claim to be rich in this world's goods, he had no gold to waste; but he had a fine mind, and was proud of it. What shall I do, he asked, to win this life which lasts be-yond the grave?

Je-sus said to him, What is in the law you teach? Let us hear how you read it. The scribe said, Thou shalt love the Lord thy God with all thy heart, and with all thy soul, and with all thy strength, and with all thy mind; and thy neigh-bor as thy-self.

Je-sus said to him, Thou hast learned it well. This do and thou shalt live. The words of the law were on his lips, he could say them all right, but they were not in his heart. He was a shrewd man and knew that this was what Je-sus meant, so to throw off the blame, as it were, he asked, Who is my neigh-bor?

Je-sus spoke to him in a par-able, so that he might with words paint a scene on the mind of this man of the

JEW-ISH PRIEST.   A LE-VITE.

law that he would not soon lose sight of. Je-sus said to him, A man went down from Je-ru-sa-lem to Jer-i-cho, and on the way he fell in-to the hands of thieves who stripped him, and beat him, and left him half dead by the roadside. By chance there came a priest that way, and when he

The Good Sa-mar-i-tan. 289

saw the poor man in so sad a plight, he did not stop, but passed by on the oth-er side.

ROB-BERS ON THE ROAD TO JER-I-CHO.

Then a Le-vite, who was well read in the law, drew near the place, and saw him, and he, too, passed by and

HALF DEAD BY THE ROAD-SIDE.

gave him no help. But a Sa-mar-i-tan, who was on his way to trade at one of the towns, came where the poor man was, and when he saw the plight he was in, his heart was sad. And he came to him, and bound up his wounds, poured on them oil and wine, set him on his own beast, and brought him to an inn, and took care of him. The next day, when he left, he took out two pence and gave them to the host, and said, Take care of him; and if thou hast need to spend more, the next time I come I will pay it back to thee.

Which of these three, dost thou think, was neigh-bor to the one who fell in the midst of thieves? And he said, He that was kind to him. And Je-sus said to him, Go, and do thou like-wise. In this way did Je-sus teach what man owes to man, and give force to the rule—Do as you would be done by.

The priest, though it was part of his work to care for the sick, and to give help to all who were in need, had not a warm heart, or he could not have passed by the poor man who had been set on by thieves. We are to do good to all, and not to stop and look at a man's clothes, or to find out to what church he goes. If he is a Jew and needs help, be quick to give it. If he is black and needs help, do not turn a-way and say, Let the black folks help him. He has been put in your way for you to help. Do good when you can, and where you can, and to whom you can. This is all God asks of us.

Near this time three-score and ten men whom Je-sus had sent out to do his work, came back, and with great joy told what they had done. And they said to him, Lord, in thy name have we had strength to cast out dev-ils. Je-sus shared in their joy, and gave thanks to God. And he said that they should do more than they had done, and he would pledge them his word to keep them from all harm. But they were not to joy in their own deeds, or what they could do in Christ's name, for the joy of joys was that their own names were writ in the Book of Life.

Je-sus then told them the par-a-ble of the Prod-i-gal Son. A prod-i-gal is one who spends all he is worth. One who wastes.

PALMS AND PLAINS OF JER-I-CHO.

Je-sus said, There was a rich man who had two sons. And one of these had no love for his home or his fath-er, and he said, Fath-er, give me my share of what will come to me as thine heir. And the fath-er did so. And in a few days this son went off in-to a far land, and led a life of sin. And when he had spent all, there came a dearth of food in the land, and he was in great want. So starved was he that he would fain have filled him-self with the husks that the swine did eat. When he saw the swine fed he craved a share of their food, but no man gave as much as this to him.

When he came to him-self, he said, The hired ser-vants of my fath-er have more bread than they can eat, while here I starve, and am like to die for want of food! I will rise and go to my fath-er, and will say un-to him, Fath-er, I have sinned a-gainst heav-en and in thy sight, and do not de-serve to be called thy son. Make me as one of thy hired ser-vants. And he rose and went to his fath-er.

While he was yet a great way off his fath-er saw him, and in the joy of his heart he ran out to meet him, and fell on his neck and kissed him. And the son said to him, Fath-er I have sinned a-gainst heav-en and in thy sight, and no more have the right to be called thy son. But the fath-er said to his ser-vants, Bring forth with haste the best robe, and put it on him; and put a ring on his hand, and shoes on his feet. And kill the fat-ted calf and let us have a feast of joy.

Now the son who did not leave his home was at this time out in the field. And as he came near the house he heard the sound of mu-sic and the dance, and called one of the ser-vants to him and asked what it meant. The man said to him, Thy bro-ther is here; and thy fath-er hath killed the fat-ted calf for joy that he hath come back safe and sound.

The son who heard these words, was so an-gry that he would not go in-to the house; and his fath-er came out and coaxed him. And he said to his fath-er, Lo, for a long term of years have I served thee, and done as thou wouldst have me; and yet thou didst not give me so much as a kid, that I might make a feast for my friends. But as soon as this thy son came, who hath led a fast life, thou didst kill for him the fat-ted calf. There was no love in this son's heart. He had done his work in hope of gain.

The fath-er said to him, Son, thou art with me all the time, and all that is mine is thine. But it was right that we should make a feast for our friends, and to be glad with a great joy. For this thy broth-er was dead and is now a-live; he was lost, and is found.

Our Lord meant to show by these two sons the two kinds of men there are in the world. Some fret at the chains, and long to be free; and they go out in the world and lead a life of sin, and are for a while like mad men. Then all at once they come to a sense of their sins, are shocked at what they have done, and full of shame. They long for the Bread of Life. They want some one to tell them what to do and to speak a kind word to them. But no one comes near them. At last in their rags and their shame they come to God, who did not cast them off, but whom they turned from of their own free will.

Do they have to wait and beg for Him to take them back? No. He sees them. He runs out to meet them. God's grace meets us more than half-way. In His love He puts on them the robe, the ring, and the shoes—the signs that mark them as the Son's of God—and all the an-gels share in His joy.

The son who staid at home is like those who go to church, keep all God's laws, and think no one is quite so good as they are. They are puffed up with pride, and love of self, and till they get rid of these sins can have no share in the joy the an-gels know.

They need a change of heart just as much as do those

who have steeped them-selves in sin. As soon as they turn to God, and ask His help, He gives them strength to do the right and shun the wrong, and they have while on earth, a joy the world can-not give.

WOM-AN OF NAZ-A-RETH.

Je-sus said to the crowd that drew near, What man of you, if he owns a hun-dred sheep and has lost one of them does not leave the nine-ty and nine in the field, and go search for the one that is lost till he find it? And when he hath found it, he bears it in his arms and brings it back with joy. And when he comes home he calls in his friends and his neigh-bors, and says to them, Be glad with me for I have found my sheep which was lost. I say un-to you that there will be more joy in heav-en when one who has been lost in sin is brought to God, than o-ver nine-ty and nine of those who have led good lives, and are in the fold.

It is said that the wom-en of Naz-a-reth still wear a head-dress of small sil-ver coins, which Je-sus had in mind when he said:

Or what wom-an who has ten sil-ver coins, if she lose one piece, doth not light a lamp, and sweep the house, and search hard till she finds it? And when she has found it, she calls in her friends and those who live near her and says to them, Be glad with me, for I have found the piece which I lost. So I say to you there is joy in heav-en when one who was lost in sin, is brought back, and strives to lead a new life.

When some of the Jews who sought to kill Je-sus asked him when the King-dom of God should come, he told them there were no signs by which men could tell. False Christs might cry out Lo, it is here! or lo, it is there! but the hopes thus raised would soon come to nought. The King-dom of God he said, is in the midst of you. He meant that the King was then with them. The King-dom of God is where Je-sus is—His throne is in the hearts of those who love Him, and who do His will.

When the Jews who sought to kill Je-sus had gone

their way, he spoke to those who were glad to be taught by him. And he said, As it was in the days of No-ah, so shall it be in the days of the Son of Man. They did eat, and drink, and made no change in their ways till the day that No-ah went in-to the ark, and the flood came and drowned them all. So it was in the days of Lot. They ate, they drank, they bought, they sold, they sowed seed, and built homes and barns. But in the day that Lot went from Sod-om God sent down fire and brim-stone and burnt up all that was in it. So shall it be in the day that the Son of Man comes. He told them to think how it was with Lot's wife. She set out all right and would have been saved, but she looked back and was lost.

Lot's wife was loath to give up the things of this world, the gay life, and the wealth that had been hers in the land of Sod-om. She looked back, and was lost! It is not meant, I think, that she was turned in-to real salt, but as salt gave a taste to food, so would this last act of hers do more good than she had done in her life. For it would stand out in the Word of God, as a sign to all, to turn from sin, and not look back lest they be lost. And Je-sus said to them, Watch, for ye know not on what day your Lord comes.

They said to him, Where Lord? Where shall this thing take place? But the words he spoke left them still in doubt.

CHAPTER XVII.

MA-RY'S CHOICE.—THEY BRING YOUNG CHIL-DREN TO JE-SUS.—THE YOUNG RU-LER.—THE WORK-MEN IN THE VINE-YARD.—THE HIGH-PRIEST TELLS THAT JE-SUS MUST DIE.

On the way to and from Je-ru-sa-lem Je-sus had to pass through Beth-a-ny. It was a small town, but an hour's walk from Je-ru-sa-lem, and here lived two sis-ters, named Mar-tha and Ma-ry. It was a great joy to them to have Je-sus for their guest, and he was glad to rest there, and feel that he was with friends. It was some time since he had been to the house, and both Mar-tha and Ma-ry were glad to see his face once more. As soon as he came in, Ma-ry sat down at the Lord's feet to hear what he had to say.

But Mar-tha kept the house, and found so much work to do that she could not sit still. There was nought too good in her house for this guest, and she wished to have the food well cooked, and all as it should be. But she found that she had more to do than she could get through with, and was in need of help. So she came to where Je-sus was, and said to him, Lord, dost thou not care that my sis-ter has left me to do all the work a-lone? Bid her come and help me.

Je-sus said to her, Mar-tha, Mar-tha, thou art full of

RUINS OF BETH-A-NY.

care, and vexed with things that take up much of thy time. There is need of but one thing; and Ma-ry chose for her-self the good part, that none shall take a-way from her.

BETH-A-NY.

Mar-tha wished to do some-thing to show her love for Je-sus, when it would have been as well for her to sit down at his feet and learn of him. He was to be at the house but a short time, and Ma-ry thought not of food or drink,

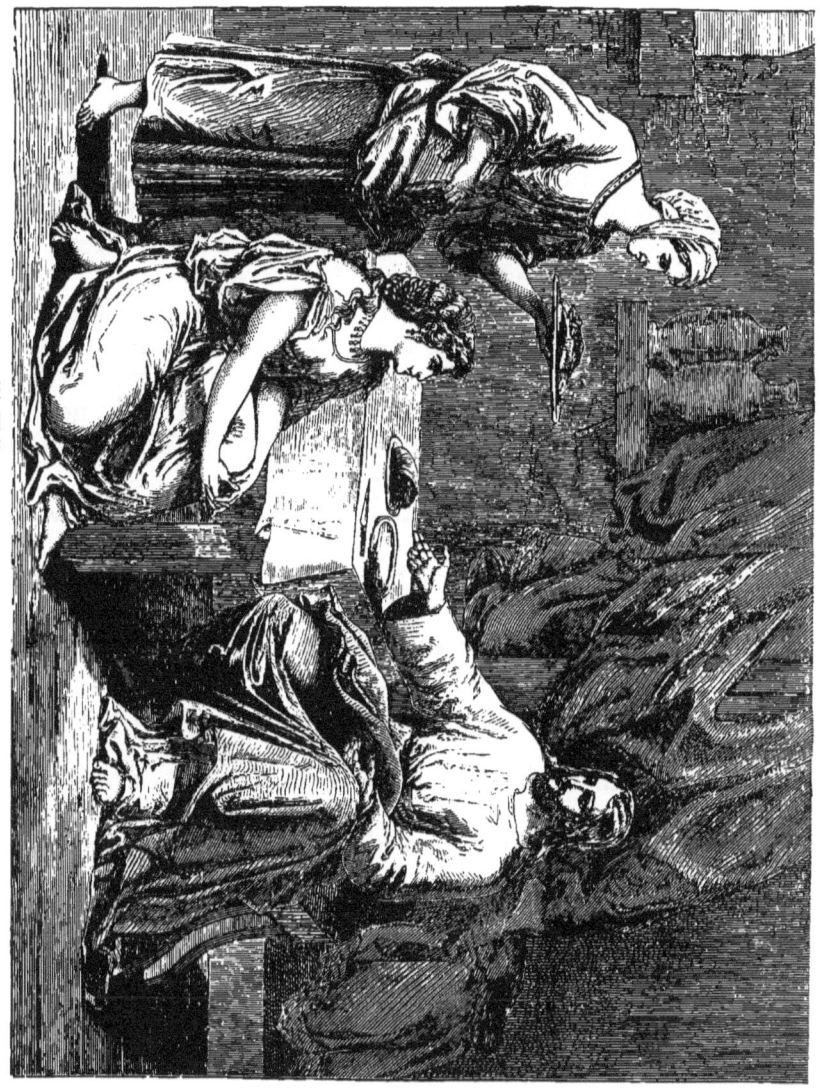

MARY HATH CHOSEN THE GOOD PART.

or the cares of the house, so great was her joy to be near her Lord.

Mar-tha takes her place with those who think more of works than of faith, Ma-ry with those who think more of faith than of works. This is what Je-sus meant when he said she chose the good part. She fed on the bread of life by faith in his word.

It is wise to make such a choice. To sit at his feet in a calm frame of mind, to do his work with-out fuss or noise. We are not to find fault with those who do not show their love for Je-sus in the same way that we do. We do not all think a-like or act a-like. Je-sus loved both Mar-tha and Ma-ry, and he knew they loved him.

There was now a feast at Je-ru-sa-lem and it was win-ter. The feast was kept up for eight days. And Je-sus walked in the courts, and in Sol-o-mon's porch, which was on the east side of the Tem-ple. There was a roof to this porch, so that at all times of the year it was a fine place to walk in. Then the Jews came round him, and said to him, How long wilt thou keep us in doubt? If thou art the Christ, tell us so in plain words.

Je-sus said, I told you, and ye be-lieve not. The works that I do in my Fath-er's name show who I am. But ye be-lieve not, be-cause ye are not of my sheep. My sheep hear my voice, and I know them, and they come with me. They are safe with me; and no one shall snatch them out of my hand. My Fath-er gave them to me; there is no one so great as He; and no one can pluck out of God's hand. I and the Fath-er are one.

The Jews took up stones that lay near to throw at him,

THEN THE JEWS TOOK UP STONES.

but were stop-ped by the words of Je-sus. For he said, Good works not a few have I showed you from the Fath-er; for which of these works do ye stone me? The Jews said, For a good work we stone thee not; but be-cause thou, who art a man, dost make thy-self one with God.

Je-sus said, If I do not the works of my Fath-er, be-lieve me not. But if I do, and ye be-lieve not me, be-lieve the works: that ye may know, and see that the Fath-er is in me, and I in the Fath-er. It was, as though he said, Look at my life, look at my works, and let them speak for me.

They dared not stone him, but they tried to seize him. But they could not. He slipped out of their hands and made his way to Beth-a-ny, where he spent some time, and taught, and wrought great works there.

When he came to Pe-re-a they brought to him young chil-dren, that he might put his hands on them and bless them. Some did not like this, and wished them sent a-way. But Je-sus said, Let the lit-tle chil-dren come to me. Do not send them a-way. None are too young to come to Christ. And he laid his hands on them, and blest them. When Je-sus went out on the road, for he did not stay long in one place, a young ru-ler ran up to him, and knelt down and asked him, Good mas-ter, what shall I do to be saved? Je-sus said, Why dost thou call me good? There is none good, but one, and that is, God. But if thou in truth wouldst be saved, keep all God's laws: Do not kill. Do not steal. Do not lie, or cheat; and do as your fath-er and moth-er tell you. The young man said to him, All these things have I kept from my youth up, and now what else do I lack? Je-sus said to him, One thing else dost thou lack. Go and sell all that thou hast and give to the poor, and thou shalt be rich in heaven, and come with me. He was to give up all things for Christ's sake. When the young man heard this, he went a-way sad at heart, for he had great wealth.

Je-sus looked round, and said to those with him, How hard it shall be for those who trust in their wealth to find their way in-to the King-dom of God. And they were a-mazed at his words. And he said to them, As hard as it would be for a cam-el—with a hump on his back, and a great load be-sides—to get through a small hole, just so hard would it be for a rich man to get through the small gate that leads to the King-dom of God.

When the Twelve heard this they said, Who then can be saved? Je-sus looked up-on them with a sad gaze, for he had thought they would not be so dull, and he said to them, What man can-not do, God can, and will do. For He can do all things.

It is not wealth that keeps men back from Christ, but the love of it. They cling to it so, and grow so fond of the things of this world, that they take no thought of the next world. And oh, how poor and mean their souls grow, and how much they miss! We can take none of our wealth out of this world. We must leave it all, when we die.

Pe-ter spoke up, and said to Je-sus, Lo, we have left all and have come with thee. Je-sus said, There is no man that hath left house and lands and kins-men for my sake, and for the sake of that which I preach, but shall have his re-ward in this world and the next. But some that are first shall be last.

Pe-ter did not mean to boast of what he had done for Je-sus, but his hopes were mixed some-what with fears, and it did him good to speak out what was in his mind. If this rich man would find it hard to get in-to heav-en, what chance would the poor man have? Je-sus made it clear to him, and to us, that heav-en joins close on to this world, and be-gins as soon as we give our hearts to Je-sus, and take him as our guard and guide. We must say as Pe-ter did, Lo, we have left all, and have come with thee; and must feel that the world is well lost for such a gain as ours.

Je-sus said, The King-dom of God is like a man who went out at day-break to hire men to work in his vine-yard. And when they said they would work for the pay he would give, he sent them out where his vines were.

At the third hour—at nine o'clock—he went out to the mar-ket place, and saw men there who were out of work. And he said to them, Go ye and work in my vine-yard. And they went and did as he told them. And at the sixth and the ninth hour—at twelve and at three o'clock—he went out and found more men who were out of work, and said the same thing to them. At five o'clock he went out for the fifth time, and found more men with nought to do. And he said to them, Why waste ye your time in this way? They said, Be-cause no one has hired us. He said to them, Go work in my vine-yard.

At the close of the day, the lord of the vine-yard said to his fore-man, Call the work-men and pay them all, from the last to the first. And when those came that were hired near six o'clock, each man was paid for a full day's work. When the first men came, they thought they would be paid

MARY BATHES THE FEET OF CHRIST.

more; but the same sum was placed in their hands. And they found fault with the good man of the house, and said to him, These last were but one hour at work, and thou hast paid them the same as us, who toiled all day long in the dust and heat.

But he said to one of them, Friend, I do thee no wrong. Didst thou not say thou wouldst do my work for so much a day? Take up that which is thine, and go thy way. It is my will to give to this last one the same that I gave to thee. Is it not right for me to do what I will with mine own? So the last shall be first, and the first last.

The vine-yard is the world. The man who owns it is God. The work-men are those who are sent out to teach and preach, and to turn men from their sins. The steward, or fore-man, is Christ, who pays off all those who work, in his name. It means, too, that all those who come to Christ late in life, shall be paid the same as those who came in their youth. We are not to count our time, nor feel that what we do is worth more than what some one else does. God knows what is best for us. We are to do His will, not ours, and to be not proud or vain. For those who put them-selves first He will put last.

Je-sus was now on his way to Je-ru-sa-lem, and for the last time. And while he still taught at Pe-re-a, word was brought to him that Laz-a-rus, the broth-er of Mar-tha and Ma-ry was sick. And the sis-ters beg-ged Je-sus to come and see him at their home in Beth-a-ny. When Je-sus heard it, he said that Laz-a-rus would not die, but was laid on a sick-bed to show forth the works of the Son of God, and by this means bring praise to God the Fath-er.

Now Je-sus loved Mar-tha, her sis-ter, and Laz-a-rus, yet when he had sent the word back to them, he staid on in the place where he was. At the end of two days he said to the Twelve, Let us go in-to Ju-de-a once more. They said to him, Mas-ter, it is not long since the Jews tried to stone thee; and wilt thou go there a-gain? Je-sus said, Is not the day twelve hours long? If a man walk in the day he makes no false step, be-cause he sees the light of this world. But if a man walk in the night he trips be-cause the light is not in him. Then he said to them, Our friend Laz-a-rus sleeps; but I go to wake him out of his sleep. They said to him, Lord, if he sleeps he shall do well.

Je-sus spoke of his death; but they thought that he spoke of the rest one takes in sleep. So he had to tell them in plain words, Laz-a-rus is dead. And I am glad, he said, for your sakes that I was not there, for now I go to bring him back to life. Then said Thom-as, one of the Twelve, Let us go, that we may die with him. Not with Laz-a-rus, but with Je-sus. It was as if he said to the rest, The Jews will be sure to put him to death this time, they hate him so. We can-not save him, but we can share his fate. Come, let us go and die with him.

When Je-sus came to Beth-a-ny he found that Laz-a-rus had lain four days in the tomb. Now Beth-a-ny was but a few miles from Je-ru-sa-lem, and the Jews came from there to see Mar-tha and Ma-ry and to weep and mourn with them. While Ma-ry sat still in the house, bowed down with grief, word came to Mar-tha that Je-sus was near at hand, and she went out at once to meet him. And she said to Je-sus, with tears in her voice, Lord, if thou hadst been here my broth-er had not died. But I know that e-ven now the things thou shalt ask of God, He will give thee.

Je-sus said to her, Laz-a-rus shall rise from the dead. Mar-tha said to him, I know that he shall rise at the Last Day. Je-sus said, I am the Life—of this world and the next. He that has faith in me, though he has died, yet shall he live. And those who live and be-lieve in me, shall not die. Christ is the Lord of Life.

Je-sus said to Mar-tha, Dost thou be-lieve this? She said to him, Yes, Lord, I be-lieve that thou art the Christ, the Son of God, who has come in-to the world. When she had said this she went in quest of her sis-ter, and said to her in a low voice, The Mas-ter is here, and asks for thee.

When Ma-ry heard this she rose in haste and went out where Je-sus was. The Jews that were with her in the house, when they saw her rise and go out, made haste to join her. For they thought that she went to the tomb to weep there. They did not know she had gone to meet her Lord.

When Ma-ry came where Je-sus was, and saw him, she feel at his feet, and said, Lord, if thou hadst been here my broth-er would not have died. When Je-sus saw how she wept, and how the Jews wept with her, his heart was moved to its depths. And he said, Where have ye laid him? They say to him, Lord, come and see. Je-sus wept. When the Jews saw him shed tears they said, See how he loved him. But some of them said, Could not he who gave the blind their sight have saved this man from death?

LAZ-A-RUS RAISED FROM THE DEAD.

Je-sus, still moved by the hate of the Jews, went out to the tomb. It was not a grave dug out of the ground, but a sort of cave cut out of the lime-stone rock. And a stone lay on top of it. Je-sus said, Take ye a-way the stone.

JEW-ISH HIGH PRIEST.

Mar-tha said, Lord, by this time he is not fit to be seen; for he hath been dead four days.

Je-sus said to her, Did I not tell thee if thou didst believe thou shouldst see the glo-ry of God? Then they took the stone from the door of the tomb. And Je-sus raised his eyes, and said, Fath-er, I thank thee that thou dost hear me. I knew that thou didst hear me at all times; but be-cause of the crowds that stand round I said it, that they might be-lieve that thou didst send me. And when he had said these words, he cried out with a loud voice, Laz-a-rus, come forth! And he that was dead came forth, bound hand and foot with the grave clothes; and his face was hid with a piece of white cloth. Je-sus said, Loose him, and let him go.

Then some of the Jews who came to the house of Ma-ry, and saw what Je-sus did, had faith in him. But the rest went a-way and told his foes what things Je-sus had done. Then the chief priests and men of the law, met, and said, What are we to do? For this man does strange signs. If we let him a-lone all men will be-lieve in him, and our down-fall will be sure.

One of them, named Ca-ia-phas, who was the high priest at that time, said to them, Ye do not know, or seem to think, that it might be well to put one man to death and so save our-selves. He was full of craft; and as all the high priests in those days could tell the things that would take place, he fore-told that Je-sus was to die for the Jews. And not for them a-lone, but that the whole world might be brought to God and known by a new name. This made the Jews hate Je-sus more and more, and from that day forth they laid their plans to seize him that they might put him to death.

Je-sus then went a-way and made his home with the Twelve in a small town at the north-east of Je-ru-sa-lem.

CHAPTER XVIII.

THE PASS-O-VER FEAST.—BLIND BAR-TI-ME-US.—ZAC-CHE-US CLIMBS A TREE.—JE-SUS ON THE WAY TO JE-RU-SA-LEM.—THE FEAST AT BETH-A-NY.

It was now the spring of the year, and near the time of the full moon. And one of the three great feasts of the Jews was close at hand. This feast was called the Feast of the Pass-o-ver, and it had been kept since the days of Mo-ses, that the Jews might bear in mind all that they owed to God, and how he led them out of the land of E-gypt. It was the law that each male Jew should go to the house of the Lord, where the feast was kept up for eight days. In all that time they were to eat no bread with yeast in it. They were to take a young lamb, and roast it whole, and this was to form the meal in each house on the eve of the feast.

The Jews were strict to keep this first great feast, and for days and days the roads were filled with the crowds on their way to Je-ru-sa-lem. Je-sus, from the small town on the hill, could see the throng as it wound through the vale that lay at his feet. The time had come for him to leave this place, and to go forth to meet his fate; and with bowed head he set out for the high road that led to Je-ru-sa-lem.

On the way he called the Twelve to him, and said, We now go up to Je-ru-sa-lem, and there by fraud I shall be led

JE-SUS ON HIS WAY TO JE-RU-SA-LEM.

to the chief priests and scribes, and they shall doom me to death. And they shall give me up to the mob, who will mock, and scourge, and spit at me. And they will hang me on the cross, but in three days I will rise from the dead.

Then the moth-er of James and John came with her two

ON THE WAY TO JE-RU-SA-LEM.

sons and bowed down at the feet of Je-sus, as those were wont to do who had some-thing to ask of a king. Jesus said to her, What dost thou wish? She said, That these my two sons may sit one on thy right hand, and one on thy left hand in thy king-dom.

The Pass-o-ver Feast. 317

Je-sus said to James and John, Ye know not what ye ask. Can ye drink of the cup that I am to drink? They said to him, We can. Then said Jesus, My cup ye shall drink—that is, he meant they should share in his pains and woes—but to sit on my right hand and on my left hand is not mine to give, but is as God wills.

JE-RU-SA-LEM FROM THE SOUTH.

When the Ten heard of it, they were not at all pleased with the two men who had shown them-selves so full of pride as to think of crowns at this time. But Je-sus called them un-to him and taught them that those who would be great in the next life, must be as ser-vants in this life. He who would take high rank there, must give up all thought of self, and serve in a low rank here. They were to do as he had done. For he had not come to be served by them, but had spent his life for the good of men, and would die that they might be set free from their guilt and sin. In times of war when the slaves of a king were seized by his foe, the king could not get them back with-out he paid a price for them. This price is called a ran-som. To ran-som is to set free. Je-sus, by his death, sets us free from the chains of sin.

As they drew near Jer-i-cho the crowd grew more and more dense. Here and there by the way-side sat the blind men, who could not work, and had to beg. One of these was named Bar-ti-me-us, who may have heard of Je-sus, and of the strange things he had done. And when he heard the noise of the crowd, and was told that it was Je-sus who had passed by, he cried out for Je-sus to help him. Those near him told him to be still, but he cried out the more, and begged Jesus to help him.

Then Je-sus stood still, and said, Call ye him. And they said to the blind man, Rise, be of good cheer, he calls thee. And the blind man sprang up and came to Je-sus. Je-sus said to him, What wilt thou that I should do to thee? And the blind man said, Master, that I may have my sight. Je-sus said to him, Go thy way; thy faith hath made thee whole. And at once his sight came to him, and he joined the crowd that went with Je-sus. And he, and all those who saw what had been done, gave thanks and praise to God.

Jer-i-cho was one of the towns where the tax was paid,

and a man named Zac-che-us lived there. He was paid to take the toll, and to see that the trade in gums and spice was well kept up. He was a rich man, and a Jew, and

SUP-POSED SITE OF JER-I-CHO.

he mass of the Jews thought that he did not make his wealth by fair means. This man had heard of Je-sus, and had a strong wish to see what kind of a man he was. But he was so short, that though he went out with the crowd, he could not catch a glimpse of him. So he ran far out on the road, and climbed up in-to a sort of wild fig-tree to see Je-sus; for he was to pass that way.

When Je-sus came to the place he looked up, and said to him, Zac-che-us, make haste, and come down; for to-day I must stop at thy house. And he made haste, and came

MOUNT AT JER-I-CHO.

down, and led the way to his house, with joy in his heart that Je-sus was to be his guest.

The crowd of Jews, most of whom were priests, raised a great hue and cry, and said, He has gone to lodge with a man that is a sin-ner! For they looked on Zac-che-us with scorn. But he stood out in their midst, and said to the Lord, with whom he wished to stand well, The half of my goods, Lord, I give to the poor; and if there is a man

ZAC-CHE-US CALLED BY CHRIST.

whom I have robbed, and charged him more than he ought to have paid, I will give him back four times what he lost.

This was proof that he would give up all that he loved best, for the sake of Him who had come to be his guest. And Je-sus said that he and his house should be saved.

SQUARE RUINS AT JER-I-CHO.

For he had owned that he was one of the lost sheep to whom the Lord was sent,

While in the house of Zac-che-us, Je-sus spoke a par-a-ble, be-cause it was thought that as he was near Je-ru-sa-lem the king-dom he had told of must be close at hand. He said, A man of high rank went in-to a far off land to be crowned king, and when this was done he would come back. And he called ten ser-vants of his and gave to them ten pounds to trade with till he came back. But those who lived in the same town with this man had no love for him, and made it known that they did not wish him to be their king. And when he came back he called the ser-vants to him that he might know how they had used the wealth he had left with them.

The first came and said, Lord, with thy pound I have made ten pounds more. And he said to him, Well done, thou good ser-vant; be-cause thou didst well with a small sum, thou shalt rule o-ver ten large towns.

Then the next one came and said, Lord, with thy one pound I have made five pounds. And he said to him, Thou shalt rule o-ver five towns. Then the third one came, and said, Lord, here is thy pound which I kept laid up in a cloth. For I feared thee, be-cause thou art a hard man, and dost take up what thou hast not laid down, and dost reap where thou hast not sown.

The mas-ter said to him, Out of thine own mouth will I judge thee, thou wick-ed ser-vant. Thou didst know I was a hard man, who took up what I laid not down, and reaped what I did not sow. Then why didst thou not put what I gave thee in the bank, that when I came back I might have had it with the sum it would have gained? And he said to those that stood by, Take from him the one pound, and give it to him that hath the ten pounds. For I say to you that he who hath shall have more; and he that hath not much, shall lose that which he hath. And those who are my foes, and who do not wish me to reign o-ver them, bring them here, and put them to death.

The king meant Je-sus, who was then on his way to a far off land, and would come back in due time. All men were his ser-vants, placed here to do his will. The pounds he left with them was the gift of faith. They were to be-lieve in Je-sus, and to serve him well, so that when he came back he would find that they had grown in grace, and were far more Christ-like than when he left.

Each one should be a king—for he would rule him-self. But the one who had hid his gift, who had done nought to spread the name and fame of his king, or to gain strength for his cause, should lose the chance of gain he had, and be poor all the rest af his days. The foes of Christ—those who did not wish him to be their king—would meet a sad fate.

Je-sus let these words sink in-to their hearts, and went out of the house, and up the rise of ground that led to Je-ru-sa-lem. He was at the head of a great crowd, some of whom gazed at him with a look of awe, for they had seen his works and heard his words, and knew not what to think of him.

He did not mean to go to Je-ru-sa-lem at this time, for the feast was yet six days off and he had need to rest. So as he drew near Beth-a-ny he left the crowd, and with the Twelve went to the house of his friends, which they reached at sun-down.

While Je-sus was at Beth-a-ny they made a feast for him, and it was a feast of joy; for Je-sus was their guest.

The Feast at Beth-a-ny.

Mar-tha served, and Laz-a-rus—whom Je-sus had raised from the dead—sat at meat with him. And there were those there, too, whom Je-sus had healed.

Ma-ry had some oil which had cost a great deal. And she took a flask of this oil and poured it on the feet of Je-sus, and she wiped his feet with the hair of her head. So

ON THE ROAD TO BETH-A-NY.

much of the oil did she use that the whole house was filled with the sweet smell.

Ju-das, one of the Twelve, who would soon give Je-sus in-to the hands of his foes, spoke up and said, Why this waste? Why was not this oil sold? for the price it brought would have done much good to the poor. This he said, not that he cared much for the poor, but be-cause he was a thief, and bore with him the bag, or box, in which the mon-ey was put. The sale of the oil would bring but ten pounds at the most, but such was his greed of gold that he could not bear to have this sum slip through his hands.

Je-sus said, Let her a-lone, for she has wrought a good work up-on me, and for the time of my death has she kept this. The poor ye have with you at all times; but me ye have not with you.

CHAPTER XIX.

JE-SUS LEAVES BETH-A-NY.—SONGS OF PRAISE AND PALMS OF JOY.—HE SPEAKS IN THE TEM-PLE.—A VOICE FROM ON HIGH.—THE FIG TREE THAT BORE NO FRUIT.

There were three roads that led from the town of Beth-a-ny up to the Mount of Ol-ives, from which a fine view could be had of the large town of Je-ru-sa-lem, with all its parks, ponds and tombs, its domes, and spires, and well-built forts, and all the signs of wealth out-spread. Two of these roads were paths, rough and hard to the feet, so Je-sus chose the main road, and led the way for those who went with him. As they drew near to Beth-page Je-sus called two of the Twelve and said to them, Go your way to the small town close at hand, and there you shall find an ass tied, with a colt near her. Loose the colt and bring him here. And if the man who owns him asks why you loose him, say, The Lord has need of him.

The two men went off and found all things as Je-sus had said. There was the ass, and near her the young colt which had not yet been used. Both were tied at the back of the house, and the men went to them to do as they were told. While they were at work, the man of the house came up to them and said, Why loose ye the colt? They said,

VIEW IN JE-RU-SA-LEM.

The Lord has need of him. And they brought him to Je-sus and threw their robes on the colt, and set Je-sus on his back.

In the East the horse was made use of when men went out to war. But when they went to trade, or to call on their friends, they rode on the mule or ass, and this was the sign that they went out for peace and not for war. The ass and the mule were beasts for the poor, for it did not cost much to keep them, and great were the loads they could bear. Je-sus came as a poor man, and not as a rich one;

BETH-PAGE.

and rode on an ass, and not on a war-horse, that all might know that he brought peace and good-will to men. As he went the crowd with him threw their robes in his way, and cut down the boughs of the palm and fig-trees to strew in the path, as they would have done to one of the kings of earth, and they cried out, Blest be the king that comes in the name of the Lord!

Ho-san-na to the most High! The day on which this scene took place is now known as Palm Sun-day; and the

WHERE BETH-PAGE ONCE STOOD.

palm is a sign of praise, or of work well done. And as the crowd went on they spoke of the great things that Je-sus had done, and more than all that he had raised Laz-a-rus from the dead. For this was fresh in their minds.

They came to a turn of the road that brought them to the brow of the hill—the Mount of Ol-ives—from whence they could look off on the far-famed town, that shone in a blaze of white and gold. All these signs of wealth were spread out to the gaze, and when Je-sus saw what Je-ru-sa-lem was, and thought of what she might be, great sobs shook his frame and he gave way to tears. He had tried to save the Jews, but they would not come to him. But his tears were not for the Jews a-lone, but for all those who turn from him and will not be saved. The shrines they set up, and the gods they bow down to will be all swept a-way and what then will they have left to cling to? If God is in the house, the house will stand; which means that if the heart—which is the true church of God—is prompt to do His will, firm in its love for Christ and its trust in Him, it will not sink though the skies should fall, but will rise and shine in white and gold that the years shall not dim.

EAST-ERN ASS-ES.

EN-TRY IN-TO JE-RU-SA-LEM.

Songs of Praise and Palms of Joy.

As soon as it was known that Je-sus was on his way to the feast, crowds went out of Je-ru-sa-lem to meet him. Some joined in the shouts, and songs of praise, which when

JE-RU-SA-LEM FROM MOUNT OF OL-IVES.

the scribes heard they called on Je-sus to put a stop to. But he said, If these shall hold their peace, the stones themselves shall cry out. As they came in-to Je-ru-sa-lem there was a great stir, and some asked, Who is this? as if they said, what has he done? What does all this fuss mean? and the crowd said, This is the proph-et, Je-sus, from Naz-a-reth of Gal-i-lee.

CHRIST WEEPING OVER JERUSALEM.

Je-sus went at once to to the Tem-ple of God, and found that men had brought their wares in-side, and bought and sold their ox-en, sheep, and doves, as they had done three years be-fore. Once more he drove them out. He could not teach the pure word of God in such a foul place, where the clink of the gold could be heard a-bove the sound of his voice. And he said to those who had sinned thus, It is set down in the Word of God—My house shall be a house of prayer, but ye have made it a den of thieves. And the blind and the lame came to him and he healed them all; and great was the throng that drew round him to hear the words that fell from his lips.

The boys in the Tem-ple cried out Ho-san-na! Ho-san-na! for so great was their joy, they could not cease their glad songs of praise.

When the chief priests and scribes saw and heard these things they ground their teeth with rage. They longed to lay hands on him, but dared not touch him, for the whole crowd seemed to be on his side. And they said to Je-sus, when the boys sang the glad song of praise, Dost thou hear what these say? Je-sus said, Yes; have ye not read that out of the mouth of babes and suck-lings hast thou brought forth praise. This was in the Psalms, and if the scribes and chief priests were as well read as they claimed to be they would know the rest of the verse, and see how the things that Da-vid fore-told had all come to pass. But these men were blind; they would not see.

There were some Greeks that had come up to the feast, and these came to Phil-ip and said, Sir, we would see Je-sus. And when word was brought to Je-sus he said,

The hour is come, that the Son of Man shall be raised up on high. If a grain of wheat falls not in the ground and dies, it comes to nought; but if it does, it will bring forth much fruit. He that lives for him-self shall lose the things he most loves; and he that gives up all thoughts of self,

SIR, WE WOULD SEE JE-SUS.

and strives to keep God's laws and to do as Christ has taught, shall win the love of men and of an-gels. If a man serve me let him walk in my foot-steps; and where I am, there shall those be who love and serve me, and they shall share my home on high where God is.

He had to do God's will; why should not they? And he said to them, How shall I find words to speak the thoughts that fill my heart? Shall I say, Fath-er save me from this hour, when from this cause came I to this hour? Fath-er, thy will be done; and to thy name be all the praise!

Then there came a voice out of the skies, so loud and strong that those who heard it were awe-struck. It did not sound the same to all, but the whole crowd felt that God was there. The voice said, I have done it in the past, and what is yet to be done will bring praise to my name.

Je-sus said, Not for my sake has this voice come but for yours. Now has the time come to judge the world: now shall the Prince of this World be cast out. Sa-tan is called the Prince of this World; he rules be-tween God and man, and tries to keep the two a-part. Je-sus the Prince of Peace, had fought with the Prince of this World, and won in the fight. And he said, I, if I be raised up on high out of the earth, will draw all men un-to me. This he said, to show forth what death he was to die.

Some in the crowd of Jews, said, We have heard out of the law that the Christ should have a long reign on the earth. How then dost thou say, The Son of Man must be raised up on high? Who is this Son of Man?

Je-sus said, that he might clear their doubts, Not long will the light be with you. Walk while the light yet shines in your midst, that ye be not caught in the dark: for he that walks in the dark knows not where he goes. Those who have faith in Christ walk in the light; those who have doubts, or care not for him, walk in the dark, and know not where they will go. He is the lamp for their feet.

And Je-sus said, As ye have the light, be-lieve in the light, that ye may be the sons of light. But their eyes were blind, their minds were dull, and their hearts were hard. Some of those who heard Je-sus scarce knew what he meant; and the few who did would not dare to let it be known that they thought he was the true Christ. They

FIG-TREE.

feared the Chief Priests and Scribes, and cared more to please men than they did to please God.

No songs of praise were now in the air. The sun sank down in the west, and soon the last ray of day-light was hid in a veil of gloom. Je-sus knew it would not be safe for him to stay in Je-ru-sa-lem, so he stole out with the crowd that went through the gate and made his way to Beth-a-ny. Here, at some way-side inn, he and the Twelve spent the night, and the next morn went back to the town to take part in the great feast.

On the way he felt the need of food, and when he saw a fig-tree by the way-side, he came to it and found nought

LOOK-ING DOWN ON BETH-A-NY.

on it but leaves. The fig tree first sends forth its flow-ers; then comes the fruit; and when the fruit is ripe the leaves form, and fill the boughs.

When Je-sus came up to the tree and found such a fair show of leaves, and no figs, he said, no more shall fruit grow on thee. And the Twelve heard him. The fig tree is a type of those who seem to be all right, but who bring forth no good fruit. They do not lead the right kind of lives. There is a blight up-on them: the blight of sin: and though they make a fair show to men, God knows their hearts, and will judge them.

The next day when they passed by the place where the fig-tree had stood, they found it dried up from the roots. And the Twelve were awe-struck at the pow-er there was in Christ. Like most men, they thought more of the strange things he did than of the truth he taught; and did not take in the fact that this was to warn them of the fate of those who led false lives, and made men think they were good by their out-side show. Je-sus had said, By their fruits—by the works they do—ye shall know if they be good or bad. When Je-sus looks for fruit, shall there be nought but leaves?

Je-sus came to the Tem-ple, and as he taught the crowd there the Chief Priests and Scribes drew near to him, and said, Tell us by what right you do these things? and who gave you this right? Je-sus said, First tell me by whom John was bap-tized? was it of God, or by man? They spoke among them-selves, and said, If we say the bap-tism came from God, he will say, Why did you not be-lieve him? But if we say, Of men, the crowd will stone us, for they are sure that John was sent from God. So, wise men as they were, they were forced to say to Je-sus, We can-not tell. Je-sus knew that they did not choose to tell, so he said to them, Nor can I tell you by what right I do these things.

Then he spoke to the crowd in this way: A man set out plants for a vine-yard; and built a wall round it; and dug a pit for the wine-press. And he built a high place for the watch-men to guard it, and then he let it out to farm-ers and went to a far land to be gone a long time.

When it was the time of the year for the grapes to be ripe, he sent some of his ser-vants to the farm-ers to get the fruit. And the farm-ers beat them, and stoned them, and one of them was killed. Then he sent out more ser-vants, and they were dealt with in the same way.

Then the lord of the vine-yard said, What shall I do? I will send my own dear son, and they will look up to him, and do him no harm. But when the farm-ers saw the son, they said among them-selves, This is the heir; come, let us kill him, and keep all his wealth. And they took him, and cast him forth out of the vine-yard, and slew him.

When the lord of the vine-yard comes, what will he do to those men? He will put them to death, and will let out his vine-yard to men who will give him the fruits in their due time. Je-sus said to the Jews, Have ye not read that the stone which the build-ers threw out was made the chief cor-ner stone? So I say to you that God shall take His King-dom from you, and shall give it to those who will bring forth the fruits of it. And he who shall fall on this stone —those who seek to harm Christ—shall meet with pain and loss; but those on whom the stone shall fall—those who shall cast him out from their hearts when he is raised up on high—shall be ground to dust.

When the Chief Priests and Scribes heard these words they knew that he spoke of them. And they would have seized him then and there, but for their fear of the crowd, so they left him and went their way.

But Je-sus still taught those who drew near to hear his words. And he said, A man that was a king made a great feast for his son, and sent forth his ser-vants to bid the guests come to the wed-ding. But they would not come. Then he sent forth more ser-vants, and said, Tell them the din-ner is laid out, the ox and the sheep are killed, and all things are made read-y; and bid them come to the feast.

But they made light of it, and went their ways, some to till their farms, and some to buy and sell; and the rest laid hold of the ser-vants and ill-used them, and at last put them to death.

The king was wroth and sent forth his armed men, who put to death those whose crimes were so great, and burned up the town in which they dwelt.

Then said he to his ser-vants, Go ye out in-to the high-ways—where the streets meet—and bring in all those ye find there. So those ser-vants went out in-to the high-ways, and brought in all they found there, the bad and the good, and the wed-ding was filled with guests.

When the king came in to look at the guests, he saw there a man who had not on a wed-ding robe. It was his own fault that he did not have one. They were there for all; a gift from the king that gave the feast. But it pleased this man to wear his own robe. And the king said to him, Friend how didst thou dare to come in here with-out a wed-ding robe? The man had not a word to say. He was dumb with shame.

Then the king said to those who stood in wait to do his will, Bind him hand and foot, and cast him out in-to the dark with those who weep and wail.

STREET IN JE-RU-SA-LEM.

The Wed-ding Feast. 343

The king means God. The feast is when Christ and his church are one. The first ser-vants are those who first went out to preach the good news. They were ill-used,

FRIEND, HOW DIDST THOU COME IN WITH-OUT A WED-DING ROBE?

were struck down with hard blows, and one of them— John the Baptist—was put to death. Christ spoke to the Jews, and it was them that God first called. But they would not come in. So God the great King of Kings, sent out to the high-ways and by-ways, and the bad and good were brought in. But they could not take part in the feast—that is, they could not share in the joys of heav-en—till they had cast out of their hearts all love of self, and put on the pure white robe which the King will give to all those who ask for it.

Men let in the bad and the good. They can-not read their hearts. But when the King comes he will judge them all, and will cast out those that have not on the robe they ought to wear. Christ Je-sus is that robe. We are to put him on so that he hides all the old rags of sin, and pride, and love of self or the world; and what does the new dress mean but a new heart? "with-out which no man can see the Lord."

CHAPTER XX.

LAST DAYS.—WHAT THE SIGN SHALL BE.—THE TEN VIR-GINS.—THE TEN TAL-ENTS.

It was now near the close of this sad week—the last that Je-sus was to spend on earth. He rose at day-break, and went with the Twelve down the slope of the hill, and through one of the gates that led in-to the town.

The crowd soon drew round Je-sus as he sat down in the courts of the Tem-ple, and the Chief Priests and Scribes sought to snare him in his speech. They meant to make him say things that would prove that he was a fraud, and give them the right to put him out of the way.

Last Days.

So they sent out spies, who came to Je-sus and said, Mas-ter we know that thou art true, and dost teach the way of God in truth, with-out fear of what men may do or say. Tell us, then, what dost thou think? Is it right, by the law of the Jews, to pay a tax to Cæ-sar, or not?

Je-sus, who read their hearts, said, Why tempt ye me

DAY-BREAK AT JE-RU-SA-LEM.

with your false way? Show me the coin with which the tax is paid. And they brought it to him. And he said to them, Whose face is this with the date it bears? They say un-to him, Cæ-sar's. Then said he, Give back to Cæ-sar the things that are Cæ-sar's; and to God the things that are God's. It is not our gold that God wants; but we are

GOLD-EN GATE.

to pay our debts to him with love. When the spies heard these words, in which there was nought they could find fault with, they left him, and went on their way.

WHOSE FACE IS ON THE COIN?

On that day there came to Je-sus the Sad-du-cces, who were the worst foes he had while on earth. They held strange views of their own, and did not be-lieve in the Word of God, or in an-gels. They said that men had no souls, and did not be-lieve that we lived on, in a home on high, when we were laid in our graves.

These men came to Je-sus, and spoke to him with a sneer, and asked him all sorts of things that they might mock at his words. But he taught them in such a way, that they were forced to hide their heads with shame. He threw new light on the law, which so pleased the Scribes that they cried out, Mas-ter, thou hast said well! And one of these asked Je-sus which, in the eyes of the law, is the great com-mand-ment? He said to him, Thou shalt love the Lord thy God with all thy heart, and with all thy mind. This is the first and great com-mand-ment. And the next is like un-to it: Thou shalt love thy neigh-bor as thy-self. The whole Word of God rests on these two com-mand-ments, and can be proved by the laws of Mo-ses, and by those who fore-told of Christ.

The Scribes moved from the place; they could think of no more to ask; but Je-sus had some-what to say to them. He asked them, What think ye of the Christ? whose Son is he? They say unto him, The son of Da-vid. He saith to them, How then doth Da-vid call him Lord, and say, The Lord said un-to my Lord, sit thou on my right hand, till I put thy foes un-der thy feet. If Da-vid calls him Lord, how is he his son? And none of them had a word to say, nor durst they from that day forth seek to snarl him up in his talk.

As the Chief Priests and Scribes left the place, Je-sus spoke to the crowd, and to the Twelve that stood near him. The Chief Priests and the Scribes, he said, sit in Mo-ses' seat. All that they bid you do, out of the Book of the Law, that give heed to and do. But do not ye as they do. For they say, and do not. They bind loads on men's backs that are hard to be borne; but they them-selves do not touch them. All their works they do to be seen of men. Small slips of parch-ment—a piece of sheep skin dried and made smooth, and on which men wrote in those days—were put in a case and worn on the left arm or fore-head in time of prayer. These slips had on them a few words of the law, and were thought by some to be a guard, or charm. The Phar-i-sees, who did all for show, and thought that no men were as good as they were, wore the badge at all hours of the day.

Je-sus said, They made broad these signs, which were worn so that all men could see them; and wide was the hem of the robe they wore out-side. The Jews had been taught how to dress. The fringe was to be of just such a length; and the blue silk that bound it of just such a width. But this did not suit these men, who were like those who have large prayer-books, and the Word of God bound in gilt, and seem to the world to be good men, while yet they have no love of Christ in their hearts.

They love the chief place at feasts, and the chief seats in the church. And they like men to greet them on the streets, and call them mas-ter. But be ye not called, mas-ter—do not have this kind of pride—for one is your Mas-ter, and that is Christ. He that is the great one in your midst shall be your ser-vant. He that is proud shall be brought low; and he that is like a child, and thinks not much of him-self, shall be raised to a high place.

But woe to you, said Je-sus, Who are not what you seem to be! For ye shut the door of heav-en in the face of men. Ye go not in your-selves, nor let those go in who would. Christ calls him-self the Door, and the Way, for by him we pass through the veil that lies be-tween this world and the next. He said they were blind guides who led men out of the right path. They took great pains to cleanse the out-side of the cup and the dish, but their hearts were full of greed and love of self. They serve me with their lips but their hearts are far from me. Cleanse the in-side of the cup and dish—cleanse the heart—so that the life may be clean, and free from stain.

Woe to you who build tombs for those who fore-told that Christ should come, and say, If we had lived in those days we would not have put such men to death. But ye prove by your own deeds that ye are the sons of those who stoned the proph-ets. And he told them that they should do the same in their day.

With a wail of grief, he cried out, O Je-ru-sa-lem, Je-ru-sa-lem, thou who dost kill the proph-ets and stone those which are sent to thee, how oft would I have drawn thy chil-dren to me as a hen draws her chick-ens un-der her wings, where they are safe from harm, but ye would not! It was left to your own free-will, and ye would not be saved.

And he spoke of the sad fate in store for her and for all those who dwelt within her walls. They should feel the weight of God's hand up-on them, but all hope should not be lost.

They might yet be saved when they should own Je-sus as their Lord, whom now they were too blind to see.

Je-sus did not leave the Tem-ple at once, but sat down in the court of the wom-en, which was near the place where

THE WIDOW'S MITE.

the great chests stood. There were thir-teen of these great brass chests with wide mouths in-to which the gifts were thrown: what each one paid for the care of God's house. Some as they went by, threw in their coins so that they would make a great noise, and Je-sus watched them, and saw that the rich cast in large sums. And there came a poor wid-ow a wom-an whose hus-band was dead and she cast in two mites. It would take four of these mites to make one cent, so the sum was not a large one; but it was all she had, and she was glad to give it. Je-sus called the Twelve to him, and said to them, I say to you this poor wid-ow has cast in more than all the rest. For they cast in of their wealth, and did not miss it, and could have spared much more. But she, poor and in need, did cast in all she had; and the gift was worth more to God, be-cause it cost more.

Then Je-sus left that part of the Tem-ple which was set a-part for the use of the Jews, and he looked round with a sad gaze. And the Twelve drew near to him to show him the large stones of great size with which the walls were built.

Je-sus said to them, As for these things that ye see, there will come a day when all these stones shall be thrown down. As they sat down on the Mount of Ol-ives, Pe-ter, James, John, and An-drew came near to Je-sus, and said to him, Tell us, when shall these things be? and what shall be the sign of the end of the world?

Je-sus said, See that you are not led off by false guides, who come in my name, and say, I am the Christ. Ye shall hear of wars, and hints of wars, but do not fear; these things must take place, but the end is not yet.

And there shall be a great lack of food, and earthquakes here and there. And men shall seize you, and ill-use you, and put you to death; and they shall hate you for my name's sake. And be-cause of the sin that is in the land, those who once loved the name of Christ, and had warm hearts, will grow cold and turn from me. But he

RU-INS OF AN ARCH, BUILT OF GREAT STONES.

whose love shall hold out to the end, the same shall be saved. And he told them more of the strange things they might look for, ere the Last Great Day. They were not to seek to know what could not be known, but to watch and pray, and wait God's time

Je-sus said to the Twelve, When the fig tree is yet young and it puts forth leaves, ye know that sum-mer is near. So shall ye, when ye see all these things, know that Christ is at your doors. The earth and the skies shall pass a-way, but my word shall not pass a-way. But of that day and hour, knows no one, not even the an-gels, nor the Son of God. But as it was in the days of No-ah, so shall it be when Christ comes. Watch then; for ye know not what hour your Lord comes. If the mas-ter of the house had known at what hour the thief would come, he would have kept watch, and would not have let him break in-to his house. Be ye on the watch—lead good and pure lives, so that ye will be fit to dwell in the home on high—for in such an hour that ye think not the Son of Man comes.

Then Je-sus spoke the par-a-ble of the Ten Vir-gins. A vir-gin is a young girl, who has not wed.

These ten were friends of the bride, and they took their lamps and went out to meet the bride-groom. And five of them were wise, and five were fool-ish. The fool-ish, when they took their lamps, took no oil with them. But the wise took oil with them to fill their lamps, in case the light went out.

The bride-groom was late; and though they kept watch for a while, and tried hard to keep a-wake, they gave up at last, and one by one dropped off to sleep. But at mid-night the cry was heard, Lo the bride-groom! come ye forth and meet him! Then all the ten vir-gins rose up to trim their lamps. And the fool-ish said to the wise, Give us of your oil, or our lamps will go out. But the wise said, Not so; for there may be no more than we shall need. Go ye to those that sell, and buy for your-selves.

The Ten Vir-gins.

While the five went off at that late hour to buy oil, the bride-groom came; and the five whose lamps were trimmed and bright went with him in-to the feast. And the door was shut.

When those who had gone off to buy oil, came back from their search, they found the door closed, and they cried out, Lord, Lord, let us in! let us in! But he said, I know you not.

The bride-groom came from a far-off land, and the vir-gins went out to meet him and bring him to the house of the bride. Christ is the bride-groom, the bride is the Church, and the vir-gins those who make up the Church of God. The lamp means the heart; the oil is the grace of God which keeps the flame bright. The grace of God, is the faith, hope, joy, strength, peace, and all that fills the soul of those who trust in Him, and seek to do His will.

LORD, LET US IN! LET US IN!

It is of no use to trim the wicks—to make a show of love to Christ—if there is no oil in our lamps. Those who went out to buy oil, may have tried hard, but the hour was late, and when they came back the door was closed, and for that time they were shut out from the feast. This Je-sus told them to warn them not to put off, but to give their hearts to Christ at once, and to turn from their sins.

Then Je-sus said, The King-dom of God, the hour when Christ comes, is like a man who, ere he set out for a far off land, called his ser-vants to him and gave his goods in-to their hands. To one he gave five tal-ents, to the next one, two; and to a third, one. A tal-ent meant in those days a large sum of wealth; but we call tal-ents the gifts of God, the skill each one has, and which God means us to use for His praise. Not all have the same gifts; some have more than the rest; but there is no one who can-not do some-thing if he will.

When the rich man had thus set a-part his great wealth, he went to the far off land. Then he who had the five tal-ents bought and sold in such a way that he gained five more tal-ents. And he that had two, did the same, so that he gained two more. But he that had but one, went off and dug a hole in the earth and hid the tal-ent the lord gave him.

When the lord of those ser-vants came back, he called them up to tell how they had made use of the wealth left in their hands. He that had five tal-ents came, and said, Lord, thou didst give me five tal-ents; lo, here are five more I have gained for thee.

His lord said to him, Well done, good and faith-ful ser-vant; thou wast faith-ful o-ver a few things, I will set thee to rule o-ver ma-ny things. Come in-to the joy of thy lord! He that had two tal-ents came and said, Lord, thou didst give me two tal-ents; and lo, here are two more tal-ents I have gained.

His lord said to him, Well done, good and faith-ful ser-vant. Thou wast faith-ful o-ver a few things, I will set thee to rule o-ver ma-ny things. Come in-to the joy of thy lord!

Then he who had but the one tal-ent, came and said, Lord, I knew that thou art a hard man, and didst reap where thou didst not sow, and didst take up what thou hadst not laid down. And I was a-fraid, and went and hid thy tal-ent in the earth: lo, here thou hast thine own. But his lord said to him, Thou wick-ed ser-vant; be-cause thou didst know that I reap where I sowed not, and take up what I laid not down, thou shouldst have put out my mo-ney so that it would have brought me in more than just what I gave thee. Take ye the tal-ent a-way from him, and give it to him which hath ten tal-ents. For he that hath—he that makes a good use of what he hath—shall have more and more. But from him that hath not shall be ta-ken a-way e-ven that which he hath. He who does not serve God well with the gift he has—small though it be—shall lose that, and all that he might have gained by it. And the doom of the lost ones shall be his if he does not turn from his sins, and pay to God the debt he owes.

Then Je-sus told how it should be when he sat on the throne on high, with all the an-gels round him. Be-fore him men shall come from all the ends of the earth, and they shall be like a great flock of sheep and goats: some mild and tame, and the rest wild and self-willed. And he shall set the sheep on his right hand, but the goats on his left. Then shall the King say to those on his right hand, Come, ye whom God has blest, come to the place set a-part for you since the world was made. For I was in need of food, and ye gave me to eat; I was a-thirst and ye gave me drink. I was in a strange land and ye took me to your homes; I was poor, and ye clothed me; sick, and ye took care of me.

I was shut up in a cell, and ye came to cheer me. Then shall the blest ones say, Lord, when saw we thee in need of food, and fed thee? or a-thirst, and gave thee drink? And when saw we thee like one in a strange land and took thee to our homes? or in need of clothes, and clothed thee? And when saw we thee sick, or in a pris-on cell, and came to nurse and to cheer thee?

And the King shall say to them, In as much as ye did it to one of the least of these who bear my name ye have done it to me. Real faith in Christ shows it-self in all our acts. The more we love him, the more good we will want to do.

Then the King shall say to those on his left hand, Go from me, ye whom God has cursed; go to the fire that burns and does not go out, which is the home of the dev-il and his an-gels. For I was hun-gry, and ye gave me no meat; I was thirst-y, and ye gave me no drink; I was in need of friends, and ye took me not in-to your homes; in rags, and ye clothed me not; sick, and in pris-on, and ye came not near me.

Then shall they say to him, Lord, when saw we thee hun-gry, or a-thirst, or in need of friends, or clothes; or sick, or in a pris-on cell, and did not do for thee? Then shall he say to them, In as much as ye did it not to one of these who bear my name, ye did it not to me. And these— the bad—shall go where grief and tears shall have no end: but the good shall live where there is no end of joy. If we treat the friends of Christ ill, we treat Him ill. We should be good and kind to all.

We are not to pick and choose, and to say, "I will do

thus and so," but are to fit our-selves for the Lord's work, and to go where He sends us. If we set out to do His work in His way, we will find all the help we need, and He will give us strength to do more than we planned. At first we may not like the work we have to do, but if we pray to Je-sus and lean up-on him, he will teach us to love the work; and tasks that seem hard and not to our taste, will seem light and sweet be-cause He is with us. "He guides our feet, He guards our way."

Then Je-sus said to the Twelve, Ye know that in two days the feast of the pass-o-ver will take place, and the Son of Man will be given in-to the hands of his foes to be hung up-on the cross. And now, as the sun had set, Je-sus rose from his seat on the Mount of Ol-ives, and went out on the road to Beth-a-ny. It was for the last time! He knew it, and was calm!

CHAPTER XXI.

JU-DAS PLOTS TO SELL HIS LORD.—THE LAST SUP-PER.—
JE-SUS WASH-ES THE DIS-CI-PLES FEET.—
LORD IS IT I.

The last talks of Je-sus had caused a great stir a-mong Jews. And the Chief Priests and Scribes met at the house of Ca-ia-phas, the High Priest, to plan how they might take Je-sus by craft, and put him to death. But they said this could not be done the week of the feast, as most of the friends of Je-sus were from Gal-i-lee, and they were so bold and full of fight, that it might be the cause of much blood-shed.

While the chief priests were in doubt as to the best move to make, there came a man to see them. This man was Ju-das, one of the Twelve. He had slunk a-way from the rest, as the shades of night came on, and made his way to the gate of the house where the high-priest lived. It was the rule that all the gates should be closed at sun-down, but when the feasts were held the rules were not so strict, as the crowd was great, and men had to go in and out at all hours.

Ju-das told the guards who he was and why he had come, and they at once made it known to the chief priests and scribes then in the house. Ju-das was sent for at once. He was just the man they wished to see. He had lived with Je-sus, had seen and heard all that he had said and done, and from him they could gain help in their base plot.

Ju-das said to them, What will you give me if I bring him in to your hands? They said they would give him thir-ty shek-els. A shek-el was a small sil-ver coin, worth not much more than fifty cents, so that for the small sum of fif-teen dol-lars, Ju-das sold his Lord. This was the price paid for a slave, and it shows what these Jews thought of Je-sus.

Ju-das was fond of wealth. What would he not do to add to his store of gold? He must have thought that the chief priests would pay him a large sum, so fierce was their hate, so glad would they be to get rid of Je-sus. But the task would not be a hard one, and he should gain friends with the rich, and add to the wealth he could call his own. Poor Ju-das! blind to all else but his love for gold! He told the chief priests that he would bring Je-sus in-to their

JU-DAS PLOTS WITH FOES OF JE-SUS.

hands for the price named, and from that time he sought for a chance to do this thing.

The first day of the feast was now at hand, and on the eve of that day each Jew who kept house took a lamb to the priests, and slew it in front of the al-tar. This lamb was to be kept for four days be-fore it was killed. There

BROOK KED-RON.

was a long row of priests, and one of these caught the blood as it flowed from the slain lamb, and passed it on in a large sil-ver bowl to the next priest. He passed it to the next in line, and so on till it reached the foot of the al-tar, where it was poured out, and ran off in-to the brook Ked-ron.

Now this was a sign, to make them think of the blood on the door-posts, when the Jews were slaves in the land of E-gypt. God had told Mo-ses that he would smite all the first-born in the land of E-gypt. Rich and poor were to be served a-like, for their sins had been great. But each Jew who kept house was to kill a lamb on this dread night, and to mark the door-posts of his house with blood. The blood of the lamb was to save them. For when God saw the blood on the door-posts he would pass by that house, and the plague should not come nigh it when he smote the land of E-gypt.

And they were to roast the flesh at night and eat it; and what was left the next day was to be thrown in-to the fire and burned. In those days they were to eat this meal in haste, with their shoes on their feet, and their staff in hand, for their lot then was to move from place to place. The Jews changed this when they came to the land of Rest.

When the day came on which the Jews were to eat the lamb—the first feast of the Pass-o-ver—Pe-ter and John came to Je-sus and asked him where they should eat this meal. Je-sus told them to go in-to the town, and they would meet a man with a jar of wa-ter. Go in-to the house where he goes, and say to the good man of the house, The Mas-ter saith, Where is the room, where I may come and eat the feast with my friends? And he will show you a large room at the top of the house: there let the feast be spread.

Pe-ter and John went forth, and found all as Je-sus had said to them. They met the man who had been to the well, and went with him to his house, and there a room was shown them where Je-sus and the Twelve could eat.

When it was night Je-sus and the Twelve went to this room where the feast was spread.

Je-sus said he was glad to eat with them once more, for it was the last time they should meet in this way on earth. On the ta-ble were bowls of broth, some loaves of bread, and some red wine—the fruit of the vine.

Je-sus took bread, and gave thanks, and brake it, and he gave to the Twelve and said, Take, eat; this is my bod-y, which is giv-en for you. This do in re-mem-brance of me. Think of me when ye eat it. And he took a cup of the wine, and gave thanks; and as he gave it to them, he said, Drink ye all of it; for this is my blood which is shed for you that your sins might be washed a-way. And they all drank of it. Je-sus said to them, I shall drink no more of this fruit of the vine till that day when I drink it with you, new, in my Fath-er's King-dom.

There had been a strife a-mong the Twelve as to which should have the chief seat at the feast; next to Je-sus of course. Each guest lay at full length on a couch, and leaned on his left el-bow, so that the right hand was free. At the right of Je-sus, was John, the one whom he loved, and his head lay near the breast of his friend and Lord. It pained Je-sus to see this strife, and to think that those who had been with him for so long a time had not yet learned the truths he sought to teach. Their hearts were full of pride; they thought but of self. Je-sus told them that they should be kings—but not like the kings of earth. He that is great a-mong you let him be as a child; and he that is chief, as one that doth serve. And he said, I am

in the midst of you as one that doth serve. Yet he was the Mas-ter of the feast and none so great as he.

As he said this, Je-sus rose from the sup-per, and threw off his loose robes, and wrapped a tow-el round his waist. And he poured wa-ter in-to a bowl, and be-gan to wash the

JE-SUS WASH-ES THE DIS-CI-PLES' FEET.

feet of those who sat at the feast with him, and to wipe them dry with the tow-el at his waist. This was the work of slaves, and as no one had come to do this for them, all had gone in to the feast with the dust of the road still on their feet, for their walk had been a long one.

The Twelve were struck dumb with awe and shame, and not a word was said till Je-sus came to where Pe-ter was. Pe-ter said to him, Lord, dost thou wash my feet? Je-sus said to him, What I do is not clear to thee now; but thou shalt know by and by. Pe-ter said to him, Thou shalt nev-er wash my feet. Je-sus said, If I wash thee not, thou hast no part with me. Pe-ter wished to be near his Lord, and if this act made him more to Him, it should be done.

So Pe-ter said to him, Lord, wash my hands and my head as well as my feet. Je-sus said, He that is bathed, needs but to wash his feet, for the rest of him is clean; and ye are clean, but not all. For he knew who should give him up to his foes; and that was why he said with a sigh, Ye are not all clean.

When Je-sus had washed the feet of the Twelve, he put on his loose robes, and took his place once more with them at the feast. And he said to them, Know ye what I have done to you? Ye call me Mas-ter and Lord, and ye say well; for so I am. If I then, your Lord and Mas-ter have done this thing, can ye not do it? I have shown you that ye should do as I have done to you. They were to make them-selves as slaves, if so they might do good in the world, and by their kind deeds prove how great was their love. And once more Je-sus warned them that they were not to look for wealth, and high rank, for the thrones that he spoke of were not of this world.

Now John was at the right hand of Je-sus so that his head lay on the breast of the Lord. Ju-das was at the left hand of Je-sus, and the two dipped out of the same dish.

In some parts of the East knives and forks are not yet in use, but a piece of bread is held in the right hand and dipped in-to the sop, or broth, and then borne to the mouth.

Je-sus was sad at heart. True, he was to part with these dear friends. It was the last night he was to spend with them on earth. But it caused him more grief to know that there was one near him, who should have been his friend and yet was one of his worst foes. The rest were true; but this one was false, and Je-sus knew it. It grieved him, and it was with pain he said, One of you shall be-tray me—shall give me up to those who seek my life.

The Twelve looked this way and that, and were in doubt as to what he meant. Each one asked, with pale cheeks, Lord is it I? There was time yet for Ju-das to own his sin, and to beg his Lord to for-give him. One word would have done, or a touch, but not a sound broke the hush that filled the room.

Then Pe-ter made a sign to John to ask who it was. John had but to lean back his head to look in the Mas-ter's face, and he said to him, Lord, who is it? Je-sus said, He it is to whom I shall give the sop, when I have dipped in the dish. And when he had dipped the bread in-to the sop, he gave it to Ju-das. And he said, The Son of Man must go the way marked out for him; but woe to that man through whom the Son of Man is led in-to the hands of his foes! It were good for that man if he had nev-er been born.

Ju-das said, Mas-ter, is it I? No need for him to ask. Well he knew his guilt. Je-sus said to him, Thou hast

IS IT I?

said it. As soon as Ju-das had ta-ken the sop he seemed to change from bad to worse. He could scarce wait for the time to come, so fierce was he to do this crime. When Sa-tan gets in-to the heart he drives out all that is good, and makes haste to bind us with his chains.

Je-sus said in a low tone, What thou hast to do, do with more speed. Those who saw him speak to Ju-das and did not hear the words, thought that as he had the bag, Je-sus had told him to buy the things they would need for the feast, or to give some-thing to the poor. For Ju-das rose at once, and left the room.

CHAPTER XXII.

WITH JE-SUS IN THE UP-PER ROOM.

Ju-das had gone out, and Je-sus was now with those whom he loved, and who loved him. There was no one near to cause a pang of grief, and joy came back, and all was light and peace. With Ju-das, the last trace of the world had gone from their midst, and it seemed as if this room, so plain and poor, was one of the rooms in God's house.

And Je-sus said, now is the time that the Son of Man shall be raised to glo-ry, and the glo-ry of God shall be shown in him. Lit-tle child-ren, for a short time I am with you. Ye shall seek me, and, as I said to the Jews, Where I go ye can-not come. So now I say to you. And he charged them to love one an-oth-er; for all men would know that they loved Christ, if they loved and were kind to each oth-er. They must walk in his steps, and they should soon find him.

Pe-ter could not bear the thought that he was to lose sight of Je-sus; so he said to him, Lord, where dost thou go a-way? Je-sus said, Where I go thou canst not go with me now, but thou shalt be with me by and by.

Pe-ter said, Lord, why can-not I go with thee now? I will lay down my life for thee. Je-sus said, Wilt thou lay down thy life for me? In truth I say to thee, The cock shall not crow till thou hast de-nied me thrice. Three times would Pe-ter be asked if he knew Je-sus, or were a friend of his, and he would say No. Pe-ter said, Though I should die with thee, I will not de-ny thee. And so said all the rest.

Je-sus then went on to teach and to train them for the work they would have to do in the world when he was gone. Be not vexed with cares, but trust in me as ye trust in God. In my Fa-ther's house are ma-ny rooms: if it were not so I would have told you. I go to make a place for you. And if I go and make a place for you, I will come back and take you to my-self; that where I am there ye may be. And where I go ye know, and the way ye know. Je-sus meant by this that he would not be far from them, and when their work on earth was done he would come and take them to his home on high, that they might dwell with him, and share in his joy.

Thom-as said, Lord, we know not to what place thou dost go; how then can we know the way? Je-sus said to him, I am the Way, and the Truth, and the Life. No

TOMB OF DA-VID.

man can come to the Father, but through me. If ye had learned to know me, ye should have learned to know my Father. From this time forth ye learn to know Him, and have seen Him.

Philip said to him, Lord, show us the Father, and we shall need no more. Jesus said, Have I been so long with you, and yet thou hast not learned to know me, Philip? He that hath seen me hath seen God. Why dost thou say, Show us the Father? Dost thou not believe that I am in the Father and the Father in me?—that God and I are one? The words that I say unto you I speak not from myself, but God who dwells in me does his own works. Believe that I am in God, and God in me; or else believe in me for the sake of the great works that I do.

In truth I say unto you, He that has faith in me, shall do the works that I do. Nay, he shall do more. He shall take my place on earth, and I will be near to help him. And all that ye shall ask in my name, that will I do. If ye love me, ye will keep my words in your hearts, and do as I have told you. And I will ask God to send some one to be with you forever.

This guest will be the spirit of truth, with whom the world will have nought to do, because it sees him not, nor learns to know him. Ye learn to know him, for he dwells with you, and is in you.

They should not see Jesus in the flesh, or hear the sound of his voice, but they should know that he was near them, to be their strength and their guide to the end of their days.

CHURCH OF THE HO-LY SEP-UL-CHRE, BUILT O-VER THE TOMB WHERE CHRIST WAS LAID.

I will not leave you a-lone, with-out one ray of hope to cheer you. I will come to you. Yet a lit-tle while, and the world sees me no more; but ye see me. And be-cause I live, ye shall live.

A watch may have all its works, all its wheels and cogs may be set just right, but if the main-spring is left out it will not go. If Christ is the main-spring in us, we will go, and keep good time. We need to be wound up with pray-er, at least once a day, and to keep our hearts—our works—oiled with faith, so that there will be no jar, or fret. If we do this we will learn the right use of time, and to the last hour of life prove our love for him, who first loved us, and gave him-self for us.

Je-sus said, He that loves me shall be loved of God, and I will love him, and will show my-self to him.

Ju-das—who was some-times called Thad-de-us—not the man of crime—said to Je-sus, Lord, how is it that thou wilt show thy-self to us, and not to the world? Je-sus said to him, If a man love me he will keep my words, and God will love him, and we will come to him, and stay with him. He that loves me not, keeps not my words; and the word which ye hear is not mine, but His that sent me.

These things have I told you while I am with you. But the spir-it whom God will send in my name, he will teach you all things, and will bring to your mind all the things that I have told you. Peace I leave with you. My peace I give un-to you. Not as the world gives, give I un-to you. Let not your heart be vexed with doubts, and cares, nor let it fear what foes can do. Ye have heard how I said, I go a-way and I come to you a-gain. If ye loved me ye would be glad that I go to the Fath-er. And now I have told you be-fore it comes to pass, that when it is come to pass ye may be-lieve. From this time forth I will not talk much with you; for the Prince of this World comes, and he hath no hold on me. But he comes that the world may know that I love God, and do His will.

At this point there was a stir in the room, and Je-sus said, Let us rise, and go from this place. And they rose, and sang a hymn, the words of which were in the Psalms of Da-vid. While yet they stood round their Lord, he once more spoke to them and said:

I am the true vine, which God has set out in the world. The world is God's vine-yard. Each branch in me which bears not fruit he cuts off; and each branch which bears fruit, he prunes, and makes clean that it may bring forth more fruit. Now ye are made clean through the words that I have taught you. Dwell in me, and I in you. I am the vine. Each one of you is a branch. He that lives in me, and I in him, the same shall bring forth much fruit; for ye can do nought with-out me. The sap flows through the vine and gives to each branch its life, and the fruit it bears is sweet to the taste.

Je-sus said, He who is not part of me, the vine, is cut off as a branch and soon dries up. And these dry twigs are cast in-to the fire and burned. If ye live in me, and my words live in you, ask what ye will and it shall be done to you. They were to ask, of course, to bear more fruit, or bet-ter fruit, and to grow more and more like the vine to which they clung. As the Fath-er loved me, so have I loved you; let my love still be with you. If ye do my will,

THE WAY OF GRIEF.

ye shall have proof of my love; e-ven as I have done the Fath-er's will, and am in his love. These things have I told you that my joy may be with you, and that your cup of joy may be filled. He bids them love as he had loved, with no thought of self. How great had his love been for them! It is a proof of great love for a man to lay down his life for a friend. Ye are my friends said Je-sus, if ye do that which I bid you. No more do I call you ser-vants; for the ser-vant knows not what his lord does. But I have called you friends; for all things that I heard from my Father, I made known un-to you.

Ye did not choose me, but I chose you, and sent you out that ye should bear fruit, and that your fruit should last, and be borne in-to God's house. These things I bid you do, and let love fill your hearts.

If the world hates you, know that it ha-ted me be-fore it ha-ted you. If ye were of the world, the world would love its own; but be-cause ye are not of the world, but I chose you out of the world, for that cause the world hates you. Bear in mind that I said to you, A ser-vant is not great-er than his lord and mas-ter. What had been done to him, would be done to them. If they ill-used me, they will ill-use you. If they kept my word, they will keep yours. But all these things will they do to you be-cause of my name, and be-cause they know not Him that sent me. If I had not come and taught them, they would have had no sin. But now they have no ex-cuse for their sin. He that hates me hates God. If I had not done in the midst of them the works that no one else did, they would not have had sin. But now they have both seen and ha-ted both me and my Fath-er. But this has been done that the word might come true which Da-vid wrote in the Book of Psalms—They hate me with-out a cause.

But when the Spir-it—the Ho-ly Ghost—is come which I will send you from the Fath-er, he shall speak well of me; and ye, too, shall tell of what I have done, for ye have been with me from the first.

These things have I told you, that ye may not trip and fall. They shall put you out of the church-es; yes, the time will come that he who kills you will think that he has done a good work for God. These things will they do to you be-cause they know not the Fath-er, nor me. But these things have I told you, that when the time shall come; ye may bear in mind that I told you of them. I spoke not of them from the first, be-cause I was with you. But now I go a-way; and none of you asks me, Where dost thou go? But be-cause I have said these things to you, your hearts are sad.

But I must tell you the truth. It is best for you that I go a-way; for if I go not a-way the Ho-ly Ghost will not come to you. But if I go a-way, I will send him to you. These words of Je-sus came true, for some-time af-ter his death on the cross, when the dis-ci-ples had met to talk of him, tongues of flame came down in-to the room, and the whole place was made bright with them. Those who saw them felt a strange glow in their heart, and with new strength they went out to preach and to teach of Him who had come in-to the world, and had died on the cross to save men from their sins.

Je-sus said, I have more things to tell you, but ye can-not

THE PLACE WHERE PI-LATE SAID THIS IS THE MAN!

bear them now. But when he is come, the Ho-ly Ghost, the spir-it of truth, he will guide you in the right way; for it is not from him-self he will speak; but what things he shall hear he will speak, and will show you the things that are to come. He shall add to the glo-ry of my name, for that which is mine will he take and show un-to you. All things that the Fath-er has are mine; and that is why I said that he shall take that which is mine and shall show it to you.

The Spir-it—which is Christ in us—will lead us to do great things, and will make clear to us the great truths of God.

A lit-tle while and ye shall not see me—I shall be gone from you; and then, in a lit-tle while ye shall see me. Some of the dis-ci-ples thought these words were strange, and they said among them-selves, What does he mean when he says, A lit-tle while, and ye shall not see me; and then a lit-tle while and ye shall see me? And what do these words mean, I go a-way to the Fath-er?

Je-sus knew that they wished to ask him of these things, so he said to them, Do ye seek to know what I mean when I say, A lit-tle while and ye shall not see me; and a lit-tle while and ye shall see me? In truth I say to you that ye will weep and grieve, but the world will be glad, and your grief will soon be turned in-to joy.

Now are ye sad, but I will come back to you, and you shall be glad, with a joy that no one can take a-way from you. These things have I taught you in par-a-bles, but an hour is near, when I shall no more speak to you in par-a-bles, but shall tell you in plain speech of the things of God. Christ in them would make clear to their minds the things that now were hid from them.

In that day ye shall ask in my name, and I say not that I will plead with God for you. There is no need, for God him-self loves you, be-cause ye have loved me, and be-lieve that I was sent forth from Him. I came forth from God, and am come in-to the world that I might lead men to Him; and I leave the world, and go back to God —that I may make a place for men in God's home on high.

The dis-ci-ples said to him, Lo, now dost thou speak in plain words, and the truth is made clear to us. Now are we sure that thou dost know all things, and by this we be-lieve that thou didst come from God. Je-sus knew that their faith was not of the right kind. They thought they knew all of Christ that they would need to know. But Je-sus knew that an hour was near which would try their faith, and prove how weak it was. And he said to them, Do ye now be-lieve? An hour will come, yes, and is now here, when each one of you will think of him-self, and leave me all a-lone in my hour of need. Yet I am not a-lone, for God is with me. These things have I told you that in me ye may have peace. In the world ye shall have much grief and care; but be of good cheer, for those who walk in the foot-steps of Je-sus, shall win the fight, and share in the joy of their Lord.

These words spoke Je-sus, and then raised his eyes, and said, Fath-er the hour is come. Let thy light shine through the Son that men may see thee as thou art. Thou didst give him pow-er o-ver all men that through him they should have life with-out end. And this is the life that dies not, that they may learn to know thee, the one true God, and Je-sus Christ, whom thou hast sent.

CARVED TOMB AT JE-RU-SA-LEM.

I have done the work thou didst give me to do; and now let it be shown to the world, O Fath-er, that I am one with thee. Let the veil be drawn that I may stand with thine own self in glo-ry that I had with thee ere the world was made. I have shown forth thy name to those thou didst give me out of the world; thine they were, and to me thou didst give them, and they have kept thy word. Be-cause the words thou didst give me I gave to them, and they have kept them in their hearts, and learned to know that I came from thee, and they be-lieve that thou didst send me. I pray for them; I pray not for the world, but for those thou didst give me; for they are thine. They have been brought back to God. And all mine are thine, and thine are mine; and my light shines in them. I am to leave the world, but these are to stay in the world, and I come to thee. Do Thou keep through thine own name those whom thou didst give me, that they may be one as we are one. While I was with them I kept them in thy name, and took care of them, and none of them is lost but one, and he chose the way of sin.

But now I come to thee, and these things I speak in the world that they may have the joy that is mine. I have taught them thy word, and the world hates them be-cause they are not of the world, as I am not of the world. I pray not that thou shouldst take them out of the world, but that thou shouldst keep them from the sin that is in the world. Set them a-part from the world and in the light of truth; thy word is truth. As thou didst send me in-to the world, so have I sent them in-to the world.

Nor for these a-lone do I pray, but for all those that

shall be-lieve in me through their word; that they all may be one, as Thou art in me and I in thee, that they may be one in us, and that the world may be-lieve that thou didst send me. The strength thou didst give to me, I have giv-en to them that they may be one with us; and that the world may learn to know, through them, that thou didst send me, and dost love them e-ven as thou dost love me.

Je-sus has left us to do his work in the world; to have no thought of self, but to strive to do all the good that we can, to lead men up and out of their sins, and to teach them of the love of God.

Je-sus said, Fath-er, I pray that those thou didst give me may be with me where I am, and see the light in which I dwell; for thou didst love me ere the world was made. The world hath not known thee, but I have known thee, and these have learned that thou hast sent me. And I made known to them thy name, and will make it known, that the love with which thou dost love me may be in them, and I in them.

If Je-sus had need to pray, how much more is there need for us to ask God to be with us and with those we love. We must pray for those who are in the world—those who are in the haunts of sin, and where the paths are rough to their feet, and where it is not so hard to do wrong as it is to do right. We must pray for these that they may have strength to walk in the foot-steps of Je-sus, and to put their trust in God. God lives with them that love him.

CHAPTER XXIII.

JE-SUS IN THE GAR-DEN OF GETH-SEM-A-NE.—THE JU-DAS KISS—IN THE HANDS OF HIS FOES.—HE IS BROUGHT BE-FORE THE HIGH-PIEST, AND THEN SENT TO PI-LATE.—PE-TER DENIES HIS LORD.

Je-sus left the room at the top of the house, and went

SLOPES A-BOVE THE KED-RON.

forth in-to the clear moon-light night. He led the way, and his friends kept near him; and he spoke to them, and said, All ye shall turn from me be-cause of what is to take

MOUNT OF OLIVES BY MOON-LIGHT.

place this night. For it was said of old, I will smite the shep-herd, and the sheep of the flock shall go from place to place. But when I am raised up I will go be-fore you in to Gal-i-lee. Pe-ter said, Though all the rest turn from thee, yet will I not leave thee. Pe-ter had a warm heart, and felt so sure of him-self. But Je-sus said to him, In this night, ere the cock crow twice, thou shalt thrice de-ny me. Pe-ter said to Je-sus, Though it cost me my life, though I

VALE OF THE KED-RON.

die with thee, I will not de-ny thee. And so said all the rest.

They had to cross a small stream called the Ked-ron, or the "black brook," which flowed through the vale, and then they came to a gar-den where there was a fine growth of ol-ive trees. There was a large trade in ol-ives, in the East as much use was made of the oil that was pressed out of this fruit. Je-sus said to eight of those with him, Sit ye here, while I go off there and pray. Out of the bright moon-light he would go, to a dark place, where he could be, as it were, shut in with God.

OL-IVE GROVE.

He took with him Pe-ter, and James, and John, and was as one borne down with a weight of woe. And he said to those with him, My soul is sick un-to death; stay here, and watch with me. He felt the need of friends in this dark hour. They were to be on their guard, and see that

Je-sus in the Gar-den of Geth-sem-a-ne.

no harm came to him. And he went on a-bout a stone's throw from them, and knelt down and prayed, O my Fath-er, if it be thy will let this cup pass a-way from me; yet, not my will, but thine be done. He left it all in God's hands, and God sent an an-gel to him to give him strength to drink the cup. We speak of the cup of woe, and the cup of joy; for when we have great grief, it is as if we drank some-thing bit-ter; and when we have great joy, it is as if we drank some-thing so sweet and good that it thrills through all our veins.

OL-IVE PRESS.

Je-sus had asked Pe-ter and James and John to keep watch; but when he rose from his knees and went to them, he found that they slept. And he said to Pe-ter, who had made such a boast of his strength, What, could ye not watch with me one hour? Watch and pray, for ye need to be on your guard: for the spir-it may be will-ing, but the flesh is weak. This was so slight a thing to ask, and yet Pe-ter had failed him.

Je-sus went a-way and prayed once more, O my Fath-er, if this cup can-not pass a-way from me ex-cept I drink it, thy will be done. And he came once more to Pe-ter,

James, and John, and found that they still slept. Then he left them and prayed for the third time and said the same words, and so fierce were the pangs that rent his heart, that the sweat poured from his face, and like great drops of blood fell down on the ground. Then full strength came to him, and he shrank no more from his fate. And he

CHRIST ON THE MOUNT OF OL-IVES.

came to Pe-ter, James, and John, and said to them, Sleep on now, and take your rest, for the hour is at hand in which the Son of Man shall be giv-en up to his foes. Rise, and let us go from this place, for he is near who is to do this thing.

GETH-SEM-A-NE.

Now Ju-das knew that Je-sus was wont to stop and rest in this gar-den, on his way to and from Je-ru-sa-lem. So he went and told the chief-priest and the Scribes, and they placed him at the head of a band of armed men, who set out with lan-terns, torch-es, swords and clubs. Though

GAR-DEN AT GETH-SEM-A-NE.

the moon shone bright, there were great trees in the gar-den that cast a broad shade, and the men thought that Je-sus might hide from them in some dark place.

But Je-sus knew all that was to take place, and when he saw the Ju-das band, he did not hide him-self but went forth to meet them. Ju-das had told the men how they were to

GARDEN AT GETH-SEM-A-NE.

know which was Je-sus. He said, The one I shall kiss is he; seize him at once, and lead him to a safe place. He then came up to Je-sus, as if he were a friend, and said, Mas-ter, Mas-ter, and kissed him on his cheek. Je-sus said to him, Was it for this that thou didst come? Pe-ter spoke up and said, Lord, shall we smite with the sword? Je-sus paid no heed to these words, but spoke to the armed men, and said, Whom do ye seek? They said Je-sus of Naz-a-reth. Je-sus said to them, I am He. Ju-das stood near them, and when Je-sus said, I am He, they were awe-struck and all went back and fell to the ground. Then Je-sus asked them once more, Whom seek ye? And they said, Je-sus of Naz-a-reth. Je-sus said, I told you that I am He. If then ye have come for me, let these go their way. He wished no harm to come to those he loved, and who had stood by him, true friends to the last.

Pe-ter, when he saw the band come near to Je-sus, to take him, drew his sword, and struck at one of the armed men and cut off his right ear. The man's name was Mal-chus. Je-sus said to Pe-ter, Put back thy sword in its sheath; for all they that take the sword shall die by the sword. Then he asked his friends if they thought he could not get free from these men if he chose. If he prayed to God, he would send him not twelve weak men, but twelve bands of an-gels. But in that case the Word of God would not come true, and these things must be. And he turned to the men who had hold of him, and said to them, Let me do this much; and he touched the ear of Mal-chus, and healed the wound. Then he said to the crowd, Have ye come out with swords and clubs to seize me, as if I were

THE JUDAS KISS.

a thief? I sat day by day, and taught in the tem-ple, and ye took me not. But this is your hour, and it is fit that such a deed should be done in the dark. Sa-tan is called the Prince of Dark-ness. Then Pe-ter, James and John, and the rest, when they heard these words felt that all hope was lost. They could not save him, and their own lives were not safe if they staid near him, so they turned from him and fled—just as Je-sus had said they would. And he was left in the midst of his foes, with his hands tied be-hind his back!

Bound in this way, they led him to the high-priest's house, where An-nas and his son-in-law, Ca-ia-phas, made their home, and where the courts of law were held. They took Je-sus first to An-nas, for he was a great man, and much thought of by the Jews. He had once been their high-priest, and though an old man, his words had still great weight with them.

The high-priest, An-nas, asked Je-sus who were his dis-ci-ples, and what he had taught them. Je-sus was calm, and showed no signs of fear. I spoke to all the world, he said. I have taught in the church, and in the courts of the Tem-ple where all the Jews go. What I have said, has been said where all could hear. Why then ask me? Ask those who have heard, what I said un-to them. These know the things that I have said.

When he had said these things, one of the armed men who stood by, struck Jes-sus a blow with his hand, and said, Dost thou dare speak thus to the high priest? Could man have borne such a blow, and yet been calm? No. Yet Je-sus with-out a frown up-on his brow, or a flash from

JESUS BEFORE THE HIGH PRIEST.

his eye, spoke to the rude wretch near him, and said, If I spoke ill, prove it; but if well, why dost thou strike me?

THE CHIEF PRIESTS TELL WHAT JE-SUS HAS DONE.

When it was found that no more could be got out of Je-sus, An-nas sent him to Ca-ia-phas, whose rooms were a-cross the court yard. For these men had great wealth, and lived like kings. Here the chief priests and Scribes had met, and they sought to find some one to speak ill of Je-sus that they might put him to death. This was a great sin for those to do who were set to judge men, and to try them for their crimes. Though men came and told false tales, they were such as they could make no use of. At last came two who said, We heard this man say he would pull down the Tem-ple of God, and build it up new in three days.

Then the high priest stood up, and said, Hast thou noth-ing to say? Is it true or false what these men say of thee? But Je-sus held his peace. Then the high priest bade him, on his oath, sworn to in the sight of God, tell those in that court of law, if he was the Christ the Son of God.

Je-sus said, I am. And I say to you that from this time forth shall ye see the Son of Man sit-ting at the right hand of God, and with his throne in the clouds. Then the high priest rent his clothes, and said, Ye have heard from his own lips that he claims to be one with God. What think ye ought to be done with him? They were not told to take time, and to look at all sides of the case ere they gave in their vote. No, it was all done in haste, that Je-sus might have no chance for his life. And they said, He ought to be put to death, and he was led out from their midst to be placed in the guard room.

It was now long past mid-night, and though it was the spring of the year, there was a chill in the air. And in the court yard was a bright fire, round which stood the ser-

PE-TER DE-NIES HIS LORD.

vants of the high priest, and some of those who had gone out with Ju-das.

Now Pe-ter and John had fled from Je-sus, but soon came back and went with the crowd to the high priest's house. John was known to the high priest, and it was no hard task for him to pass in to the court. But Pe-ter was stopped at the door. As soon as John found this out, he spoke to the maid that kept the door, and went and brought Pe-ter in. By this time Je-sus was out of sight, and in one of the court rooms in the high priest's house; so Pe-ter walked off by the fire, and stood there to warm him-self.

While he was there, the maid who had been at the door drew near, and looked at Pe-ter, and said, Art thou not one of this man's friends? Pe-ter said, I am not. He went out for a while on the porch, and while he was there the cock crew.

In a short time the same maid passed by Pe-ter a-gain; and she said to those who stood by, This man is one of them. And Pe-ter said, I am not. It was not long ere one of those who stood by the fire, and had heard Pe-ter speak, turned to him, and said, Thou must be one of them, for thou dost come from Gal-i-lee. Then Pe-ter, thrown off his guard, swore with an oath that he knew not this man of whom they spoke. And just then the crow of the cock was heard.

At the same time Je-sus was led by the group round the fire, and and on the way he turned and gave Pe-ter a look that smote him to the heart. It was a look of love, but oh, so sad! And it brought back to Pe-ter's mind the words of the Lord, Be-fore the cock crows twice thou shalt

THE PRICE OF BLOOD.

de-ny me three times. It had come true. And when Pe-ter tnought of what he had done, and of the boast that he had made, he hid his face that his tears might not be seen, and rushed forth in-to the night.

When Je-sus was placed in the guard room, the men in whose charge he was, did mock at him, and strike at him with their fists; and they did blind-fold him, and struck him in the face, and said, Tell us who it is that struck thee. And he bore it all, and said not a word.

At day-break, the chief priests and Scribes, the four-score and ten that made up the San-he-drin met in their large hall, and Je-sus was brought in to them. They said to him, If thou art the Christ, tell us. Je-sus said to them, If I tell you, ye will not be-lieve me. He knew that all he could say would have no weight, for they were bent up-on his death.

Then said they all, Art thou then the Son of God? He said to them, Ye say it, for I am. And they said, What do we need more? Out of his own mouth we can judge him. And they all rose from their seats, and went out to give Je-sus in-to the hands of Pi-late, who dwelt near the Tem-ple in the house that King Her-od had built.

When Ju-das saw the crowd on its way to Pi-late, he was grieved for what he had done. And he took back to the chief priests the price they had paid him, and said to them, I sinned in that I did charge a man with crime who had done no wrong. They said to him, What is that to us? see thou to it. And he flung down the mon-ey in the ho-ly place, and went out and hung him-self. The chief priests took up the sil-ver and said, We can-not put this

THE FIELD OF BLOOD.

with the church fund since it is the price of blood. So
they bought with it a piece of land, which from that day
was known as, The field of blood.

The chief priests and Scribes did not go in-to the court
room them-selves, but sat down out-side. Pi-late went out
to meet them, and said, Why have ye brought this man
here? What has he done? They said, If he had not
done wrong we would not have brought him to thee.

Pi-late said to them, Take him, and judge him by your
own law. The Jews said, We have no law that will let us
put a man to death. Then Pi-late went back to the court-
room, and called Je-sus and said to him, Art thou the
King of the Jews? Je-sus said, Didst thou ask this thing of
thy-self, or wert thou told to ask me? Pi-late said, Am I
a Jew? Men of thine own race have brought thee to me.
What hast thou done?

Je-sus said, My King-dom is not of this world, else would
my ser-vants strive to keep me from the hands of the Jews.
Pi-late said, Art thou then a king? Je-sus said, I am a King.
To this end was I born, and for this cause came I in-to the
world, that I should prove the truth. Those that are of the
truth hear my voice. Pi-late said to him, What is truth? He
said this as one might say, How hard it is to find out what is
the truth! For he went out at once to the Jews, and said
to them, I find in him no crime. He saw in him no signs of
guilt, and thought it was as well to let him go. So he said to
the Jews, Ye know at this feast I have been wont to set
free one of those shut up in jail. And there was at this
time in one of the cells a bad man named Ba-rab-bas. And
he said to the Jews, Which of the two shall I set free, Je-

WHAT THEN SHALL I DO WITH JE-SUS?

sus or Ba-rab-bas? And he left them, that they might take time to think, and make up their minds.

In the mean-time, ere Pi-late went back to the hall, where Je-sus stood bound in the midst of the rough crowd, his wife sent for him, and said, Have nought to do with this good man; for I have been in great grief be-cause of a dream I have had of him.

But the chief priests and Scribes had talked with the mob and told them what to say. And when Pi-late took his seat, and asked, Which of the two will ye that I set free? They cried out, Ba-rab-bas! Pi-late said, What then shall be done to Je-sus which is called Christ? They all said, Let him be put to death on the cross.

Pi-late said, Why, what crime hath he done?—for none but the worst of men, those who had done the worst of crimes, were put to death in this way. But they cried out all the more, that he should be put to death on the cross.

When Pi-late saw that the mob would have its way, and that his words were lost on them, he took wa-ter and washed his hands and said, I am not to blame for the death of this just man; see ye to it. Then they all cried out and said, His blood be on us, and on our chil-dren. Since the days of Mo-ses the Jews had made use of this sign, and knew well what it meant; and to this day men say, I wash my hands of this thing, and mean to have it known that they do not share in the guilt of those who may have done a wrong deed. But in the sight of God Pi-late had done a great sin. He could not wash from his hands the blood red stain.

That he might please the Jews, and be at peace with

SCOURG-ING CHRIST.

them, he set Ba-rab-bas free; and when Je-sus had been scourged, he was led off to be put to death on the cross. None but slaves were scourged. The back was bare, and the man made to stoop so that the skin would stretch. The whips were thongs made of strips of tough hide, with bits of lead or bones at the end of each lash. These cut through the skin and drew blood, and some-times caused the death of the poor slaves. The men who had mocked Je-sus and spat in his face, would not be mild in the use of the lash. With his stripes are we healed.

When the men had scourged Je-sus, they led him off to the guard room, and the whole band of troops were there to watch him. And they took off his clothes, and put on him a red robe. And they wove a crown of thorns, and put it on his head, and a reed in his right hand. And they bowed the knee be-fore him, and mocked him as they said, Hail, King of the Jews! And they spat up-on him, and took the reed and struck him on the head.

Pi-late went out once more, and told the Jews that he found that Je-sus had done no crime. Je-sus then came forth, and he still wore the crown of thorns and the red robe that had been put on him to mock him. When the chief priests, and the armed men saw him they cried out, Cru-ci-fy him! cru-ci-fy him!

Pi-late said to them, Take him your-selves, and put him to death on the cross, for I find no crime in him. The Jews said, We have a law, and by the law he ought to die, be-cause he made him-self the Son of God. When Pi-late heard that he was the more a-fraid, and he went back to the court room, and said to Je-sus, Where dost thou come

CROWN OF THORNS.

from? But Je-sus spoke not a word. Pi-late said, Wilt thou not speak to me? Dost thou not know that I have pow-er to put thee to death or to set thee free?

Je-sus said, Thou wouldst have no power to harm me if God did not give it to thee. For this cause he that gave me in-to thy hands has sinned far more than thou. Then Pi-late tried to set Je-sus free; but the Jews cried out, and said, If thou let this man go, thou art not Cæ-sar's friend. He who makes him-self a king treads on the rights of Cæ-sar. Now it was the aim of Pi-late to stand well in the eyes of the king whom he served, and to be known as Cæ-sar's friend. So when the Jews spoke thus, he brought Je-sus out and sat down in the place where he was wont to judge those who were brought to him. And he said to the Jews, This is the man. Be-hold your King! But they cried out, A-way with him! a-way with him! cru-ci-fy him! Pi-late said to them, Shall I cru-ci-fy your King? The chief priests said, We have no king but Cæ-sar! Then Pi-late gave Je-sus in-to their hands to be put to death on the cross. And they took Je-sus and led him a-way.

When Je-ru-sa-lem was built up, the place wher Pi-late stood, when he said, This is the man! was marked by an arch-way of stone, which stands to this day.

But it is not in piles of stone, and rich gifts, that we best show our love for the Lord, but in kind deeds, and the pains we take to put down self, and to be more and more like Je-sus.

THEN CAME JESUS FORTH.

CHAPTER XXIV.

JE-SUS ON THE CROSS—AND IN THE GRAVE.—AN AN-GEL ROLLS THE STONE A-WAY.—"HE IS NOT HERE.—HE HAS RIS-EN."

It was now Fri-day morn, and the sun shone down on men who were to do such a base deed that the blood runs cold at thought of it. None but those who had done the worst of crimes were put to death on the cross. The cross was made of a long piece of wood, with a short piece a-cross it near the top. It was first laid on the ground, and then the man who was to be hanged was nailed to it through his hands and feet, the hands stretched out on the cross beam. When this was done the cross was raised and let fall with a shock in-to the hole dug for it, and the whole weight of the poor man doomed to such a death, was on the hands, through whose palms the wounds were made.

When the Jews hung those whom they had stoned to death, they took care to have the corpse laid in the ground the same day. But the Ro-mans let those who were hung on the cross die a slow death; some-times they were left for three days, and the birds and the beasts fed on their flesh.

The Jews were not quite so cru-el, for if death was slow they broke the legs of those who hung on the cross, or pierced their side to make sure that no life was left in them. And both Ro-mans and Jews shrank from the shame and

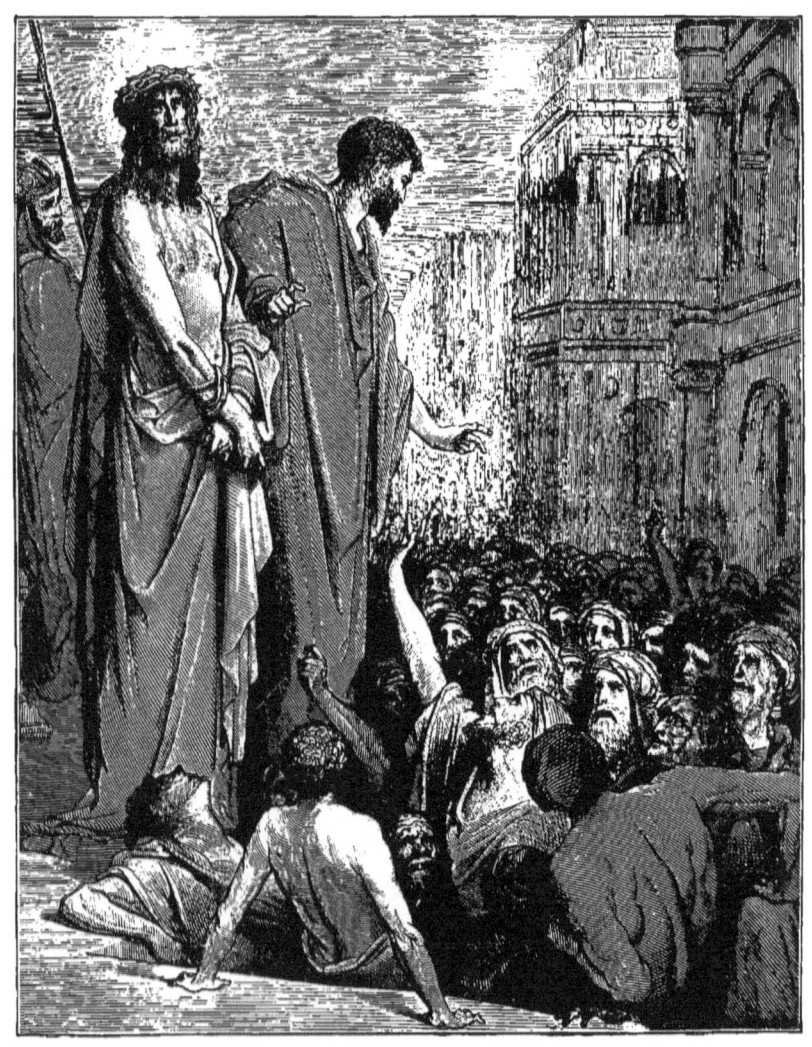

NOT THIS MAN, BUT BA-RAB-BAS.

the pain of this the worst form of death—death on the cross.

The place where the cross was to be set up was out side of the town, and the troops led Je-sus out to meet this death of shame. At first Je-sus bore his own cross, but the weight of it was too great for him, and so a black man named Si-mon, was called out of the crowd, and made to bear one end of it. The road which Je-sus took to the cross is now known as the way of grief.

Then they went on till they came to a hill shaped like a skull, from whence it took the name of Gol-go-tha. Here they brought Je-sus some sour wine mixed with gall, to keep up his strength, but when he had put it to his lips he would not drink it. At nine o'clock they nailed him to the cross, and Pi-late wrote out in three forms, so that it might be read by all, the sign that was set up o-ver the head of our Lord. It told that he was, JE-SUS OF NAZ-A-RETH THE KING OF THE JEWS.

The chief priests of the Jews said to Pi-late, Write not The King of the Jews, but this man said I am the King of the Jews. But Pi-late said that what he had done was done, and he could make no change. And the Jews and the Greeks and the Ro-mans could all read the words, THIS IS JE-SUS THE KING OF THE JEWS. Pi-late had meant but to mock at the Jews, but the hand of God was in this thing, and those who sought to bring shame on Christ, had crowned him King of the whole wide world.

The Jews, as they passed by this place, wagged their heads, and said, Thou that canst pull down the Tem-ple, and build it up in three days, save thy-self. If thou art the

JESUS FALLS BENEATH THE WEIGHT OF THE CROSS.

Son of God, come down from the cross. And the chief priests and Scribes said, He saved oth-ers; him-self he can-not save. If he is the King of the Jews, let him come down from the cross, and we will be-lieve in him. His trust was in God; let him save him now if he cares for him; for he said, I am the Son of God. With such taunts and gibes they showed their hate for him who for three long hours hung up-on the cross, and felt a weight of woe in which no one on earth could share.

Four men—part of the Ro-man guard—were set to watch Je-sus, lest some of his friends should come and take him down from the cross. And these men took his clothes, which had been stripped from him, and made them in-to four parts, so that each one could have the same share. But there was one long robe, such as was worn by the high priest, and it had no seam in it, but from the top through-out was in one piece. The men looked at it, and said, Let us not tear it, but cast lots for it, to see whose it shall be. And this was done.

Now at the time that Je-sus was put to death on the cross, two thieves were put to death in the same way near him, one on his right hand, and one on his left. This was done to cast more shame on Him, who knew no sin.

The thief on the left hand, to add to the taunts of the crowd, said to Je-sus so that all could hear him, If thou art the Christ, save thy-self and us. But the thief on the right hand, said to him, Dost thou not fear God, as thou art to be judged for thy sins? It is just that we be put to death for our crimes, but this man has done no wrong. And he turned his face to Je-sus and said, Lord, bear me in mind when thou dost come in-to thy King-dom.

ON THE CROSS.

Je-sus said to him, To-day shalt thou be with me in the home of the blest. This was the thief's last chance; his last hope. He was vile and full of sin, but at the last hour of his life, ere the breath left him, he came to Je-sus and was saved.

Now there stood by the cross of Je-sus four wom-en, and one of them was his moth-er. When Je-sus saw her, and that John whom he loved stood near her, he said to his moth-er, Wom-an, be-hold, thy son! And he said to John, Be-hold, thy moth-er! And from that hour John was as a son to her; and he took her to his own home and took care of her.

Je-sus was nailed to the cross at nine o'clock, and from the hour of noon till three o'clock the light of the sun was put out, and the whole land was as dark as night. Not a sigh, nor a groan, was heard from the cross where Je-sus hung. All was still. The light of the world had been put out by the hand of man, and the sun hid its face be-hind a cloud. This was a sure sign that God was not pleased with what had been done, and must have brought fear and dread to those who had had a hand in the death of Je-sus.

At three o'clock, when Je-sus had been on the cross for six hours, he cried out to God with a loud voice. He felt the pains of the flesh, and so sharp were they and so hard to bear it seemed as if God had left him. So he laid hold on God for fresh strength, to teach us what we must do in the last hour when flesh and heart fail us.

The guards heard the cry of Je-sus and thought that he called for E-li-jah, and they said, let us see if E-li-jah comes to save him. Then Je-sus gave a sigh, and said, I thirst. And one of the men took a sponge and filled it

THE MA-RYS AT THE CROSS.

with sour wine and put it up-on a reed, so that Je-sus could quench his thirst. It touched his lips, and he said: The work Thou didst give me to do, is done. And he bowed his head and gave up the ghost.

Then the veil of the Tem-ple was torn in two, and the earth did quake, and the rocks were rent. The stone doors fell from the tombs, and some of the saints which slept there were raised from the dead. When the men who were on guard, and kept watch of Je-sus saw the earth quake and the things that were done, they said, Of a truth this was the Son of God.

As the next day was the Sab-bath, and the first of this great fast of the church, the Jews sent to Pi-late and beg-ged him to have the guard break the legs of those that

VEIL OF TEM-PLE RENT IN TWAIN.

THEY TOOK JE-SUS DOWN FROM THE CROSS.

hung on the cross, that they might be put in-to their graves. Then came the armed men, and first broke the legs of the thieves that were on the right hand and left hand of Je-sus. When they came to Je-sus and saw that he was dead they brake not his legs; but to make sure that life had left him, one of the men thrust a spear in-to his side, the heart was pierced, and the blood flowed out.

These things were done, that all that was fore-told of Christ might come true. For Mo-ses had told the Jews that the bones of the Lamb that was slain for the feast must not be crushed. And it was said in the Psalms, A bone of him shall not be crushed. And else-where it was said, They shall look on me whom they have pierced. Je-sus was the Lamb whom God had sent, but whom the Jews would not have. The Lamb of God that takes a-way the sins of the world.

Now there was in Je-ru-sa-lem, a rich man from Ar-i-ma-the-a, named Jo-seph. He had faith in Je-sus, and thought that he was all that he claimed to be; but for fear of the Jews he had not let this be known. He was a good and just man, and well read in the law, and had no hand in the death of Je-sus.

It was three o'clock when our Lord drew his last breath, and at sun-down Jo-seph grown more bold went to Pi-late and beg-ged that he might take Je-sus from the cross. Pi-late did not think he could be dead so soon, but when he learned that the breath had left him, he bade his men give the corpse in-to the hands of Jo-seph to do with as he would. He came then, and took Je-sus a-way; and there was with him one Nic-o-de-mus, the same who came to Je-sus by

CHRIST IS BORNE TO THE TOMB.

night, and he brought with him more than four-score pounds of mixed gums and spice to spread on the cloths in which the form of Je-sus was to be wrapped.

SEP-UL-CHRE, OR TOMB.

Then they took Je-sus down from the cross and wrap-ped him in the fine white lin-en cloths that Jo-seph

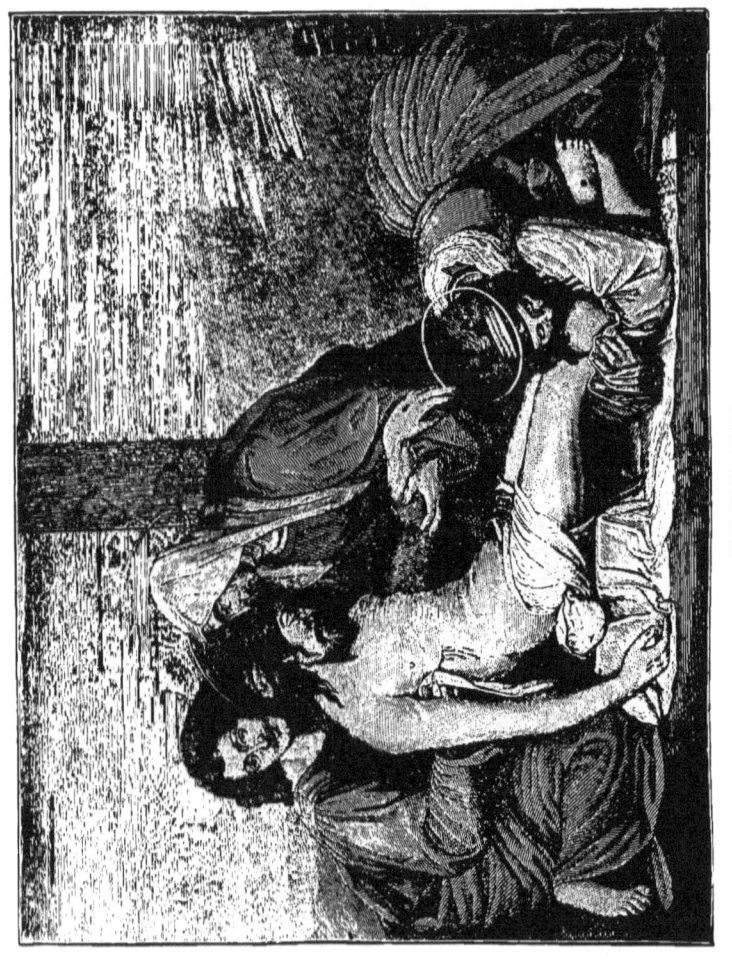

FRIENDS OF JE-SUS.

had bought, and they laid him in Jo-seph's own tomb in a gar-den close at hand. This tomb was cut out of a rock, at great cost, and in it no man had yet been laid. And when they had rolled a great stone up to the door of the tomb, they left the place, and went back in-to the town.

THE GUARDS AT THE TOMB.

Some of the rich men spent a great deal of their wealth on their tombs, the place where they were to lie when they were dead. They felt great pride in this, and much skill was shown in the way the tombs were built, and not a few of them stood forth as great works of art.

The next day—which we would call the last day of the week—was, with the Jews, the great Sab-bath of the year. And the chief priests and Scribes came to Pi-late and said, Sir, it is in our minds that that man said, while he was yet a-live, At the end of three days I shall rise from the dead. Let a guard keep watch of the tomb till the third day, lest his friends come by night and steal him a-way, and claim that he rose him-self from the dead.

Pi-late said to them, Ye have a guard of your own; go your way, and use such means as you think best to make it safe. So they went and stretched a string a-cross the great stone door, and made it fast to the rock with seals of wax, or clay. And when this was done they placed a guard of armed men there to keep watch, and see that no one broke the seals.

At sun-set of that day—for no work could be done on the Day of Rest from sun-rise to sun-set—Ma-ry of Mag-da-la, and Ma-ry the moth-er of James, and her sis-ter Sa-lo-me, bought spice and gums that they might come and lay out Je-sus for the grave, for what Nic-o-de-mus had done was done in haste.

Ere the sun rose on the first day of the week, these three wom-en set out for the tomb, and on the way they said, Who shall roll us a-way the stone from the door of the tomb? And there came a great earth-quake. And an an-gel of the Lord came down from on high, and rolled back the stone from the tomb, and sat up-on it. His face shone as the sun, and his robes were as white as snow; and for fear of him the watch-men did quake, and were as dead men. This was not known to those who came with sad hearts at the dusk of dawn to mourn their loss. They were the last to leave the cross, and were now the first at the grave.

As soon as Ma-ry of Mag-da-la saw that the stone had been rolled from the door of the tomb, she ran to Pe-ter and John and said to them, They have ta-ken the Lord out of the tomb, and we do not know where they have laid him. Pe-ter and John set out at once for the tomb, but as John was a young man, and light of foot, he out-ran Pe-ter and reached there the first. And he stooped down, and looked in, and saw the cloths that had been wrapped round Je-sus, but dared not go in-to the tomb.

Pe-ter was more bold; for as soon as he came up, he went in-to the tomb, and saw the cloths that lay there. And the square piece that was on the face of Je-sus did not lie with the rest of the cloths, but was rolled up in a place by it-self.

Then John went in, and when he saw these signs he knew that no one had robbed the grave, but that Je-sus had left the tomb him-self, and it was vain to search for him. All doubts and fears were at rest, and yet in a strange frame of mind Pe-ter and John went back to their own homes.

Ma-ry had run with them part of the way, but by the time she reached the tomb, they had left, and she stood out-side and wept. Her sole thought was, They have ta-ken my Lord a-way from the tomb, and I know not where they have laid him. With her eyes filled with tears she stooped down, and gazed in-to the tomb, and saw there two an-gels in white, one at the head and one at the feet, where the form of Je-sus had lain.

JE-SUS SHOWS HIM-SELF TO MA-RY.

They said to her, Why dost thou weep? She said, They have ta-ken a-way my Lord, and I know not where they have laid him. When she had thus said she turned round, and saw that some one stood near her, but did not know that it was Je-sus.

Je-sus said to her, Why dost thou weep? Whom dost thou seek? She thought that he was the man who had charge of the grounds, and that he might tell her what she longed to know. So she said to him, Sir, if thou didst bear him from this place, tell me where thou hast laid him, and I will take him a-way.

Je-sus said to her, "MA-RY!" She turned and said to him, "O my Mas-ter!" and would have thrown her-self at the feet of the Lord, and held him fast. But Je-sus said, Touch me not! Cling not to me! but go to my breth-ren and say to them, I go to my Fa-ther and your Fath-er; and to my God and your God. The time would come when men should see him, and touch him, and cling to him, and hear his voice—as we do now by faith—but then it was too soon to look for such a state of things.

Awe struck: Ma-ry went her way to bear the word that Je-sus had sent, and to tell all whom she met, "I have seen the Lord!" And the tears she now wept were those of joy.

When the wom-en came up who had brought the rich gums and the spice, they found the stone rolled a-way from the door of the tomb; and as they went in-to the tomb they saw a young man at the right side of it, clothed in a long white robe, and were awe-struck at the sight. The an-gel said to them, Fear not; for I know ye seek

HE IS NOT HERE.

Je-sus who was put to death on the cross. He is not here. He is ris-en. Come, see the place where they laid him.

Then go with speed and tell Pe-ter and the rest that he will meet them in Gal-i-lee. There shall ye see him, as he said un-to you. And they went out from the tomb with fear and great joy, and ran to take the word to those who had been left to do the Lord's work on earth.

On the way Je-sus met them, and said to them, All hail! And they came and took hold of his feet, and bowed down be-fore him. Then said Je-sus to them, Fear not. Go and tell Pe-ter and the rest to go in-to Gal-i-lee, and there they shall see me.

Then Pe-ter and the rest went in-to Gal-i-lee, and to the mount where Je-sus had said he would meet them. And when they saw him, they bowed down be-fore him; though some had doubts if this was the right thing to do. And Je-sus came still more near, and spoke to them, and said, All pow-er is giv-en to me in heav-en and on earth. Go ye, then, and teach all the world, and bap-tize them in the name of the Fath-er, and of the Son, and of the Ho-ly Ghost. Teach them to do all things that I have taught you; and be sure that from day to day I will be with you to the end of the world.

In the mean-time some of the watch-men came in to the town, and told the chief priests all that had been done. And when they heard of it, they paid a large sum to the watch-men, and told them to say, The friends of Je-sus came by night, and stole him a-way while we slept. Now it was a crime for a man on guard to sleep at his post; and these men, who were part of an armed band, knew that they would be put to death if it was found out. So to quell their fears the chief priests said if it came to the ears of Pilate they would make it all right with him, and no harm should be done them. So they took the price that was paid them and did as they were told; and for long years it was thought that what they said of Je-sus was true, and that he did not rise from the dead.

CHAPTER XXV.

THE WALK TO EM-MA-US.—JE-SUS IS SEEN BY THOSE WHO LOVE HIM.—THE LAST FARE-WELL.—A CLOUD HIDES HIM FROM SIGHT.

The same day that Je-sus rose from the tomb, two of those who had been with him, and were taught by him, set out for a small town called Em-ma-us, which was less than eight miles from Je-ru-sa-lem. And as they went on their way they spoke of all these strange things which had been done. And while they thus talked, Je-sus him-self drew near and went with them. And they did not know him. It is so at times with those who love Je-sus the most. They are sad, and the light seems gone out of life, and there is no hope in their hearts. But Je-sus is near though they do not see him. He leaves them in the dark a while, that he may bless them more and more.

And as he drew near these two, he said to them, What things do ye talk of as ye walk? and why are ye sad? and

The Walk to Em-ma-us.

one of them named Cle-o-pas, said un-to him, Art thou but just come to Je-ru-sa-lem, that thou dost not know the things which have come to pass there in these days? He said un-to them, what things? They said, The things a-bout Je-sus of Naz-a-reth, who was a great proph-et in deed and in word be-fore God and all the world: and how

EM-MA-US.

the chief priests and Scribes gave him up to be put to death, and hanged him on the cross.

But we put great trust in him, and hoped that it was he who should save our race from their sins. And now it is the third day since these things took place. Yes, and some wom-en of our band who went to the tomb at day break told us strange news. For when they found He was not there, they came back and said they had seen some an-gels who told them he was a-live. And some of those who were with us went to the tomb, and found that what the wom-en said was true: but him they saw not.

Then Je-sus told them if they had read the Word of God as they should have done, they would have learned what Mo-ses and all the proph-ets had fore-told. For all these things must take place, and Christ must bear the load of grief and pain, and be put to death on the cross ere he could reach his home on high, and shine down on the hearts of men. And he made clear to their minds all that had been said of him—in the Psalms, and else-where in the Word of God.

As they drew near to the small town, for which they had set out, Je-sus made as if he would go on and leave them. And they begged him not to do so, and said, Come and stay with us, for the day is now far spent, and it will soon be dark. And he went in to stay with them. And when he had sat down to sup with them, he took the bread and gave thanks, and broke it and gave to them. And then they knew him. And as they gazed awe-struck up-on him he passed out of their sight.

When speech came back to them, they said, Did not our hearts burn with-in us while he talked with us on the way, and while he made plain to us the Word of God? and they rose at once, and went back to Je-ru-sa-lem, and found Peter, John and the rest in the room where they were wont to meet. And they told them all the things

JE-SUS SHOWS HIM-SELF TO HIS DIS-CI-PLES.

that took place on the way to Em-ma-us, and how Je-sus was made known to them as he broke the bread.

They were met with joy, and those who heard the good news had good news to tell, for Je-sus had in-deed left the tomb and had been seen by Pe-ter.

At the close of that same day Ten of them sat in this room with closed doors, for fear of the Jews. And as they talked of the things that had made glad their hearts, and turned their grief to joy, Je-sus came and stood in the midst of them, and said, Peace be with you. But they were scared, and thought they saw a ghost. Je-sus said to them, Why are ye scared? and why do doubts a-rise in your hearts? See my hands and my feet, that it is I. Touch me, and see for your-selves; for a ghost hath not flesh and bones as ye see me have. And while they were yet in such a state of joy that they could scarce be-lieve it was not all a dream, Je-sus said, Have ye here some food? And they gave him a piece of a boiled fish. And he took it and did eat be-fore them.

And he said to them once more, Peace be with you. As the Fath-er hath sent me, so do I send you. And when he had said this he breathed on them, and said, The Ho-ly Gost be up-on you! He gave them, as it were, new life, and they were to go out and build up His church on earth, and teach men how they could be saved from their sins.

Now Thom-as, one of the Twelve, was not with the rest when Je-sus came, and when he heard the news it seemed to him too good to be true. In vain did the rest say to him, We have seen the Lord.

He thought their grief had crazed them. As for himself, the death on the cross crushed out all hopes that he had that Je-sus would save the race, and set the Jews free from the yoke, that made them slaves to the King of Rome.

So Thom-as could not share in the joy that filled the hearts of the rest, and he said to them, If I cannot see in his hands the prints of the nails, and put my fin-ger in-to the print of the nails, and put my hand in-to his side, I will not be-lieve. At the close of that week these friends of Je-sus met in the same room, and Thom-as was with them. And when the doors were shut Je-sus came and stood in their midst, and said, Peace be un-to you. Then he called Thom-as to him, and bade him stretch forth his finger and put it in the wounds in his hands; and to stretch out his hand, and thrust it in the spear-wound in his side. And he told him not to be so weak in faith, but to be-lieve that he was the same Je-sus who had died on the cross, and now reigned on high.

He had put all foes under his feet; and the last foe of all was Death.

When Thom-as saw Je-sus him-self, and heard these words, all doubts fled a-way, and he cried out with a burst of joy, My Lord, and my God! Je-sus said to him, Be-cause thou hast seen me thou dost be-lieve; blest are they that have not seen me, and yet have faith in me.

The next time that Je-sus was seen on earth, was by the Sea of Gal-i-lee. Pe-ter was there, and Thom-as, and five more of those whom Je-sus had first called. They had lived for some time from one purse, but now as there was

HE SHOWED THEM HIS HANDS.

no one to be at their head, each one must shift for him-self. They talked for some time of their plans, and at last Pe-ter made up his mind to go back to his old trade. The rest might do as they pleased, but Pe-ter said, I go to catch

SEA OF GAL-I-LEE.

fish! The rest said, We will go with thee.

They set sail the same night—for night is the best time to catch fish—and though they toiled all night long not one fish did they catch. At the break of day, while yet the mist was on the sea, some one stood on the shore, but those on the boat did not guess who it was.

And a voice called to them, and said, Have ye caught any fish? They said, No. The voice said to them, Cast the net on the right side of the boat, and ye shall find. They cast the net as they were told, and had scarce strength to draw it, so great was the haul of fish. Then John said to Pe-ter in a low voice, It is the Lord.

At once Pe-ter tied his coat a-round his thighs for he had no clothes on, and leaped in-to the sea, to swim the

CAST-ING THE NET.

space that lay be-tween him and his Lord, and to throw him-self at his feet. The rest came in a small boat—for they were not far from land—and dragged the net with them.

As they came to land they saw a wood fire there, and a piece of fish had been laid on the coals to broil, and near at hand was a loaf of bread. And He who stood there bade them bring some of the fish which they had caught. Pe-ter sprang up at once, and went to help them, with his strong arm, to drag the net to shore, and though there were 153 large and small fish-es, not a rent was made in the net, and not one fish was lost.

THE NET DID NOT BREAK.

The Church of Christ is like a net. Those who go out to fish, are those who go to seek and to save those who are lost; the fish that swim in a sea of sin. They toil in the night, that the lamp they bear with them may shine the more bright, and may toil for hours in vain. But when they hear the voice of the Lord, they must at once do as he bids them. The right side of the boat is the Lord's side, and when the net is cast, such crowds—the great and the small—will be brought in-to the church, that there will seem to be scarce room for them. If you will look at a net you will find it is made up of small holes. Each hole is called a nesle, or a snare. Here and there are knots that keep the snares a-part and add strength to the net; and the whole is made up of one cord—the cord of God's love—which will not break though all the fish in all the seas were caught in the net.

When Pe-ter and the rest had brought the fish to shore, Je-sus said to them, Come and break-fast. So awed were they by the sight of his face, and the sound of his voice, whom they knew to be the Lord, that they dared not speak one word. And he came and gave them of the bread and the fish, and they did eat.

When souls are brought in-to the Church of Christ, Je-sus bids them sit down to a feast with him. The fare is plain, but with Je-sus there we feed on an-gels' food, and He gives us strength for our life work.

When the meal was at an end, Je-sus said to Pe-ter, Dost thou love me more than all the rest? Pe-ter said, Yes, Lord; thou know-est that I love thee. Je-sus said to him, Feed my lambs. Then in a short time he asked Pe-ter a-gain if he loved him. And Pe-ter said, Yes, Lord; thou know-est that I love thee. Je-sus said to him, Feed my sheep.

The young are the lambs of God's flock; and Je-sus

meant that Pe-ter was to teach and to preach to these, and not to let them stray from the fold. The old-er ones are

JE-SUS TAKES BREAD AND GIVES TO THEM.

the sheep, whom he was to care for with wise thought, and to be their guide and friend, that they might not fall in-to the pits dug for their feet, or be seized by beasts of prey.

And Je-sus said to Pe-ter, When thou wast a young man thou didst gird thy-self, and walk here and there of thine own free will. But when thou shalt be old, thou shalt stretch forth thy hands, and some one else shall gird thee and bring thee where thou wouldst not go. These words he said to show forth to Pe-ter the death he should die. When he was an old man, he would be bound, and his hands stretched out, and nailed to the cross. All this took place as Je-sus had said, and Pe-ter at his death, begged to be hung with his head down-ward that he might bear more shame than his Lord and Mas-ter.

He was to do God's will, and to walk in the foot-steps of Je-sus—to bear all that he bore on earth—and at last to die a death of shame up-on the Cross.

While Je-sus spoke these words, Pe-ter walked by his side, and a few steps in front of the rest of the fish-er-men. And he looked back and saw John, and said to Je-sus, Lord, and what shall this man do?

Je-sus said, If I will that he stay till I come, what is that to thee? Thy path is made clear to thee. Walk in my foot-steps.

Each one of us has his own work to do in the world. It may not be just what suits us, but if it is the Lord's will we must do it. It is thus we show our love for Him, and he will give us strength and joy. We must not ask what this one is to do, and why we must tread such a rough way, and have such a hard lot, where some that we know lead a life of ease, and walk in a smooth path. God knows what is best for us, and it is not for us to find fault with Him. If we raise our hearts to Him He will give us all the

The Last Fare-well.

help we need; and all the ills of life that seem so hard to bear, will be sure to turn out for our good.

More than a month had now passed since Je-sus was put to death on the Cross, and we are told that he had been seen on the earth at least nine times since he rose from the dead. He had made it known, that on a mount

BROW OF THE MOUNT OF OL-IVES.

in Gal-i-lee he would meet with all who knew and loved him, for the last time.

He met them in Je-ru-sa-lem, and led them to the brow of the Mount of Ol-ives, and called to their minds all that he had taught them when he was with them on earth. He made clear to them the Word of God, and showed them how all things that Mo-ses and Da-vid had said of him, the Christ, had come to pass. He told them to preach and to teach In His Name, not the Jews alone but all the whole world, that men might lead new lives, and give their hearts to God.

And to cheer them, Je-sus said, Lo, I am with you all your days, e-ven un-to the end of the world. And he bade them stay in Je-ru-sa-lem till pow-er came down to them from on high, that they might have strength and skill to preach the Word of God. For those who had seen him with their own eyes had a great work to do, and must tell of Je-sus to all the ends of the earth.

Then he raised his hands and blest them; and while they looked at him, he was borne up from the ground as on wings, and as he rose a bright cloud hid him from their sight. While their gaze was yet fixed on the sky, in the hope that Je-sus would come back to them, two men clothed in white came and stood by them. And they said, Ye men of Gal-i-lee, why stand and gaze up in-to heav-en? this same Je-sus shall come down from his home on high in the same way that ye have seen him go up to heav-en.

They were not to fold their hands, and watch and wait for him, but to go at once and do the work that he had laid out for them to do.

And they went back to Je-ru-sa-lem with hearts filled with joy, and gave thanks and praise to God, for this sign that Je-sus was not lost to them, but that they should see his face once more.

Je-sus is with those who love him. They see him with the eye of faith. He is near them at all times. He knows

THE AS-CEN-SION.

their grief and pain, and gives them strength to bear them. He has balm for all our wounds.

In a few years Je-ru-sa-lem was a great heap of stones; its walls were torn down, and the whole race of Jews put to flight, and charged not to come near the place or they would be put to death. For a long time it was the scene of great wars, and at last fell in-to the hands of the Turks, whose King or Ca-liph had a mosque built on the

MOSQUE OF O-MAR.

site, or place, where once stood the great Tem-ple of Sol-o-mon.

A mosque is a place of pray-er. The Turks have faith in God, but their be-lief is a strange one, and their mode of wor-ship not at all like ours. They say, There is no god but God; and Mo-ham-med is his proph-et. They have faith in him, and not in our Lord, Je-sus Christ.

But it is on him we lean. There is no friend like

HE HAS BALM FOR ALL OUR WOUNDS.

Je-sus. He knows our hearts. He sees our tears. He knows what we would ask for, though our lips are dumb. There is not one of us but needs to say, Care for me, Lord, for I can-not take care of my-self. I am poor and weak. I need a strong friend near me night and day. Make

JESUS MY KING.

thy home in my heart. Drive out all thy foes. Let me be on the watch to hear the sound of thy voice.

I am here to do thy will, and not my own will; to please God, and not to please my-self. There is not an hour of my life that I do not need thee. Thou who didst go out to seek and to save those who were lost, search me out when I stray from the right path, and save me from those who would drag me down to shame and death.

Oft I do wrong when I do not mean to do wrong. Teach me to so hate sin as to fight it on all sides, and give it no chance to find a weak spot in my heart. If once in, it is hard to get it out.

Je-sus was thir-ty-three years old at the time of his death, and had taught but three years; yet the seed he sowed has sprung up and borne rich fruit, and will go on, and grow, till all the world shall know his name, and all hearts shall bow down and serve him. For he is King of Kings—Lord of Lords—and Prince of Peace.

He came on earth to bring peace and good-will to men: peace with God, whose good will it is that all men shall be saved. He died on the cross to save them from the curse due to their sins, and now lives and reigns in the bright home on high, where life and love shall have no end. Those who shut him out of their hearts, and walk in a dark path, do it of their own free-will; for Je-sus stands at the door of their hearts at all hours of the day and night.

And he says to you and to me—Come, learn of me. Walk in my foot-steps. I AM THE LIGHT OF THE WORLD.

THE END.

www.ingramcontent.com/pod-product-compliance
Lightning Source LLC
Chambersburg PA
CBHW022148300426
44115CB00006B/405